this

and Other Plays

this

and Other Plays

Melissa James Gibson

THEATRE COMMUNICATIONS GROUP
NEW YORK
2013

This and Other Plays is published by Theatre Communications Group, Inc., 520 Eighth Avenue, 24th Floor, New York, NY 10018-4156

The publication of *This and Other Plays*, by Melissa James Gibson, through TCG's Book Program, is made possible in part by the New York State Council on the Arts with the support of Governor Andrew Cuomo and the New York State Legislature.

TCG books are exclusively distributed to the book trade by Consortium Book Sales and Distribution.

LIBRARY OF CONGRESS CATALOGING-IN-PUBLICATION DATA

Gibson, Melissa James.
[Plays. Selections]
This and other plays / Melissa James Gibson.—First edition.
pages ; cm.
ISBN 978-1-55936-379-2 (trade paper)
I. Gibson, Melissa James. This. II. Title.
PS3607.I27T48   2013
812'.6—dc23   2013001991

Book design and composition by Lisa Govan
Cover design by Yentus & Booher, cover photo by Jason Fulford,
author photo by Heather Weston

First Edition, June 2013

For Celia and Griffin

Acknowledgments

Deepest thanks to my collaborators: the actors, designers and theaters that first brought these plays to life, as well as to the mentors and friends who provided fuel along the way. In particular, I'd like to thank Daniel Aukin, who directed six productions of these four plays and nourished my thinking on their trajectories at every juncture. I am also grateful for the wisdom, generosity and support of the following: Todd London, Mac Wellman, Anna D. Shapiro, Martha Lavey, Michele Volansky, Melissa Kievman, Linsay Firman, Alexandra Conley, Alaine Alldaffer, Christina Kirk, Elissa Adams, Peter Brosius, Barbara Brousal, Adam Greenfield, Tim Sanford, Michael Friedman, Louisa Thompson and lastly, lastingly, Matt Frey.

Table of Contents

this

Production History

This was originally commissioned by Playwrights Horizons with funds provided by the Doris Duke Charitable Foundation/Andrew W. Mellon Foundation Leading National Theatres Program. The world premiere of *This* was produced by Playwrights Horizons (Tim Sanford, Artistic Director; Leslie Marcus, Managing Director) in New York on December 2, 2009. It was directed by Daniel Aukin; set design was by Louisa Thompson, costume design was by Maiko Matsushima, lighting design was by Matt Frey, sound design was by Matt Tierney, original music was by Peter Eldridge; the production stage manager was Kasey Ostopchuck. The cast included:

JANE	Julianne Nicholson
MARRELL	Eisa Davis
TOM	Darren Pettie
ALAN	Glenn Fitzgerald
JEAN-PIERRE	Louis Cancelmi

This received its west coast premiere at Center Theatre Group (Michael Ritchie, Artistic Director; Edward L. Rada, Managing Director; Gordon Davidson, Founding Artistic Director) in Los Angeles, California, on July 30, 2011. It was directed by Daniel Aukin; set design was by Louisa Thompson, costume design was by Jessica Pabst, lighting design was by Matt Frey, sound design was by Matt Tierney, original music was by Peter Eldridge; the production stage manager was Elle Aghabala. The cast included:

JANE	Saffron Burrows
MARRELL	Eisa Davis
TOM	Darren Pettie
ALAN	Glenn Fitzgerald
JEAN-PIERRE	Gilles Marini

Characters

JANE, Caucasian, thirty-eight
MARRELL, African American, thirty-eight
TOM, Caucasian, early forties
ALAN, Jewish, forty
JEAN-PIERRE, French, late thirties

About the Language

The line breaks, internal capitalizations and lack of punctuation in general are intended as guidelines to the characters' thought processes, in terms of emphasis, pattern and rhythm; they should be honored, but should not feel enslaving.

When a line is indented, it indicates a line break. When there is no indentation, it indicates a continuation of the previous line. When a forward slash (" / ") appears within the dialogue, it indicates that the next line should begin, creating an overlap with the previous line.

Tom and Marrell's living room, after the dinner part of the dinner party.

TOM: Jane
JANE: No
ALAN *(Walking into the room)*: Yes Jane
TOM: Jane
MARRELL *(To Tom)*: Shhh
TOM: JANE
JANE: Not Jane
TOM: Come on Jane
JANE: Jane is a terrible idea
ALAN: Come On Jane
MARRELL *(To Alan)*: Shhh
ALAN *(To the others)*: What are we trying to get her to do
TOM: The game
JANE: I don't want to
MARRELL: It'll be fun
    (To Alan) Where were you
ALAN *(To Marrell)*: The bathroom
TOM: Jane you'll love this game

ALAN AND JANE: Jane hates games
TOM: Be a sport
MARRELL: Did you tiptoe
JANE *(To Tom)*: I can't /
    I'm not
ALAN *(To Marrell)*: What
MARRELL: Did you wake him
JANE: I hate sports and games
ALAN AND TOM: I didn't know you hated sports
JANE: So we got that straightened out
MARRELL: DID YOU WAKE THE BABY Alan
ALAN: No but I bet you just did
TOM *(To Marrell)*: Keep your voice down
    (To Jane) You're Being Closed-Minded
MARRELL: Keep Your voice down Tom
JANE: The rules are over my head
TOM: They're Simple

TOM:	MARRELL:
I AM keeping my voice down	Keep Your Voice Down

TOM: Tell her the rules are simple Alan
ALAN: The rules are simple
JANE: No they Sound simple which means
    they're not
ALAN *(To Tom)*: What are the rules
    I was in / the bathroom
TOM: You leave the room
    We make up a story
    You come back
    You ask us questions to try to figure out the story
    Simple
JANE: I have to get home
MARRELL *(Lowered voice)*: Jean-Pierre hasn't even arrived
TOM: It's still early
JANE *(Looking at her watch, lowered voice)*: Isn't he late
TOM: It's a quick game

MARRELL *(Lowered voice)*: He called
    He was stuck at a fundraiser
    He promised to make it for a drink
ALAN: Can I put on some music
JANE: I promised Maude's babysitter
MARRELL *(To Alan)*: How many times do I have to tell you
TOM *(To Alan)*: She just got the baby down
    (To Jane) So how about it Jane
JANE: Why don't you do it Tom
TOM *(To Jane)*: I can't
ALAN: All these funny expressions
    Just Got The Baby Down
    It's like the baby's depressed or
    or like you've finally succeeded in oppressing the baby
    I Just Got The Baby Down
    I Just Got The Baby Down
MARRELL: Do you think there are too many toys in this room
TOM: Everyone keeps changing the subject
    C'mon Jane
JANE *(To Tom)*: I already said I think you should be the one to play
the game
TOM: I can't

TOM:	MARRELL:
It's my game	It's his game

*(The doorbell rings. Tom and Marrell immediately turn to the bed-
room door, expecting crying. Marrell goes to answer the front door.)*

MARRELL *(On the way to the door, to Tom)*: What Happened To
The Please Knock Sign
TOM: It fell down
MARRELL: Why didn't you tape it back up
TOM: I was going to but the baby started crying on my way to /
the tape
MARRELL *(As she answers the door)*: Jean-Pierre

(They kiss hello, on both cheeks.)

I'm so glad you made it Did someone let you in downstairs
JEAN-PIERRE: A lady with a cat I'm sorry I'm late
MARRELL: It's fine You're here You're here This is my husband Tom
This is our friend Alan and
    (With a little too much emphasis) This Is Our Dear Friend Jane
JEAN-PIERRE: Hello

TOM:	JANE:	ALAN:
Nice to meet you /	Hello	I didn't get Dear Friend
		(To Jane) Did you notice that

MARRELL *(To Jean-Pierre)*: Let me take your coat
JANE *(To Alan)*: No
MARRELL *(To Jean-Pierre)*: What would you like to drink
ALAN: There's nothing left
MARRELL: What
ALAN: The wine's gone
    The beer's gone
    And I just killed that old bottle of Drambuie you keep next to
the expired baby formula
MARRELL: I need to make a sign a reminder sign I keep
    meaning to throw that out
JEAN-PIERRE: I brought some wine
ALAN: Yay
MARRELL: Are you hungry
JEAN-PIERRE: No thank you I'm fine
MARRELL: Tom could you pour Jean-Pierre a glass of wine
JEAN-PIERRE: Actually water would be great
ALAN: That we have
    I mean They have I don't live here actually And
    whatever you do Do Not
    Mistake Me For A Dear Friend
MARRELL: Tom could you pour Jean-Pierre a cold glass of water
please

(Tom turns on the tap.)

From the fridge please

(Tom opens the fridge.)

(Pronouncing it like rhymes with "Rita") From the Brita please
ALAN *(Pronouncing it like rhymes with "it-ta")*: I always thought
it was Brita
MARRELL *(Like "Rita")*: It's a Brita
    (To Jean-Pierre) So This Is Jane
JANE: We met Marrell
ALAN *(To Tom)*: Do you say Britta or Breeta
JEAN-PIERRE: You're the poet
TOM *(To Alan)*: I don't
JANE: More of a standardized test proctor these days actually
    And I teach a bit
MARRELL: She's being modest Don't be modest
JANE: I'm an aMAZing standardized test proctor
TOM *(Like "it-ta")*: I think it Is a Brita Marrell
MARRELL: I think it's my water thing Tom so I can call it whatever
I want
ALAN: Do you think it's a Britta or a Breeta
MARRELL: Leave Jean-Pierre alone Alan
ALAN: I was hoping to get the European perspective
JEAN-PIERRE *(Pronouncing it like rhymes with "Rita")*: I dated a
girl name Brita once actually
MARRELL *(To Alan)*: See I was right
ALAN *(Like "Rita")*: You knew he dated a girl named Brita once
TOM: We were about to play a game
ALAN *(To Jean-Pierre)*: Was she well-hydrated
MARRELL: Not now Tom Jean-Pierre just got here
TOM *(To Marrell, regarding the Brita)*: I don't think that filter's
been changed in about a year
MARRELL *(?!)*: What
JEAN-PIERRE: It must be hard to teach poetry
JANE: Easy actually because it's impossible
MARRELL: That's not funny Tom That's one of your Only Jobs
    Is it too much to depend on you to change the filter
TOM: I believe in tap water
JEAN-PIERRE *(To Jane)*: Who are your favorites
JANE *(?)*: Poets

JEAN-PIERRE: Yes

JANE: Oh you know Stevens

    Rich

    Oliver

    Donne and

    a bunch of much more obscure people

TOM: How did that become my job I never even use that thing

MARRELL: You must use it because I keep finding it with the water line below the filter

    Are you aware that it doesn't even work when the water line falls below the filter

JEAN-PIERRE: I wish I had more time to read for pleasure

MARRELL: It's like an open invitation to bacteria

ALAN *(To Marrell, finishing a glass of water)*: I didn't know that

(Slightest pause.)

MARRELL: Jean-Pierre's a doctor

    (With emphasis) Without Borders

ALAN: I always think that sounds like the doctor has a messy personal life

JEAN-PIERRE: That's frequently the case actually

TOM: I'm a cabinetmaker without borders

ALAN *(Musing as he opens the wine and pours himself a glass)*: But I mean don't you hate that question

JANE: What question

ALAN: The What Do You Do question

    Why do you need to know what I do

    Because you don't really mean What Do You Do what you really mean is

    How Much Money Do You Make and

    Do You Make More Money Than I Do and

    Could You Possibly Be Of Use To Me As I Continue On My Path Of Attempting To Make More Money and really the

    What Do You Do question is just a shortcut to the unspoken ranking system that's going on in all interpersonal situations at all times

    What Do You Do

I'll tell you What I Do
I drink a lot I read a lot and I jerk off with an Olympic frequency you know
I mean THAT'S What I Do

(Slight pause, as Alan takes a large sip of wine. Jean-Pierre's cell phone rings. He looks at the caller ID.)

JEAN-PIERRE: Excuse me

(Jean-Pierre moves over to the side of the room and answers the phone.)

(In French) Oui, allô
     Oui Bob m'a appelé il y a une heure et demie Qu'est-ce qui se passe?
     Ils ont quoi La ligne est très mauvaise Tu dis qu'ils
     Qu'ils ont Tiré Sur Une Ambulance?
     Oui? Ils ont C'est bien ça que t'as dit?
     Merde alors Ces salopards d'animaux C'est totalement contre ce qui était convenu
     Ils nous ont regardés droit dans les yeux en disant Pas de Violence Contre les Missions Humanitaires
     Ce mec Adou le chef de ces bandits, il m'a promis que ça n'aurait pas
     As-tu parlé à Bob?
     Il faut que tu parles à Bob
     Est-ce qu'ils ont essayé de pénétrer dans le camp?
     Okay, il faut que tu parles à Bob parce que
     C'est complètement Complètement scandaleux On va fermer tous les dispensaires mobiles de la région jusqu'à ce qu'ils acceptent
     Jusqu'à ce qu'ils jurent sur les culs de leurs putains de mères qu'ils ne porteront pas atteinte à la sécurité de notre personnel ni surtout de nos patients
     Okay, rappelles-moi dès que tu auras parlé à Bob
     Ne t'en fais pas, je serai éveillé

(English translation:
     Hi
     Yes Bob called me an hour and a half ago What's happening now?

They what This line is very bad Did you just say
Did you say they Fired On An Ambulance?
Yes they did You said yes?
Holy shit they are Animals This is totally against what we agreed
They looked us in the eye and said No Violence Toward Huma-
nitarian Missions
That guy that head bandit Adou promised me that this wouldn't
Have you talked to Bob?
You need to talk to Bob
Have they tried to enter the IDP camp?
Okay, you need to talk to Bob because
this is totally Totally outrageous We're going to have to shut
down all mobile clinics in the area until they agree
Until they swear on their mothers' assholes that they will not vio-
late the safety of our staff and especially our patients
Okay, call me after you talk to Bob
Don't worry about it I'll be up)

(Jean-Pierre hangs up.)

(In English, to all) Sorry
MARRELL *(Don't worry about it)*: Please

(Slight pause.)

ALAN: Maybe you should
   call them back

*(The residue of the mysteriously seductive French words still hanging
in the air, everyone in the room silently agrees that Alan's idea is an
excellent one.)*

TOM: Time for the game
   Time for you to leave the room Jane
JANE: Aw Tom I told you I don't want to play
TOM: It's a fast-moving game
JANE *(Giving in and grabbing her coat)*: I'm putting on my coat and
I'm leaving in ten minutes

Even if the game's not over
I Promised Maude's Babysitter
MARRELL *(To Jane)*: Don't put on your coat
TOM: Just leave the room and we'll
    make up our story
JANE: Where should I go to leave the room
MARRELL: The bedroom I guess /
    Oh no
TOM AND MARRELL: Not The Bedroom
MARRELL *(To Jean-Pierre)*: We have a baby
    who sleeps in fifteen-minute increments

(She laughs an insane, sleep-deprived mother's laugh.)

But it's okay A baby doesn't mean your life stops We still have
dinner parties
TOM *(?, to Marrell)*: We do
MARRELL: Well this is our first actually but we'll
    probably make this a weekly thing
ALAN: GREAT I'm Free For All Foreseeable Weeks
TOM AND MARRELL: Shhh
JANE: I'll wait in the hall
TOM AND MARRELL: Okay
JANE: When do I come back in
TOM: We'll call you

(Jane leaves.)

MARRELL *(To Jean-Pierre)*: Isn't she great
TOM *(To the French guy)*: Have you ever played this game Pierre
JEAN-PIERRE: Jean-Pierre
    No
TOM AND MARRELL: What
JEAN-PIERRE: I've never played this game
MARRELL: Oh
TOM: It's a great game
JEAN-PIERRE: Great
    Are you sure she want to play

TOM: Do people call you anything for short

JEAN-PIERRE: Like what

TOM: JP

PJ

JEAN-PIERRE: PJ

No

MARRELL: I'm glad to hear that

JEAN-PIERRE: How do you people know each other

MARRELL: Alan and Jane and I went to college together

And Tom was there too actually

TOM: She means I worked there

JEAN-PIERRE: Where

TOM: At the college

I mowed the ivy

MARRELL: I hate it when you make that joke

TOM: It's not a joke

MARRELL: Yes it is

It's some kind of horticultural-slash-socioeconomic joke

ALAN: Oh man I Hate

horticultural-slash-socioeconomic jokes

TOM *(To Jean-Pierre)*: Their good fortune embarrasses them

ALAN: You spent more time in the library than I did Tom

TOM: I was quite happy to better myself by inhaling their privileged carbon dioxide

MARRELL: That sounds so bitter / why do you sound so bitter

TOM: I'm not bitter I'm grateful

(To Jean-Pierre) Through the ivy I met my wife

MARRELL *(To Jean-Pierre)*: The four of us have known each other forever

ALAN: That sounds bleak Marrell

MARRELL *(?)*: Forever

Since when did Forever become bleak Tom

(Pointing across the room) where did that plank come from

TOM: That's not a plank Marrell That's black maple

MARRELL: Why is it here

TOM: I'm going to use it for something

(Slightest pause.)

MARRELL: I guess I'm sort of begging you Tom that
    before you bring any more things you're Going To Use For
Something into our home you first use all the things you're Going
To Use For Something that are already here

(Slight pause.)

JEAN-PIERRE: So do we make up a story now
ALAN: Yes What's our story
TOM: What
MARRELL: Oh Right Here's the thing
TOM: There is no story
JEAN-PIERRE: I thought you said we make up a story
MARRELL: That's just what you say
TOM: That's what the person's supposed to think /
    That's part of the fun
MARRELL: It's confusing until you do it but it's fun
    We played it one night at a friend's house
ALAN *(?)*: Was it at a Dear Friend's house
MARRELL *(Ignoring Alan)*: This was before we had the baby
TOM: That's the game
ALAN: I don't get it
TOM: There's nothing not to get
    That's the game
    There's no story
MARRELL: That's the point
JEAN-PIERRE: What's the point
TOM: It's an interesting psychological exercise because
    the player writes her own story
ALAN: Oh but Jane hates games
MARRELL: This one is fun
    and funny
ALAN: Jane could use some funny fun
TOM: Jane'll be great
JEAN-PIERRE *(?)*: But she thinks we've made up a story
TOM: Yes
ALAN *(Looking through the cupboards)*: Are you sure you don't
have anything else that's not wine to drink

MARRELL: No
ALAN: No you're not sure
MARRELL *(In lowered tones)*: I thought you were cutting back
ALAN *(In lowered tones)*: It's still in the planning stages She
    looks sad
MARRELL *(?)*: Jane
    Because it's only been a year
ALAN *(In lowered tones, indicating Jean-Pierre)*: So why are you
setting her up
MARRELL *(Lowered tones)*: I'm not setting her up
ALAN *(Lowered tones)*: Marrell
MARRELL *(Lowered tones)*: Because it's been a whole year

(Jean-Pierre has lit up a cigarette and everyone stares at him. He puts out the cigarette.)

JEAN-PIERRE: I'm sorry
    I should have asked I'm
    so used to being in places where everyone smokes
TOM: Well our infant son is trying to kick nicotine so
MARRELL: Tom
    I'm sorry Jean-Pierre
    I should make a sign
TOM: How many signs do you think we should have in the apartment Marrell
JEAN-PIERRE: I'm sorry

(Jane knocks on the door.)

JANE *(From off)*: Can I come back inside yet
TOM *(Calling to Jane)*: Yes
ALAN *(Calling to Jane)*: Hi Jane
TOM *(Calling to Jane)*: No
    Wait
    (To the people in the room) Did I explain the rules
MARRELL AND ALAN: No
TOM: If she asks a question that ends in a vowel we say No
    If she asks a question that ends in a consonant we say Yes
    If she asks a question that ends in a Y we say maybe

JEAN-PIERRE: Vowel Yes
    Consonant No
    Y Maybe
ALAN *(Correcting Jean-Pierre)*: Other way around
    Vowel No
    Consonant Yes
    Y Maybe
TOM: Right That's it
    Jane you can come in

(Jane reenters through the front door.)

JANE: Your neighbor wants to know if you can feed her cat for a
few days next week
ALAN *(?)*: The super intense one
JEAN-PIERRE *(?)*: The cat
ALAN: The neighbor She's
    one of those people you'd rather talk about than to
MARRELL: But she's a very destabilizing person because just when
you've
    written her off she'll suddenly tell you your sweater's really
cute
ALAN: She's an evil genius
MARRELL: So what did you tell her
JANE: I smiled and nodded
MARRELL *(?)*: You nodded
    So now I have to feed her cat in addition to feeding our baby
TOM: Uh are you equating the two responsibilities Marrell
JANE: I didn't say yes I just smiled and nodded
ALAN: Well noncommitally done Jane
JANE *(Looking at her watch)*: Thank you So
    I'm just supposed to start asking questions
TOM: Uh-huh
JANE: Are you going to tell me when to start
MARRELL: Just start
TOM: Wait Did we tell you that you can only
    ask Yes or No questions
JANE: No

ALAN: You can only ask Yes or No questions
JANE: Really That seems so
TOM: What
JANE *(?)*: This is the fun game
MARRELL: Just Start
JANE: Okay I'm starting
    Is the story real
ALL EXCEPT JANE *(Though Alan's response is always very slightly delayed)*: Yes
JANE: Okay
    Is the story about a man
ALL EXCEPT JANE: Yes
JANE: Okay
    About him um
    only
ALL EXCEPT JANE: Maybe
JANE: Oh Is the story about a woman
ALL EXCEPT JANE: Yes
JANE: So it's about a man and a woman
ALL EXCEPT JANE: Yes
JANE: I got that right Okay do
    they know each other
ALL EXCEPT JANE: Yes
JANE: Are they close
ALL EXCEPT JANE: No
JANE: But they've met
ALL EXCEPT JANE: Yes
JANE: Would they like to know each other better
ALL EXCEPT JANE: Yes
ALAN *(Admonishing)*: Were you listening at the door
JANE: Just lucky I guess Would they like to know each other
    in a romantic way
ALL EXCEPT JANE: Maybe
JANE *(?)*: They're not sure
ALL EXCEPT JANE: No
JANE: Or is one of them unaware of the attraction
ALL EXCEPT JANE: Yes
JANE: Is it the man

ALL EXCEPT JANE: Yes

JANE: So the man doesn't know about the woman's feelings

ALL EXCEPT JANE: Yes

JANE: Am I especially good at this game

ALL EXCEPT JANE: No

JANE: Okay uh
    is the man married

ALL EXCEPT JANE: Yes

JANE: All right
    Is the woman married

ALL EXCEPT JANE: Yes

JANE: I can't believe you don't think I'm good at this game

(Everyone, except Alan, gets that this isn't really a question.)

ALAN: No

JANE: Okay so the woman is she
    married um
    happily

ALL EXCEPT JANE: Maybe

JANE: That's confusing And she's attracted to this other man

ALL EXCEPT JANE: Yes

JANE: Okay Well
    does her spouse know about his wife's attraction to a
married man

ALL EXCEPT JANE: Yes

JANE: Does this bother her spouse

ALL EXCEPT JANE: No

JANE: Is he extraordinarily mature

ALL EXCEPT JANE: No

JANE: He sounds evolved

ALL EXCEPT JANE: Yes

JANE: He's evolved but not mature That seems contradictory

ALL EXCEPT JANE: Maybe

JANE: Maybe
    It sounds like you're all going easy on this woman It sounds
like she should pay more attention to her husband instead of fan-
tasizing about this other guy

ALL EXCEPT JANE: Maybe
TOM: These aren't yes or no questions
JANE: Sorry Is this woman twenty
ALL EXCEPT JANE: Maybe
JANE: Is she thirty
ALL EXCEPT JANE: Maybe
JANE: You're not giving me yes or no answers You're not making
any sense
    Is she thirty-five
ALL EXCEPT JANE: No
JANE: Is she forty
ALL EXCEPT JANE: Maybe
JANE: Stop it Is she thirty-eight
ALL EXCEPT JANE: Yes
JANE: Finally

(Slight pause.)

Wait a minute Is her husband alive
ALL EXCEPT JANE: No

(Slight pause.)

JANE: Is this woman someone we know
ALL EXCEPT JANE: Yes
JANE: Someone we know very well
ALL EXCEPT JANE: Yes
JANE: Someone in this room
ALL EXCEPT JANE: Yes
JANE: Someone called
    what I'm called
ALL EXCEPT JANE: Yes

(Slight pause.)

JANE: Is this supposed to be funny
ALAN *(Before he understands it's a real question)*: Maybe

(Slight pause. Jane gets up to leave.)

TOM: Where are you going
JANE: Home
MARRELL: Don't go Jane
TOM *(Trying to grab her arm):* No no It was just a game Jane /
    There was no story
    You made it up yourself
    It's just a fun
    game
MARRELL: Come on Jane
ALAN *(Punctuating the above after Jane gets up)*: Jane Jane Jane
JANE *(As she grabs her bag and exits in a hurry)*: How Many Times
Do I have To Tell You
    Jane Hates Games
ALAN: Yes

The next day. The hallway outside of Jane's apartment. She answers the door. There is the sound of piano practicing in the background.

TOM *(Softly)*: So
JANE: What
TOM: Sorry
JANE: Okay
TOM: Are you
JANE *(?)*: Sorry
TOM *(Clarifying)*: Okay
JANE: I don't feel like talking Tom
TOM: It was supposed to be fun
      I would never uh / intentionally
JANE *(Cutting him off)*: Maude's practicing
      and I'm in the middle of something
TOM: Sorry
JANE: No it's good for me to be in the middle of something I usually
never get past the beginning of something these days so you know
TOM: This is harder than I thought
JANE: Apologizing
TOM: Talking to you

JANE: Good because I don't want you to
    apologize anymore
TOM: I thought you were going to say talk to me
JANE: What
TOM: That you didn't want to talk to me anymore
JANE: I'm just tired of I'm Sorry In general In life It's all I've
heard for the past year I'm cranky
    I'm sorry
TOM: Did you say that as a joke
JANE: No They're necessary little words I'm Sorry Just like Please
and Thank You but just like Please and Thank You I'm Sorry gets
old you know
TOM: Did he catch up with you
JANE: Who
TOM: The Doctor Without Borders
JANE *(?)*: Jean-Pierre
    walked me to the subway
TOM: Did you know you were being / set up
JANE: I knew Marrell wanted me to meet him
TOM: I didn't know you were being set up
JANE: Why should you know
TOM: Because it's my
    house
JANE *(?)*: So
TOM *(Referring to what Maude is playing)*: I know this song
JANE: Everyone knows this song
TOM: What do you think of him
JANE *(?)*: Bach
TOM: The doctor
JANE: I don't know Why do you ask
TOM: Because I'm interested
    Because you deserve to
JANE *(?)*: have sex again
    you were going to say
TOM: Be with someone I was
    going to say
JANE: He's nice he seems nice
TOM: He seems French

JANE: He is French
    (Starting to close the door) Tell Marrell I'll see her tomorrow
TOM: He's not your type
JANE: What's my type
TOM: He's not like Roy
JANE: He's not black you mean
TOM: No
    that's not what I mean
JANE *(Apologizing)*: See I'm too cranky to be anybody's type

(She tries to close the door again.)

TOM: Were you thinking about me
JANE: What
TOM: In the game
JANE: I don't want to talk about the game
TOM: I'm / sorry
JANE: Stop Apologizing
TOM: I don't know what I'm saying
JANE: You and Marrell are tired When they're not making you
happy babies make a person /
    tired
TOM: I was jealous
JANE *(?)*: Of the baby
TOM: The borderless doctor
JANE: Why
    Because he's French
TOM: No
JANE: Because he's a doctor
TOM: No
JANE: Because he doesn't have borders
TOM: Because he has access
    to you
JANE: That's so uh silly
TOM: I wanted to
    tell you something
JANE *(Closing the door)*: Good night Tom
TOM: I've wanted to tell you something for a long time

(Slight pause.)

JANE: I don't want you to
TOM: Why
JANE: I don't know
     Good night
TOM: Why
JANE: Because I don't quite know what you're talking about
TOM: You know exactly what I'm not quite talking about
JANE: I have to go assign grades to creative writing
TOM: You have
     invaded my psyche Jane
JANE: Stop it / Stop this
TOM: You think it's because I'm tired
     It's not because I'm tired
JANE: Stop this Tom
TOM: I'm sorry about the game / Wait Wait
JANE: STOP IT
TOM: I think about you Jane
     You invade perfectly benign thoughts all the time
     I'll be buying bread trying to figure out the optimal number
of grains and there you will be with your hand clasping the back
of your neck lost in thought
JANE: In your bread Tom
TOM: In my head Jane
     There you'll be standing with your hand on your hip and
your scrunched-up smile
     and I'll think about how I want to touch you
     I watch you I've been watching you
     for years and
     I'm not stupid I know I'm going through something and I
     know it's partly adjusting to having a child and nothing will
be the same and I know it's
     partly the stress of my close-but-never-a-cigar business and
     it's also just this feeling that I'm the guy who never gets in
the door
     never gets past the waiting area
     and the chairs are uncomfortable in the waiting area

and I don't know what I'm saying except that I feel the only thing
that gives me any pleasure lately
and I know this is a terrible thing to say
especially because Marrell and I have just been given the gift
of this boy but
the only thing that gives me any pleasure
is the thought of touching you Jane
some day and
sometimes I hear
these voice-overs in my head narrating my life and it's true
that sometimes the voice just sounds like bad advertising copy but
sometimes the voice says things that feel very
compelling and that voice
has started narrating some things I'm finding very very hard
to resist
and the other thing I think about as I think about touching
you is that I've thought about touching you for so long and forgive me for saying this but when Roy
when Roy died
and I know this is shameful but when he died I thought
Oh maybe it could be me now Maybe I could
and I know I know
I'm sorry
but Jane there's a small part of me that always wondered
what if
what if
(An actual proposition) What If Jane
I'm sorry
JANE: PLEASE STOP
APOLOGIZING Tom

*(Tom leans in to kiss Jane. She shoves him. He leans in to kiss her
again. She resists at first. Then she doesn't. Their kiss turns into grop-
ing that brings them to the other side of the open door. As Maude
continues to practice the piano in the other room, Jane and Tom have
upright sex behind the door.)*

The next day. Marrell and Jane are sitting in a public place. Jane is very nervous. Marrell has a stroller beside her and is pushing it back and forth periodically throughout the scene to make sure the baby stays asleep. Marrell and Jane each hold freshly purchased ice-cream cones. Marrell eats hers throughout the scene, while Jane just holds hers.

MARRELL: I'm unhappy
JANE: You are
MARRELL: Did you mean to say that as a question
JANE: What did I say
MARRELL: You said You Are like a
    statement
    You said You Are
    Like You Are Unhappy
JANE: I meant to say
    (?) You Are
MARRELL: Yes I am
JANE: I'm sorry
MARRELL: It's not your fault
    You should take a lick you know

JANE: I'm sorry

MARRELL: It's your cone Don't you want to know
    what kind of unhappy I am

JANE *(?)*: There are kinds

MARRELL *(Explaining the categories)*: Personal Marital Professional
Existential or Interdisciplinary

JANE *(?)*: Interdisciplinary

MARRELL: Marital
    Why did you guess interdisciplinary

JANE: I don't know
    Isn't most people's unhappiness interdisciplinary
    How do you delineate the precise source of your unhappiness

MARRELL: I've been thinking very clearly lately

JANE: That's great

MARRELL: You sound surprised

JANE: Just jealous

MARRELL: Do you think everybody knows
    about my marital unhappiness

JANE: No I mean I doubt it No no

MARRELL: Tom knows
    Don't you think Tom knows he's unhappy

JANE: How would I know

MARRELL: Because you know us
    together

JANE: But I'm not alone with you together

MARRELL: You're alone with us all the time

JANE: But not alone alone

MARRELL: Does that matter

JANE: Doesn't it

MARRELL: But you're alone with us individually

JANE: What do you mean

MARRELL: I don't know Tom's
    perpetually unhappy That's his schtick

JANE: Tom has a schtick

MARRELL: Everybody has a schtick
    His is the brooding craftsman
    The stoic woodworker
    The martyred artist

JANE: That's a complicated schtick

MARRELL: Tom stopped voting

JANE *(?)*: He did

MARRELL: I don't know who he is anymore
   He blogs about Scandinavian spoon carving instead of
   building the nursery we need

JANE: I hate that word blog
   It sounds like a large accumulation of snot

MARRELL: What do you think I should do

JANE: I think you should talk to someone

MARRELL: That's what I'm doing

JANE: Together I mean
   To a professional person

MARRELL: He always thinks he's smarter than the therapist
   Oh wait a minute I'm thinking of me
   He's never actually been in therapy
   What I can't tell is if we're unhappy Together
   Individually
   or Both Of The Above

JANE: I
   don't know what to say

MARRELL: I don't really know how he feels
   He's a patient man
   He can spend four weeks installing a hinge
   Maybe it's just me

JANE: Probably

MARRELL *(?)*: I love my husband

JANE: Don't say it as a question

MARRELL *(!)*: I Love My Husband

JANE: Don't say it like it's aberrant

MARRELL *(Truly)*: I love my husband

JANE: Yes and vice versa emphatically yes

MARRELL: And the baby

JANE: Of course the baby

MARRELL: I've been reading about postpartum depression

JANE: Maybe you should talk to your doctor

MARRELL: How many doctors do you want me to
   talk to Jane

JANE: I'm sorry
  I thought you said you were thinking clearly
MARRELL: Maybe I meant I'm thinking
  differently and stop saying you're sorry for things that aren't
your fault
JANE: If you're having a hard time connecting with your baby /
then maybe you should
MARRELL: That's not what I said
JANE: Okay
MARRELL: So what do you think of him
JANE: I love Henry
MARRELL: I know you love my son You don't have a choice I'm
  talking about Jean-Pierre
JANE: Oh He seems nice
MARRELL: That's it
JANE: I only just met him
MARRELL: Tom never wants to have sex
JANE: Where did that come from
MARRELL: Maybe it's to do with the baby but frankly it predates
the baby by a long time
JANE: No Why
  are you telling me this
MARRELL: Because you're my best friend and I need some
  help
JANE: I'm sorry I
  want to help
MARRELL: You never questioned your marriage
JANE: Are you asking me or telling me
MARRELL: Can we stop talking about punctuation You never
  said to yourself
  What If I Made A Terrible Mistake
  You never said to yourself
  What if instead of my husband I was supposed to marry
  (Pointing randomly at a man in the street) That Guy There
JANE: I've never thought I should marry That Guy There
MARRELL: You know what I mean
JANE: You're tired You're both tired
MARRELL: That's your diagnosis for everything

JANE: It explains a lot don't you think
MARRELL: When I met Tom I thought Oh
    There it is This is it that
    chemical dialogue that defies words or logic
    Oh
    And now I can't feel it anymore
JANE: It's still there
MARRELL: Where

(Pause.)

I thought The Whole Point is that you make each other
    Feel Better in a marriage
JANE: You do
MARRELL: Not lately
JANE: That doesn't mean you can't
MARRELL: Too often we make each other feel worse
JANE: Because
    You're Tired
MARRELL: I think you might be tired Jane
JANE: I think I am yes
MARRELL: Do you think I should leave him
JANE: NO
    Why would you do that
MARRELL: I wouldn't
    I don't think
    I was just saying it out loud
JANE: Don't Do That
MARRELL: Say things out loud
JANE: Leave him
    I mean Don't Leave Him
    That's a dumb thing to say
    You love each other
MARRELL: We have arguments that go from zero to sixty in seconds flat
JANE: Big deal
MARRELL: He constantly points out my patterns in public He's a pattern-pointer-outer

JANE: So what

MARRELL: He never wants to have sex
    I want to have sex
    I want to have sex with other men

JANE: Don't Do That

MARRELL: Why are you getting so upset It's just an idea

JANE: Adultery is not the answer

MARRELL: That sounds like a bumper sticker

JANE: It's the truth You're / just

MARRELL: I'm / tired of you saying I'm tired

JANE: Okay I won't say it but
    you're not leaving him
    You're not
    Make a pro/con chart
    You'll see
    All the good outweighs the bad

MARRELL: I HATE
    pro/con charts

JANE: You've Been Together Since You Were Twenty

MARRELL: Exactly
    And Was There A Time When I Was Dumber Than I Was
When I was Twenty
    with the possible exception of right now

(Slight pause.)

What's wrong

JANE: I'm not feeling very well

MARRELL: It's melting all over your hand

(The ice cream falls onto the ground, leaving Jane holding the cone.)

JANE: I'm sorry

MARRELL *(Regarding the cone)*: Oops

*(While still pushing the stroller back and forth, Marrell puts the rest
of her own cone in her mouth, so that it's sticking out, freeing up a
hand to reach for a baby wipe, which she hands to Jane. Jane picks up*

the fallen ice cream with the wipe and throws it in a trashcan, while Marrell finishes her cone.)

How do you do it
JANE: What
MARRELL: You just
    don't allow yourself to make bad decisions
    Your moral compass is
    true
JANE: Why are you saying that
MARRELL: Because it's true that it's true
JANE: Stop it Marrell
MARRELL: It is It's
    one of my favorite things about you You
    know how to keep the wolf away from the door
JANE: The wolf is never away from the door The wolf IS the door
Marrell
MARRELL: He's going to call you
JANE: Tell Him Not To
MARRELL: Who
JANE: Who do you mean
MARRELL: Jean-Pierre He's going to
    ask you out on a date

(Slight pause.)

Someone should have sex with him I mean he's
    Someone Who Should Be Slept With I mean he
    Should Not Be Left Unslept With
JANE: I'm not feeling well Marrell
    I'm sorry

(Jane leaves abruptly.)

Tom and Marrell's apartment. It's the middle of the night. Marrell is composing a song on the piano. Tom is sanding a piece of wood.

MARRELL *(Singing)*:
> I know
> You think
> More than you say
> I think
> You know
> At the end of the day
> One of us will be left
> La la la la bereft
> One of us will leave
> One of us left
> Who knows
> Who's who

(In the bedroom, about halfway through the song—Marrell won't actually get through the whole song—the baby wakes up. In the living room a silent negotiation ensues to determine: whose turn it is to go in; whose work is more important; and when will this ever get easier?)

Jane unlocks the door and enters her apartment. Alan is sitting in a chair in the relative dark, staring at his hands.

JANE: Is she asleep
ALAN: Uh-huh
JANE: Why are you sitting in the almost dark
ALAN: Shouldn't they match
JANE: What
ALAN: Shouldn't the veins in a person's hands be symmetrical I mean they're both
    hands They should look alike
JANE: I think it's okay

(Jane unzips her coat, but then has to step out of it, because the zipper is broken at the bottom.)

ALAN *(Regarding her coat)*: You haven't fixed that yet
JANE: No Mom I haven't
ALAN: What did that zipper ever do to you
JANE: It broke
ALAN: How was work

JANE: Which work

ALAN: Both works

JANE: Only three of my poetry students showed up and
     then when I was proctoring I caught two kids cheating

ALAN: What did you do

JANE: Nothing It was a practice test

ALAN: So they were only practicing cheating

JANE: And they definitely need more practice Did
     Maude have homework

ALAN: I was
     reading over her shoulder and
     the book about Troy they're reading in her class
     says Patroklos and Achilles are "cousins"

JANE: They're lovers

ALAN: Her textbook says they're "cousins"

JANE: Did you set her straight

ALAN: So to speak I thought that was your job

JANE: I'll write a letter to the Board of Ed

ALAN: I told her they weren't cousins

JANE: What did she say

ALAN: She said that was confusing because
     it said so right there in the book that they were cousins

JANE: What did you say

ALAN: I said sometimes books are wrong

JANE: I've been down that road with her
     That's when she says
     Sometimes Mothers Are Wrong
     and then when I say That's True
     But Not This Time
     and then when she says You Always Say That
     and then when I say You're Right

(Slight pause.)

ALAN: Pretty much

JANE: I'm telling you Very Soon she'll be wearing the pants in this
household and it's All My Fault

The other night she was taking forever to get into bed and
I couldn't even think of a proper threat
ALAN: You threaten your daughter Jane
JANE: All I could come up with was
    You Get In Bed Right Now Young Lady Or A Really Bad
Threat
ALAN: Scary
JANE: Right I didn't even have the presence of mind to go with
Or Else
    which at least has a little mystique to it
    Did you eat anything
ALAN: Your cupboard is bare
JANE: I'm sorry What did you give Maude
ALAN: Mac and cheese and frozen peas
JANE: That's poetic and
    you didn't answer my question
ALAN: Mac and Cheese / Mac and Cheese
JANE: No why are you sitting in the almost dark
ALAN: It's the human condition Jane in case you haven't noticed

(Jane turns on a light. Alan's flask rests at the foot of his chair. Jane looks around at her messy house.)

JANE: This place is a disaster

(Jane starts to "clean," but really just moves things to different piles.)

ALAN: I know I was almost moved to do something about it

(Jane turns off a light.)

JANE: But you got distracted by your physical asymmetry
    Can I have a sip
ALAN: You next to never drink What's the occasion
JANE: It's next to never

(Jane takes a swig and sits down. Slight pause.)

ALAN: I'm thinking of adding a second L to my name
JANE: Why
ALAN: Like Ginsberg
    Shake things up
JANE: Why
ALAN: Stop analyzing
JANE: If you want to be like Ginsberg you also need to change the
second A to an E
ALAN: I bet my life would have been different with two L's and
an E
    Or do you think the problem is more systemic than that
because
    Alan is somebody's uncle Alan's got Hush Puppies written
all over it
JANE: So try adding an I
    Pronounce it the French way
ALAN *(?)*: Alain
JANE: Uh-huh
ALAN: Did you get that idea from
    (Overly pronounced) Jean-Pierre
JANE: No

(They overlap through the following:)

ALAN: I bet you did
JANE: No
    I didn't
ALAN: I bet you did
JANE: I didn't
ALAN: Did
JANE: Didn't
ALAN *(Sung)*:
    I BET YOU DID

(Jane stops.)

JANE: What is wrong with you
    exactly

(Slight pause before Alan gives the question a thorough and silently enumerated answer.)

ALAN: Um
    I'm somewhat shallow
    as far as the casual observer is concerned
    I spend the better part of my life waiting for a wake-up call
    you know the thing that will make everything come into focus
and that I can point to later when I'm writing my memoir
    I habitually press Reply All
    A fair number of my sentences begin with When I Almost
Joined The Peace Corps
    I'm subversive by impulse but lazy by nature
    I fall in love with people serially for the length of a long
weekend
    I'm a latenik
    If there's a downside I find its underbelly
    I can't stop myself from pressing elevator buttons that have
already been pressed
    I haven't flossed my teeth in weeks
    And
    oh I don't know should I go on

(Slight pause, during which Jane turns the light back on again.)

JANE *(?)*: You're a Reply All-er

(Slight pause, during which Alan affirms that he is.)

Some people might say you have a problem with self-involvement
ALAN: I have no problem with self-involvement
    except in others
JANE: Nice outfit
ALAN: Really I don't stand behind it
JANE: Why not
ALAN: I don't know I just don't I
    don't find it convincing
JANE: Of what

ALAN: My undeniable allure

JANE: It is hard to deny

ALAN: Not a laughing matter Jane Outfits

are important when you can't rely on other things I mean you're lucky You

still have two or three years left when you can attract people By Looks Alone

JANE: Gee thanks Alan

ALAN: Whereas I'm not that fortunate

I don't have that option I've

never had that option

I've always had to reel them in with my humor and intellect that together work to obscure my physical shortcomings and

it's Completely Exhausting

JANE: Alan

You're very

handsome

ALAN: You know what Really tires me out

I mean Really Really

When attractive people don't acknowledge the edge they have in Every Single Situation In Life with the sole exception of when rapists are selecting their prey

That's pretty much the only circumstance I can think of when it's

bad to be hot

The pretty people and the likable people have a much easier time of it on this planet

And don't even get me started on the likable pretty people

Like You You're a person whose name people regularly precede with Everybody Loves

whereas I'm a person whose name people regularly precede with Everybody Could Take Or Leave

I say when are the unlikable unattractive people ever gonna catch a break

When is it gonna be Our Turn

JANE: Okay but sometimes there's a difference Alan between how the world sees you and how you wish the world would see you

ALAN: How do you wish the world would see you Jane

JANE: I would like the world to say that
    Jane has a ready smile
ALAN: But you don't have a ready smile
JANE: I know but that's what I wish
ALAN: I actually think you have a reluctant smile
JANE: Jane Has A Ready Smile
ALAN: You can't expect the world to say it if it's not true
JANE: Maybe I'll make it true

(Slight pause before Jane fashions a laborious smile.)

ALAN: That's a fake smile

(Jane tries again.)

That's a crazed smile

(Jane tries again.)

That's a forced smile

(Again.)

That's a crying-on-the-inside smile

(Again.)

That's an Alan-inadvertently-hit-a-chord smile

(Again.)

That's a lame-attempt-to-dispute-the-fact smile

(Again, but utterly unsuccessful.)

I don't know what that is except the opposite of a ready smile

(Jane is crying. Pause.)

JANE: I've done something stupid

ALAN: But you're in luck because you're pretty and likable so it'll all be fine

JANE: I don't think it will

ALAN: What did you do

JANE: I don't think I can tell you

ALAN: Was it that bad

JANE: Yes

ALAN: You feel shame

JANE: Yes

ALAN: You should be like me I can turn my shame on and off

JANE: Then I don't think it qualifies

ALAN: Why is shame such an exalted concept

JANE: Because it means you have a gauge

for conduct for

behavior

People do stupid things when they ignore the gauge

ALAN: Wow what did you do

JANE: I just told you that I'm not going to tell you

ALAN: So you're going out of your way to tell me that there's something huge you're keeping from me

JANE: A PERSON CAN OFFER HELP WITHOUT KNOWING WHAT THE PROBLEM IS ALAN

ALAN: Oh so it's blind help you're after Why didn't you say so

Is it something you can't undo

JANE: Yes

ALAN: So don't do it again

JANE: I won't I really won't

ALAN: So what do you want from me Absolution

JANE: Please don't mock me right now

ALAN: I was mocking me The problem is

you're probably not capable of pretending whatever it was never happened and acting normal

Anyway you need to stop this

JANE: What

ALAN *(Gesturing around)*: This

This way of being

You need to clean your house and buy some groceries and
repair your coat and fix your life
　　And whatever you did It's Done

(Slight pause.)

Speaking of Jean-Pierre
JANE: This is not about Jean-Pierre

(Slight pause.)

Tell me this will be all right Alan
ALAN: Lots of things will be all right Jane and there's no reason
this couldn't be one of them

(Slight pause.)

JANE: You know
　　I've always wanted to be the woman gay men would want to
have sex with if they wanted to have sex with women and weren't
gay
　　Maybe you should fall in love with me Alan
　　Maybe that will fix everything
　　Maybe it's not too late
　　Vaginas aren't that bad
ALAN *(Sincerely)*: I wish

(Slight pause.)

Do nothing Jane
　　That's usually the best thing
JANE: Except when it isn't

Alan appears on a talk show. Applause before the voice of the Talk Show Host greets him warmly, amplified over speakers. Note: the Host's Voice should be read live, offstage.

HOST'S VOICE: Alan Stimple ladies and gentlemen
    Good to see you again sir
ALAN: Nice to be here How have you been
HOST'S VOICE: Don't you know
    I always feel like you should know that already
ALAN: But remember I'm a mnemonist not a mentalist Jim
    I don't predict the future I recall the past
HOST'S VOICE: That's right Just to remind everyone of Mr. Stimple's skill He is able to reproduce
    (?) verbatim right
ALAN: Verbatim yes
HOST'S VOICE: exactly
    things he has heard only one time
ALAN: It's a blessing and a curse
    I mean there's what you want to remember
    and there's what you want to forget
    I can't forget to save my life

HOST'S VOICE: Man is that
    fun or or just a giant pain in / the
ALAN *(Forgetting that he's on TV by the end of the speech)*: It's you
know it's
    complicated It's I
    do enjoy the broad perspective I'm able to maintain but
    at times I must admit I sort of dream of
    I really kind of dream of
    of of
    trying to recall the
    color of the sky the day my parents got divorced
    or the content of the speech I gave at my sister's wedding
    or the nutritional information on the cereal box I was holding
this morning and not being able to
    I would give almost anything in fact
    Anything
    I would
    to draw a blank
    to find my hands
    and head
    full of nothing
    you know where I could start from some sort of
    scratch
HOST'S VOICE: Well we have a surprise for you
ALAN: Okay
HOST'S VOICE: When you were in the green room chatting with
our producer Mandy we caught the whole thing on tape

*(Alan nods his head and smiles painfully. He can no longer bear being
a dancing bear.)*

So what we're going to do is we're going to test you by having you
repeat that
    conversation
    and then we'll watch the film to check your accuracy
ALAN: Okay
HOST'S VOICE: Please tell us about your exchange with Mandy

ALAN: Mandy said
    Hello Alan We're Glad You Made It
    I said
    I Almost Didn't Something Was Going On With The Subways
    Mandy said
    What Do You Want To Uh Cover This Time
    I said
    Well Last Time I Was On We Did A Night Before The First
Day Of School From My Childhood So Maybe We Should Do
Something From My College Years A Lecture Or Something Like
That
    Mandy said
    Or Maybe We'll Uh You Know Maybe We'll Surprise You
    I said
    Okay Mandy Knock Yourselves Out
    Mandy said
    Five Minutes Until Airtime
    I said
    The Bathroom Is This Way Right
    Mandy smiled and said Don't You Remember Alan and
I laughed politely and that was it
HOST'S VOICE: Okay great Now let's watch the tape

(The tape is played. Alan has remembered the exchange perfectly. Applause.)

(In amaᴣement) Alan Stimple ladies and gentlemen

A jazz club. Marrell sits at a piano and sings "After All." Jean-Pierre sits at a table.

MARRELL *(Singing)*:
How long
Is too long
Who's the first to know
The one who says stop
Or the one who's first to go
See you
Seeing me
What do you perceive
A book left open
Or a penchant to deceive
And after all
Is said and undone
I wonder who's the lucky one
After all
A mess
I confess
What's it going to be

On again off again
No lifetime guarantee
And after all
Is said and undone
I wonder who's the guilty one
After all
Don't walk
Away my dear
Come back and catch my eye
I dare you to tell me
It's worth another try
And after all
Is said and undone
I wonder who's the lonely one
After all

(Jean-Pierre applauds.)

(Into the mike) Thank you I'll be
    (Starts to walk away before realizing she didn't finish, then into mike) back

(Marrell walks backstage. Jean-Pierre takes a sip of his drink and Marrell emerges from backstage, joining Jean-Pierre at the table. She leans over and kisses him hello.)

JEAN-PIERRE: Fantastic
MARRELL: I'm glad you made it

(Jane enters from outside, a bit breathless, clapping.)

JANE: I missed your first set didn't I
MARRELL: So why are you applauding
JANE: I bet it was great
MARRELL: What do you call that
    speculative applause
JEAN-PIERRE *(To Jane, about Marrell)*: Fantastic
MARRELL: You remember Jean-Pierre

JANE: Yes Marrell Hello
JEAN-PIERRE: Hello
JANE *(Leaning in and kissing Marrell)*: Hello
MARRELL: Hello
JANE: My babysitter's babysitter was late
MARRELL: My babysitter was snoring on the couch
    What can I get you to drink

JEAN-PIERRE:	JANE:
I'll go	No you sit I'll go

MARRELL: No no I Want You Two To Have A Chance To Talk
JEAN-PIERRE: The woman who sing like that does not buy the drinks
JANE: He's right
MARRELL: Okay okay sparkling water
JANE: Two please

(Jean-Pierre exits to get the drinks.)

MARRELL: Is he gallant or is he is gallant
JANE: Um the first one

(Slight pause.)

MARRELL: Are you all right
JANE: I'm just sorry I was late
MARRELL: I meant the date
JANE *(Referring to Jean-Pierre)*: With him you mean
MARRELL: No the calendar date
JANE *(No clue)*: The calendar date
MARRELL: It's been a year
    today
JANE: What's been a year today

(Slight pause.)

Oh My God
MARRELL: Fast wasn't it

JANE: I can't believe I
    forgot
MARRELL: You were probably blocking it out
JANE: How could I block it out
MARRELL: It's human
JANE: I'm sick of being human
    I'm a bad widow
MARRELL: I'm a bad wife
JANE: You're not a bad wife
MARRELL: I'm a mad housewife
JANE: You're not a housewife
MARRELL: But you agree that I'm mad
JANE: I'm more mad than you are
MARRELL: You don't Seem more mad
JANE: Or should it be madder /
    I think it should be madder
MARRELL: And you certainly aren't Perceived as more mad madder / whatever
JANE: It's always the ones who don't seem more mad and aren't perceived as more mad who are the maddest of all I'm a bad person Marrell
MARRELL: No You're Not
JANE: Yes I Am Marrell I just realized that I've Been Fooling All Of The People All Of The Time
MARRELL: Or
    maybe
    you're tired

(Alan enters holding a drink.)

ALAN: Good evening

JANE:	MARRELL:
Hello	Hi

JANE: I didn't know you were going to be here
ALAN: Me neither I like to keep us guessing

(Jean-Pierre returns with drinks.)

JEAN-PIERRE: Here we go

JANE: Thank you You remember Alan

JEAN-PIERRE: Hello

ALAN: Well I'm glad to see you because
    I wanted to talk to you about something Somewhat Pressing
    I'm actually trying to make a career move
    but all the good jobs have been taken
    you know what I mean

MARRELL: What's a good job

ALAN: The good jobs the good jobs I
    did some research you know
    trying to determine how I could get to be the guy who chooses
the colors of the lights on the top of the Empire State Building
    Guess what
    They already have a guy who does that

JANE: Oh I love that guy's work

ALAN *(Slamming his hand on the table)*: I could be that guy
    But actually scratch that because
    That Guy just has a
    (Thumbs up) good job
    whereas what I'm after is a
    (Hand thumping chest) Good Job

JEAN-PIERRE: I thought you were an entertainer

MARRELL: He's a mnemonist

JEAN-PIERRE: What's that

JANE: He remembers things
    in public

ALAN: You've seen me
    on television

JEAN-PIERRE: I don't have a television

ALAN: Oh Don't Tell Me You're One Of Those

JEAN-PIERRE *(To Jane)*: I don't understand

MARRELL *(Not now)*: Alan

JEAN-PIERRE: What

JANE: He thinks the I-Don't-Have-A-Television people are smug
and superior Just ignore him

JEAN-PIERRE: But I don't

JANE: It's fine

JEAN-PIERRE: I mean to say I don't have a television
It's just a fact
ALAN: Listen
You can't be a Doctor Without Borders Without A Television
It's too goddamned much

(Slight pause.)

JANE: Do you like being a doctor
JEAN-PIERRE: Yes
JANE: That was my dream when I was a kid
To be a doctor
JEAN-PIERRE: So why are you not a doctor
JANE: I have issues with reaction time I'm one of those people who if I
spill a glass of water on myself it goes like this
Spill water
Oh I think I've spilled water
Oh I've spilled it on myself
Oh I can feel the wetness
Oh I should probably do something about this
Oh I should wipe it up
You know on and on like that
Patient would be dead right
JEAN-PIERRE: Actually it's harder than you think
JANE: Killing patients
JEAN-PIERRE: I am amazed sometime at the human body's
what's the word
JANE *(?)*: Resilience
MARRELL: How do you say that in French
JEAN-PIERRE: Résilience
ALAN *(To Jean-Pierre)*: What if you wake up and discover you've been living a dinky life you know
JEAN-PIERRE: A What life
ALAN: Dinky / dinky
JEAN-PIERRE: I don't know this word Dinky
ALAN *(Defining the word)*: Of no importance
JEAN-PIERRE: Dinky

ALAN: Like when
    you're in the middle of telling someone a story and as you're
telling it say
    midway through
    you realize that your story isn't as good as you thought it was
but
    It's Too Late To Go Back
    Do you ever fear that your life is like that
    Do you ever fear that your life has gone a little l-i-t-e if you
know what I mean
MARRELL *(To Alan)*: Yes
ALAN *(To Jean-Pierre)*: My life
    is an American Movie
    and what I've just now realized is
    my life Wants To Be a
    Foreign Film
    Don't be scared J-P I just want to pick your brain
JEAN-PIERRE *(To Marrell)*: That sounds messy
MARRELL *(To Alan)*: Pick his brain about what
ALAN: About doing good What do you think
JEAN-PIERRE: I
    have a hard time understanding you
ALAN: Okay forget the foreign film
    The thing is I put all my eggs in one basket
    Because actually I only had one basket
    I'm looking for another basket

(No response.)

How Does A Person Break Into Doing Good
JANE *(Quietly to Marrell)*: What if I had sex with Tom
ALAN: The field The world of Doing Good Is there like a
    job fair or something
MARRELL *(To Jane)*: What
JEAN-PIERRE: I don't know

(Jean-Pierre turns to the women.)

ALAN: Take microfinancing

JANE: Are you shocked or didn't you hear me

ALAN: Are you listening Take microfinancing

MARRELL: I didn't hear you

JEAN-PIERRE: What about it

JANE: Nothing

ALAN: How hard would microfinancing be to break into

JEAN-PIERRE: I don't know I'm a doctor

MARRELL *(To Jane)*: Tell Me What You Said

JANE: It was nothing

ALAN: But I thought you were without borders

MARRELL *(To Jane)*: You've got to stop censoring yourself

This passive behavior is taking a toll on you

I'm sorry I shouldn't / have said that

JANE: Don't apologize

ALAN *(To Jean-Pierre)*: Are you straight

MARRELL: What did you just ask him

ALAN: If he was straight Is he straight Are you straight

MARRELL, JEAN-PIERRE AND JANE: Why

ALAN: I'm just more comfortable when I know the sexual orientation of the whole group

JANE: What whole group

ALAN: Of everyone I'm dealing with in a given moment

MARRELL: It's none of your / business Alan

JANE: Why does it matter Alan

ALAN: It just helps me to have a context in my mind

MARRELL: He's not interested in sleeping with you

ALAN: That's Not

Why I Was Asking

JEAN-PIERRE: Given your secret powers shouldn't you know if I'm straight or not already

ALAN: They're not secret powers I'm not a psychic I just happen to have a superb memory and don't think the inflection with which you said the words Secret Powers escaped my notice

(Referring to Marrell and Jane) So you're saying you want to sleep with one of them

JEAN-PIERRE, MARRELL AND JANE: NO

JEAN-PIERRE: Both

(Jean-Pierre, Marrell and Jane laugh—because he's kidding, right—and Jean-Pierre finishes off his drink.)

I need another drink
ALAN: Thanks I'd love one
JEAN-PIERRE *(?)*: Marrell Jane Drink

MARRELL:	JANE:
I'm good	No thanks

ALAN *(Grabbing Jean-Pierre's arm)*: I mean I know it's not like you get a good do-gooding job and then Bang you're a better person
I know it's more complicated than that
I actually have an acquaintance who works at the Sierra Club who's quite open about the fact that she doesn't recycle
I Mean She Does Not Recycle
Anything
Paper metal OR plastic
Plus she has a hard time connecting to animals because she's allergic to cats and horses
All I can tell you is a variety of signs lately have been working together to push me in the do-good direction
Give me an example Alan
Okay
I've had mothers
Jane for instance
tell me that they can always discern their own child's cry in a playground full of children
Mama Mama
Well
True story here
I myself was passing a playground the other day and somewhere from amongst the frolicsome din of youngsters at play emerged a very Very Tiny voice calling out
Alan Alan
and then I started to think
and I hope you're not going to think I'm sick
Then I Started To Think

maybe what I was actually hearing were
dying babies calling out to me from a foreign land

(Pause.)

JEAN-PIERRE: Excuse me

(Jean-Pierre walks off toward the bar.)

ALAN: That guy's an asshole
JANE *(To Alan)*: Are you all right
MARRELL: Can you believe it's been a year
JANE: I should mark this occasion
MARRELL: It's not really a should thing
JANE: You think I should I can tell
MARRELL: No I think I would There's a difference You should do
what feels right
JANE: Not forgetting in the first place feels right
ALAN: What did you wind up doing with Roy's ashes
JANE: They're still on top of the fridge

(Slightest pause.)

I like to imagine he enjoys the hum
MARRELL: You could do something with them
JANE: I should do something with them
MARRELL: I said could
ALAN: Spread them somewhere maybe
MARRELL: In a place that he loved
JANE *(Nodding her head)*: That isn't the top of the fridge
MARRELL: It should be somewhere beautiful
ALAN *(?)*: Should be
MARRELL: I mean could be
JANE: It could be somewhere beautiful
    Who am I trying to make feel better
    It's not Roy
ALAN: You and Maude
JANE: I don't think that will make us feel better

MARRELL: The memory of him then

(Jean-Pierre returns with a fresh drink.)

JANE *(?)*: I'm trying to make the memory of Roy feel better
MARRELL: I'm talking about rituals Jane about
    rituals that are rituals for a reason
JEAN-PIERRE: Who's Roy
ALAN: Her dead husband
JEAN-PIERRE: I'm sorry

(Pause.)

JANE: Death is such a killjoy
MARRELL: Let people express their feelings Jane
JANE: Knock yourself out just don't feel sorry for me
MARRELL: I'm sorry doesn't mean we feel sorry for you It means
we feel sorry that it happened
JANE: I'm sorry

(Pause.)

ALAN: What are you going to do to mark the occasion Jane
JANE: Maybe nothing
ALAN: You can't do nothing
JANE: Why can't I
ALAN: You don't want a reputation as a ball-dropper
JANE *(Sort of horrified)*: Do I have a reputation as a ball-dropper
ALAN: NO Well as a small ball-dropper / It's understandable
MARRELL *(Agreeing with Alan)*: Just as a small one
JANE *(!, to Alan and Marrell)*: I have a reputation as an under-
standably small ball-dropper
    But why
ALAN: Um
MARRELL: Well
ALAN: You forget about plans
MARRELL: Occasionally
    And birthdays

ALAN: Here and there
and the three hundred *francs* I lent you at that Swiss youth
hostel the summer after junior year
MARRELL *(Pronouncing it the French way, as Alan did)*: Did you just
say *francs*
ALAN *(?)*: That's how you say it right Pierre
JANE *(An idea)*: I know
the Brooklyn Bridge
JEAN-PIERRE: Fantastic
ALAN: What about it
JANE: As a place from which to throw his ashes
MARRELL: He didn't swim
JANE: He's dead
MARRELL: You shouldn't throw a person's ashes into a situation he
would have found scary when he was alive
JANE *(?)*: Shouldn't
MARRELL *(Sticking to the word this time)*: That's right Shouldn't
JANE: He's been through cremation Marrell
MARRELL *(?!)*: How cold is that
ALAN: And hot I would imagine
JANE: It's not cold It's honest Just like Roy was
He's laughing somewhere right now
MARRELL: No he's terrified you're going to throw him off a bridge
JANE: DO NOT TELL ME WHAT MY DEAD HUSBAND'S
THINKING MARRELL
MARRELL: I'm sorry

(Slightest pause.)

JANE: I'm sorry

(Pause of uncomfortable length.)

ALAN: Socrates was right

(Everyone turns to look at Alan.)

Examine life at your peril

JEAN-PIERRE: That's not what he said
ALAN: But that's what he MEANT
    I'm Just Feeling
    a sudden sense of urgency mixed with intense exhaustion
MARRELL: That's called middle age Alan
ALAN *(Taken aback)*: Uh I am not
    Middle-aged
MARRELL: That's also called middle age
ALAN: I'm not middle-aged
JANE AND MARRELL: Yes you are
ALAN: Middle age starts at sixty
MARRELL: Forty
    Sixty is like
JANE: approaching old age
ALAN: So I'm approaching middle age
JANE: No you've arrived You ARE middle-aged

(Tom arrives with the baby in the Bjorn.)

ALAN: Hi Tom
    you're just in time for the name-calling
MARRELL: What are you doing here
TOM: I came to see you
MARRELL *(?!)*: With the baby
TOM: With the baby in the Bjorn
MARRELL: I can't believe they let you in
TOM: I don't think they noticed
MARRELL: He should be at home
TOM: He's fine
    He's sleeping in the Bjorn
MARRELL: He should be sleeping at home
TOM: He doesn't care He's actually almost slept for More than
fifteen minutes
    He loves the Bjorn
MARRELL: Stop saying Bjorn
TOM: What did you say
MARRELL: Nothing
TOM: That's what it's called

MARRELL: He shouldn't be here
TOM: Bjorn
    Bjorn
    Bjorn /
    Bjorn
    Bjorn
MARRELL *(Overlap)*: That's so mature Tom
    (Then) You're absurd
TOM: You are

(Marrell looks at her watch.)

MARRELL: Excuse me
    I have to go sing about the letdown waiting to happen that
is love
TOM: You do that Marrell

(Slight pause.)

MARRELL:	TOM:
I will	You do that

(Marrell crosses to the stage and sings "Here's My Chance.")

MARRELL *(Singing)*:
        I looked up
        And caught your
        Sideways glance
        I looked up
        And I thought
        Here's my chance
        I'm off-kilter
        You've lost track
        Of all the things
        You meant to take back
        Here we are in this
        Circumstance
        Here we are
        Here's our chance

The hallway outside of Jane's apartment. She answers the door. Pause.

JANE: Where are you
    in theory
TOM: I'm at the Y
JANE *(Closing the door and pointing)*: It's that way

(Tom puts his foot in the door.)

TOM: I need to / talk
JANE: Move your foot please
TOM: Don't you think we should talk
JANE: I think we should the opposite of talk
TOM: I've been thinking about you
JANE: I've been thinking about me too and how much
    I wouldn't want to be my friend

(He touches her face.)

Or your friend
    Or your wife

(He takes his hand away. Pause.)

TOM: You mean Marrell or married to me
JANE: You know what I mean
TOM: We're going through a bad time
JANE: I know that
TOM: I mean Marrell and I
JANE: I Know That
TOM: You know that I love her it's / just
JANE: Please don't give me your perspective on your marriage
Tom I need to maintain the purity of my bias
TOM: There don't have to be sides Jane
JANE: There are always sides Tom and I'm on hers
     Especially Now That You've Cheated On Her
TOM: I didn't know you were so angry with me
JANE: Didn't you hear me I'm angry with me Tom Now go
TOM: Was that a
     date you were on the other night
JANE: GO
TOM *(To himself, sort of anguished)*: I'm sorry I thought you would
resist me

(Slight pause, before the door swings open.)

JANE: What did you just say
TOM: Nothing
JANE: Yes you did
TOM: I didn't mean this to get further than my mind's eye
JANE *(?)*: This
TOM: What should I call it then
JANE: I'm the one who didn't mean it to happen Tom
TOM: It
JANE: It came out of nowhere
     You show up at my door with
     I don't know what to call it
TOM *(?)*: Feelings
JANE: Okay feelings projected from your mind's eye I guess and
     I let it happen and I'm full of self-hatred for it

TOM *(?)*: You Let it happen
JANE *(?)*: You thought I would Resist you
TOM: I'm sorry I'm not
    sleeping
JANE: Do you think I'm sleeping because I'm not
    sleeping
    I almost told her
TOM: Don't do that Jane
JANE: It's not up to you
TOM: She'd leave me
JANE: I don't think so
TOM: I know her
JANE: I've known her longer
TOM: I have a child with her
JANE: We tell each other everything
TOM: I doubt that
JANE: You shouldn't
TOM: She never wants to have sex
JANE: You mean you don't
TOM: What
JANE: I thought you said that to me
TOM: No
    I didn't

(Slight pause.)

What about your mind's eye Jane
JANE: My mind is blind Tom
    and also deaf
    and really dumb
TOM: So I'm the only one who imagined this

(Slight pause.)

JANE: Why did you come here
TOM: To
    figure out what we're telling ourselves

(Slight pause.)

JANE: If we stop acknowledging its existence maybe we won't
have to suffer its consequences
TOM: Which means you can't tell her
JANE: Tell her what
TOM *(Quietly, as he exits)*: Okay
JANE *(As she closes the door)*: Okay

(Tom is gone.)

Jane and Alan and Marrell at Marrell's. Marrell walks in and out of the room, gathering things—a baby bath or basin and a towel, etcetera. At some point she will fill the basin with water. Jean-Pierre is asleep on the couch.

JANE: I'm not sure you should do this
MARRELL: He leaves me no choice
ALAN: Who
JANE *(Keep up!)*: Alan
JANE AND MARRELL: Tom

(Slight pause.)

ALAN: I asked him if he would take me back to Africa with him
JANE AND MARRELL *(?, confused)*: Tom
ALAN: Jean-Pierre Why is he
    asleep on your couch
MARRELL: He's exhausted
    He says the situation over there is ongoing
JANE: Isn't Every
    situation ongoing

ALAN: Why is he sleeping Here Marrell

MARRELL: He came by to pick up a bunch of CDs of my last recording

> To give as gifts to his co-workers
>
> He's exhausted I said take a nap

ALAN: Oh

JANE: Marrell doesn't have to apologize for offering rest to a French national who's weary Alan

MARRELL: What did Jean-Pierre say Alan

ALAN: I don't know I wasn't here

MARRELL: No when you asked him about taking you to Africa

ALAN: No

MARRELL *(?)*: He said / no

JANE: Did he give you a reason

ALAN: He said they're fully staffed

> and I annoy him

MARRELL: He said that

ALAN: I can tell

MARRELL *(Annoyed)*: There are tons of places to volunteer Alan

ALAN: Remember when my periodic helplessness used to endear

MARRELL AND JANE: Yes

(Marrell walks over to the fridge and takes out the Brita.)

ALAN: Now people find it annoying

> and cloying
>
> All the oyings

MARRELL *(Holding the Brita, as in "Rita")*: Now someone's started doing a thing where they pour out just enough water so the Brita filter is BARELY submerged just to avoid being the one to refill it

JANE: That is So rude

(Marrell pours herself a glass of water and fills up the Brita tank as Alan finishes up the glass of water he had poured himself earlier.)

MARRELL: Should I wake him up

ALAN *(?)*: Jean-Pierre

JANE AND MARRELL: The baby

JANE: Don't wake him up

MARRELL: Tom will be back soon

JANE *(To Marrell)*: You don't want him to be crying during

MARRELL: You're right we'll wait a little longer

JANE: I mean this should be joyous shouldn't it

(Marrell nods. Jane picks up a magazine and Alan looks over her shoulder at the cover.)

ALAN: I thought that guy was dead

JANE: You always think people are dead

(Jane starts fanning herself with the magazine.)

ALAN: A lot of people are

JANE *(Still fanning herself)*: Speaking of dead people I brought Roy

MARRELL: You brought Roy where

JANE: Here

He's in that paper bag by the door

(Jane and Alan look over at the paper bag.)

MARRELL: You took him on the subway

JANE: He wasn't afraid of subways Marrell

ALAN: I hated taking the subway with him

Remember how he used to do that thing

JANE *(It was awful)*: Yes

MARRELL: What thing

JANE: The seating thing

ALAN: He used to try to police the seating as people got on and off

So that it was first-come first-served

MARRELL: Oh right

JANE: He was all about good citizenship

ALAN: Drove me nuts

But now I'm all about good citizenship too

MARRELL: Why did you bring him here

JANE *(?)*: Roy

I thought you could help me take him somewhere beautiful that isn't by the front door

(Jane has been fanning herself all this time.)

ALAN *(To Jane, regarding the fanning)*: What's the matter with you

JANE: I don't know I feel
    schvitzy

ALAN: You can't feel schvitzy

JANE: Why not

ALAN: You're not Jewish

JANE: But I am

MARRELL *(?)*: Jewish

JANE: Schvitzy

ALAN: Are you going to start saying verklempt and mischegoss

JANE: I wasn't planning on it but why
    are you telling me they're off-limits

ALAN: You can be sweaty if you want

JANE: I'm not sweaty I'm schvitzy

ALAN: It's up to you

JANE: Yes it is
    I'm the captain of my own glandular experience Alan and
what I am is
    Schvitzy

ALAN: No offense but it just doesn't sound right coming out of
your mouth

JANE: That's racist or something Alan

ALAN: That's ridiculous

JANE: That's like me telling you to stop using all the WASPy words

ALAN: Like what

JANE: I don't know like
    like wainscoting

ALAN: Wainscoting

JANE: Yes I'd like you to stop saying wainscoting

ALAN: Okay
    It'll be tough
    But I'm going to
    make that adjustment

(Slight pause.)

JANE: I'm serious sometimes I get
    a little tired of all the clubs I can't join
ALAN: Are you kidding me
    (To Marrell) Is she kidding
    Come on Jane
    You Are The Club
JANE: A woman can't be The Club Alan
ALAN: You're white
JANE: I'm more female than I am white
ALAN: Interesting
JANE: You're white
ALAN: White with a twist
JANE *(?)*: You're using your dormant Judaism to Other yourself
ALAN *(?)*: That's a verb now
JANE *(?)*: Other
    It's a verb It's a noun It's a fact
ALAN: But the thing is Jane one doesn't Other oneself that's the
whole point Anyway weren't you just using your gender
JANE: I'm not using it It's a fact
ALAN: Another fact
JANE: Yes
ALAN: And so is my ethnic identification
    I'm not trying to offend you Jane
JANE: Ever notice that whenever people say that they're right in
the middle of being Really Offensive Do
    you want to weigh in here Marrell
MARRELL *(Offhandedly, as she crosses the room looking for a towel)*:
It sounds like it's hard to be white
ALAN: I guess I just sort of feel certain words and expressions Are
    unofficially off-limits if you didn't grow up in the culture
JANE *(?)*: So our roles are to reinforce the insanely entrenched
expectations of our culture
    That's like saying you should be a merchant because you're
Jewish
    That's like saying Marrell should be a jazz singer because
she's black
MARRELL AND ALAN: Marrell is a jazz singer

JANE *(To Alan)*: But not Because she's black
(To Marrell) You're a jazz singer because you're a great singer
and you like jazz
(To Alan) Unofficially Off-Limits
Do you hear yourself
ALAN: I don't know maybe I Should Be
a merchant
I think maybe I'd make a Great Merchant
Or or I know
A Moneylender
Or a
Moneylender Without Borders
JANE: I can recite the Kaddish Alan
Can you recite the Kaddish Alan
ALAN AND JANE *(Reciting—at racing speed—in Hebrew)*: Yeet-
gadal v'yeet-kadash shmei rabah
bi-al-mah dee vrah chir-oo-tey
v'am-lich mal-chu-tey b-chai-yay-chon oov-yo-may-chon
oov-chay-yay di-chol beit yis-ro-el
ba-a-gah-la ooh-viz-mahn kar-eev v'eem-ru amein
yi-heysh mei raba me-varach le-oh-lam ul-may-al-maya
MARRELL *(Cutting them off before they're done)*: Can we talk about
something else
JANE: Yes let's talk about Caucasians with dreadlocks
MARRELL: Let's not
ALAN: That's not fair
That was a very short two-year stint in college
JANE: By your standards Alan your dreadlocks were
culturally dishonest or
or fraudulent even
MARRELL: No they just looked bad but
Come On Now
(Gesturing to all three of them) our friendships have sustained
a number of indefensible hairdos over the decades so
maybe we should move on
JANE: Yes to T-shirts
MARRELL AND ALAN: What
JANE: What about all those T-shirts of yours Alan

ALAN: What T-shirts

JANE: Your John Coltrane T-shirt

    Or your Miles Davis T-shirt

    Or your Malcolm X T-shirt

ALAN: It's not a Malcolm T-shirt It's a half Martin half Malcolm T-shirt It's a

    Marmal T-shirt

JANE: What's the difference between you wearing your T-shirts and me feeling schvitzy

ALAN: I wear those T-shirts as a sign of respect to some of my heroes

MARRELL: As the black person on call I doubt Malcolm would want you wearing his face on your T-shirt

ALAN: Well Martin would like it

MARRELL: And I don't think Malcolm would appreciate you calling him Malcolm

ALAN: Well Martin wouldn't mind

MARRELL: Who Dr. King

ALAN: Are you on her side

MARRELL: I'm on the side of the baby waking up

    This is the longest he's ever slept in his entire little life

    The one time I want him to wake up he stays asleep longer than fifteen minutes

JANE AND ALAN: The One Time You Want Him To Wake Up

MARRELL: You know what I mean

ALAN: I don't even know what a godfather does

JANE: That's great news Alan seeing as you've been Maude's for the past nine years

ALAN: I just look out for her

MARRELL: Exactly that's all I'm asking

    If anything happens to me the two of you will help Tom out

    He would be horrified if he knew I was doing this

ALAN: Why is he so opposed

MARRELL: He's decided that when you stack Something

    i.e. my mildly religious inclinations vs Nothing

    i.e. his deeply felt agnosticism something will inevitably beat nothing in the eyes of a child

    He thinks the playing field's unfair so he doesn't want to play

JANE: So what are you going to do
 secretly take Henry to church
MARRELL: No I
 think if I just Do This
 I'll feel better
ALAN: I didn't know it counted when you did it at home
MARRELL: It counts as long as God sees it
 If we do this God will watch Henry's back
JANE: Don't you think an all-loving God should watch every-
body's back regardless of whether or not they do this
MARRELL: Of course
 This is just like
 divine life insurance
 I'm going to wake him up
ALAN *(?)*: God
JANE *(Ignoring Alan)*: You don't want to do that Marrell
MARRELL: Tom's on his way home I can feel it
 I'll give Henry three more minutes

(Pause.)

ALAN: I wish this room had more wainscoting

(Marrell laughs.)

JANE: I don't find it funny Alan I mean do you think people should
only be friends with people exactly like themselves
ALAN: Obviously not Jane
 as my T-shirts attest
 Despite my tenacious despair I Am An Aspiring Optimist
 about race relations Among Other Things
 I mean it's not like I don't have two biracial godchildren to
backseat raise

*(The baby starts crying. Marrell exits into the bedroom. Marrell
enters with the baby wrapped up in a blanket.)*

MARRELL: Okay he's basically still asleep but let's do this
 Stand on either side of us and create a circle around us

(Jane and Alan do as they are told, holding hands and creating a ring around mother and child. Marrell, with her back to us, takes the blanket off the baby and then dips him in the water. The smallest cry. She wraps him up again.)

ALAN: Aren't you going to say anything

MARRELL: I did

ALAN: I didn't hear anything

MARRELL: It was a silent conversation between me and Henry and God Alan

ALAN: What did God say

MARRELL: He blessed Henry and told me to take good care of him He told me that parenthood is a long road and it's important to pace oneself He said to trust my instincts and let my conscience be my gauge He said to strive to provide an example of an honest life and to instill in Henry a respect for and a belief in the inherent goodness of people He said to teach him to embrace the world and to honor the bounteous harvest that is life itself He said even when life seems hard and I know life is hard for you right now Marrell it's important to hold fast to what you know is the proper course for you and your family He said he knew there were distractions including the hot Frenchman who comes to watch you sing but that hot Frenchmen will come and hot Frenchmen will go while your family is forever

ALAN: He said all that

(Marrell nods.)

MARRELL: Okay you can let go

(Jane doesn't let go.)

ALAN *(?)*: What

MARRELL *(?)*: What

(Alan and Jane continue to hold hands, containing Marrell in the circle. Pause.)

JANE: I did something to hurt you even though I never would

ALAN AND MARRELL *(?)*: What
JANE: I don't think I can say it
MARRELL: Does it involve me
JANE: Yes
MARRELL: Does it involve you
JANE: Yes
MARRELL: Does it involve race relations
JANE: NO
MARRELL: Are you just saying that because the first two sentences ended in vowels and the third in a consonant
JANE: No
MARRELL: Does it involve Alan
JANE: No
ALAN: As usual
MARRELL: Does it involve Tom
JANE: Yes
MARRELL: But not Alan
JANE: No
ALAN: Why would anything involve Alan
MARRELL: Has something bad happened
JANE: Yes
MARRELL: Is it my fault
JANE: NO
MARRELL: Is it Tom's fault
JANE: Partly
MARRELL: I'm tempted to say the possibilities are endless Is it
    your fault
JANE: Yes
MARRELL: So it's your fault and Tom's fault and not my fault
JANE: Yes
MARRELL *(!)*: Don't Tell Me You Had Sex With My Husband Jane
JANE: Okay

(Pause, during which Alan laughs and Marrell realizes she guessed right.)

MARRELL *(?, to Jane)*: You did
    You did

(Jane doesn't deny it. Pause. Marrell breaks through the clasped hands as Tom walks in the front door, with groceries. Apparently he forgot to remove the Bjorn earlier, and still wears it, partially unsnapped. Marrell hands the baby to Alan and walks over to the side of the room.)

TOM: Hey
    Are you staying for dinner
ALAN: Not Jane I'm guessing but I'm
    totally free

(Longish pause, during which no one knows what to do. Then, Jean-Pierre wakes up on the couch and sits up.)

JEAN-PIERRE *(Looking around the room)*: Oh
    Marrell
    It's all your friends

(Alan has been rocking the baby.)

ALAN: Hi Jean-Pierre
JEAN-PIERRE: I should go
    (Noticing Jane, who has started moving toward the door) Oh hello
Jane
JANE: Hello Jean-Pierre
JEAN-PIERRE *(To all)*: Are you making up stories again
MARRELL *(To Jean-Pierre)*: Jane Just Told Us A Great Story
JEAN-PIERRE: Was the story funny
MARRELL: Hilarious
JEAN-PIERRE: Fantastic
JANE: Marrell please I hate myself I
    don't know what else to do right now

(Slight pause, during which Tom reaches out to take the baby from Alan.)

MARRELL: KEEP YOUR HANDS OFF HIM

(Alan retains hold of the baby, and with his free hand begins searching through the cupboards.)

TOM: I think we need to talk Marrell
MARRELL: I think we need to divorce Tom

(Jane has reached the door.)

You're Not Leaving Jane
JANE *(?)*: You don't want me to leave

(Alan has successfully located a bottle of wine.)

ALAN *(Holding up the bottle)*: Anyone mind if I open this
MARRELL: I could leave Want to go get a drink Jean-Pierre
JEAN-PIERRE: I'd love to but I've got to get to a pre-conference
    Has anyone seen a manila folder
MARRELL *(To Jean-Pierre)*: Are you sure you brought it with you
JANE: Pour me some please
JEAN-PIERRE *(To Marrell)*: Yes because I was on my way there
MARRELL *(Louder than necessary)*: Jean-Pierre and I need a glass
Alan

(Still holding the baby, Alan has poured four glasses. As the conversation continues, he brings one glass each to Marrell, Jean-Pierre and Jane. By the time he returns for his glass he finds that Tom has taken it. Throughout the rest of the scene he proceeds to sneak sips from whoever's glass is nearest.)

TOM *(Pointing to the baby)*: Keep your voice down Marrell
MARRELL: Keep your pants on Tom
JANE: Marrell please it was a terrible mistake
ALAN: Terribly mistaken sex is on the rise
JEAN-PIERRE: Worldwide as a matter of fact
MARRELL *(To Jean-Pierre)*: When's the actual conference
JEAN-PIERRE: It starts tomorrow
MARRELL: I'd love to watch your speech
JEAN-PIERRE: I'm just a panelist
ALAN *(To Marrell)*: I offered to volunteer on his next mission
JEAN-PIERRE: I told him we need trained physicians
ALAN: You also need Water and Sanitation Logisticians I read it
on the website

JEAN-PIERRE: Are you an engineer
JANE, TOM AND MARRELL: No
ALAN: I know you need people to do the clerical stuff as well
JEAN-PIERRE: It's essential that these people have superb communication skills okay
    that they are able to pick up on all manner of social cues okay and
    that they are extraordinarily adaptable
ALAN: Of course

(Awkward pause.)

Jean-Pierre is homophobic
JEAN-PIERRE: Jean-Pierre is bisexual
TOM, JANE, ALAN AND MARRELL *(?)*: He is
JEAN-PIERRE: I love people I love sex
ALAN: I love people and sex
JEAN-PIERRE: But you're annoying
JANE: No he's not
ALAN *(To Jean-Pierre)*: You can't stop me from going you know
TOM: Please Marrell Talk to me
ALAN: You're Not The Boss Of Africa
MARRELL *(Referring to the groceries, as in "Rita")*: Did you buy more Brita filters

(Slight pause.)

Of course you didn't
    And By The Way Tom
    God just watched me baptize our son this afternoon and
    he told me he's going to stop watching your back
TOM: Marrell WE REALLY NEED TO TALK
MARRELL: Talk away Tom
TOM: I'd prefer to talk in the other room
MARRELL: And I'd prefer to talk here
    in front of our dear friends
    (Pointing at Jane) Except her
    and well you too of course

ALAN *(Perking up)*: Did you just call me a dear friend Marrell
TOM *(Pointing at Jean-Pierre)*: He's not my dear friend
JANE: I need more wine
ALAN: This is empty

(Jane gets up.)

Where are you going
JANE: To raid the cat lady's liquor cabinet

(Jane walks out the front door. Jean-Pierre goes back to searching for his folder.)

ALAN *(Calling to her)*: Good thinking Jane

(Alan walks around with the baby, who has started to fuss a little. Pause.)

TOM: Okay
    You want to talk here Marrell
    You know when things really started to go off track Twelve
    months ago in this very room we were having a conversation
about Roy and Jane and you said
    in this very offhanded way
    you said
    I can't imagine being that much in love
ALAN *(Walking past with the baby)*: I was there for that
    (Pointing to the Bjorn) Can I borrow that thing
TOM *(?)*: You were Oh right
    (Pointing) And I was standing there and Marrell was
sitting there
ALAN *(Pointing)*: No you were sitting there and Marrell was leaning against the counter over there
    (Pointing to the Bjorn again) Can I borrow that thing Tom

(Jane returns carrying two bottles.)

TOM *(To Alan)*: What

MARRELL: I don't remember saying that

TOM *(To Marrell)*: You did

>*(To Alan)* And you know what it's called Alan

JANE *(To Alan)*: She doesn't remember saying what

ALAN *(To Tom)*: I know what it's called but I don't want to say it

JANE *(To Marrell)*: You don't remember saying what

ALAN *(To Jane)*: You weren't there

>*(?)* No wine

JANE *(Shaking her head)*: It's Peppermint Schnapps or Triple Sec

TOM *(To Alan)*: It's a Bjorn

ALAN *(To Tom)*: I'm Not Saying It

(Slightest pause.)

TOM *(To Alan, referring to the Bjorn)*: Not gonna say it Not gonna wear it

JANE *(?)*: Marrell Doesn't Remember Saying What

JEAN-PIERRE *(Updating Jane)*: She told him she didn't love him

(Jean-Pierre, still looking for his folder, walks into the bedroom.)

MARRELL: That's not what I said

JANE: Marrell wouldn't say that

TOM: Actually

>that's essentially what you said but

>let's talk about this later Marrell

MARRELL: THERE MIGHT NOT BE A LATER TOM

TOM: COME ON MARRELL

(Slight pause.)

MARRELL: No No No

>I want to talk about it now

TOM: No one could ever compete with the perfect couple

JANE: What perfect couple

TOM, MARRELL AND ALAN: You and Roy

JANE: We weren't the perfect couple

MARRELL: Maybe you and Tom will be

TOM AND JANE: Stop It Marrell

ALAN: Marrell didn't say I Can't Imagine Being That Much In Love
     She said Don't You Wish We Were That Much In Love

TOM: That's worse

MARRELL: I don't remember saying that

ALAN: You don't remember how old you are half the time

MARRELL: Thirty-seven

(Alan shakes his head.)

JANE: We weren't the perfect couple

MARRELL *(?)*: Thirty-eight

ALAN *(To Tom, as he gives Marrell the thumb's up on her age)*: And
then in response you said I Can't Imagine

MARRELL *(?, to Alan)*: He said I Can't Imagine like he couldn't
imagine being that much in love

JANE *(Trying to get his attention)*: Alan
     (Making a pouring-drink gesture) Triple Sec please

TOM: Ironically
     I said it ironically in response to the sting of your barb

MARRELL: How about the sting of your extramarital sex

TOM: That predates this by twelve months

JEAN-PIERRE *(Walking back into the room, empty-handed)*: Who
had extramarital sex

(Alan subtly motions to Tom and Jane.)

Fantastic

TOM *(To Jean-Pierre)*: What were you doing in there

JEAN-PIERRE: Looking for my manila folder

TOM *(To Marrell)*: Why would it be in the bedroom

JEAN-PIERRE: I thought maybe Marrell move it

TOM *(?, to Jean-Pierre)*: To the bedroom

MARRELL: Oh please Tom I'm not like you

TOM: Oh please Marrell YOU'D LOVE TO HAVE SEX WITH
HIM except now you're
     weirded-out by the bisexual thing I know you

ALAN: And then Marrell said I Wonder What It's Like To Have The Perfect Life
  (Making a list) Passionate Marriage
  Beautiful And Bright Daughter
  Fulfilling Career
  Jane And Roy Have It All
JANE *(?!)*: Fulfilling Career
  I don't have
  nor have I ever had
  a fulfilling career
MARRELL: You Had A Book Of Poems Published
JANE: Fifteen Years Ago
MARRELL *(!)*: That's like yesterday for a poet
ALAN: And then Tom said I Don't Know Marrell Why Don't You Ask Jane Why Don't You Ask Roy Why Don't You Marry Jane And Roy
TOM *(To Jean-Pierre)*: Again irony
  in response to the second barb
MARRELL: Okay I remember now because
  then I found out I was pregnant
JANE *(To Jean-Pierre)*: We weren't the perfect couple
MARRELL *(To Tom)*: Because I screamed back at you I Would If I Could
ALAN *(For general clarification)*: i.e. marry Jane and Roy
MARRELL: And then I went into the bathroom and then I remembered I'd just bought a pregnancy test and I took the pregnancy test and lo and behold
TOM: You didn't tell me you were pregnant that day
MARRELL: I was too mad at you I told you later
TOM: Two weeks later
MARRELL: I needed time to think
TOM *(To Jane)*: When did she tell you
JANE: I don't remember
MARRELL: Yes you do I called you from the bathroom
TOM *(!)*: You called her from the bathroom
JANE *(Referring to Marrell)*: She wasn't mad at me then
MARRELL *(Referring to Jane)*: It was before you fucked her
JANE: Please don't say that Marrell

TOM *(?)*: So you were mad at me because it bothered me that you called our marriage loveless

MARRELL: I never said loveless

ALAN: She never said loveless

TOM: She said loveless without saying loveless

MARRELL: Not Loveless just not Perfect

(Pointing to Jane) like theirs

JANE: OUR MARRIAGE WAS NOT PERFECT

    I don't know why people insist on clinging to this fiction

    Sure Roy was a Great Guy but ours was a Regular Marriage

    We had Ups we had Downs most recently we were in a Down but

    he got sick so it never did have a chance to fall apart and maybe it never would have fallen apart but we'll never know and I got all the glory

    I wanted to tell people I Don't Warrant Your Commiseration

    But without my having done anything to deserve it my stock went up after I became a widow

    And surviving spouses become blank slates onto which those around them project this

    this Tragic Sheen they secretly hope their own deaths will one day engender

    And people can become extremely Entitled when it comes to their commiseration and can be extremely Forceful in their efforts to make you accept it

    Really people have such tiresome fantasies about the dead

    They romanticize final conversations

    They become exhilarated by their own grief

    They feel a sudden compulsion to belong to the inner circle of the dead person's ex-life

    It's bizarre

    People started talking about Roy like he was Desmond fucking Tutu and you know what He wasn't Desmond fucking Tutu

    He was just a Regular Great Guy who we all wish didn't die fifty years prematurely

    Why can't that be enough

(Slightest pause.)

ALAN: Are you done
JANE: No
    Pass the Triple Sec

(Alan passes the bottle of Triple Sec.)

(?!, to Alan) WHAT
ALAN *(Quietly)*: I just wanted to say Hear hear

(Pause.)

JANE *(Waving the bottle of Triple Sec to Tom and Marrell)*: Sorry to interrupt Go on
TOM *(To Marrell, picking up right where he left off)*: And then when you came out of the bathroom that day it was clear that you had been crying so I said I Didn't Mean For Things To Escalate Like This
ALAN: No you said Why Do You Always Overreact
MARRELL: And I said I'm Just Not Feeling Well
ALAN: No you said Fuck Off And Die
TOM: And I said Let's Talk About This Later When You're Feeling Better
ALAN: No you said I'll Fuck Off And Die After You Fuck Off And Die First
MARRELL: And then I turned to Alan and said It's Better Than Cable Isn't It
ALAN: And I said Yes
JEAN-PIERRE: Ah

(Jean-Pierre crosses to the door and lifts up the paper bag containing Roy's ashes. His folder is on the floor underneath.)

My manila folder
ALAN: Fantastic

(Jean-Pierre finishes his drink and leaves his glass on the counter.)

MARRELL: Don't go Jean-Pierre

JEAN-PIERRE: I have to
Everything of substance happens at the pre-conference
MARRELL: Tell Me What To Do Before You Go
JEAN-PIERRE: About what
MARRELL *(Gesturing toward Tom and Jane)*: About this
JEAN-PIERRE: Why Americans are so threatened by nature
So you have a body and you have another body and these
bodies do what bodies do
Fantastic

(He starts to leave.)

MARRELL: But this is upsetting
JEAN-PIERRE *(Lifting up his manila folder)*: Non
THIS
is upsetting
This
*(Pointing vaguely in the direction of Jane and Tom before asking
Alan)* What's that word you taught me
about your life
ALAN *(?)*: Dinky

(Jean-Pierre smiles and walks to the door, then exits.)

Oh no
JANE: What
ALAN: All the alcohol is gone
JANE *(Really drunk by now)*: Oh no
MARRELL *(To Tom and Jane)*: Where When How many times Was
it fun
TOM: The other day
JANE: Once

(Slight pause.)

MARRELL: Why

(Tom moves toward Marrell, but she avoids him and goes to Alan for comfort instead. Jane crawls over to the door. She picks up the paper bag containing Roy's ashes and then crawls into the kitchen. She struggles to stand up, succeeds, and then manages to put the paper bag up on top of the fridge.)

What are you doing
JANE: He's better off on top of your fridge Marrell
TOM: Who
MARRELL, JANE AND ALAN: Roy
MARRELL: Get your husband off my fridge Jane
JANE: Please Marrell Your fridge is so much more of a beautiful place than mine
TOM *(?)*: Roy's in there
JANE: Please take him
MARRELL: No
JANE: I'm begging you Marrell
MARRELL: Don't do that Jane
JANE: This is horrible

(Slight pause.)

MARRELL: Fine Roy can stay but you're out
JANE: I'm out
MARRELL: Yes
    you're out

(Pause. Marrell passes the paper bag back to Jane, who accepts it.)

You should take Roy home
JANE: I'm sorry
MARRELL: You should give him a proper place to spend eternity
JANE: I know
    I know
    but
MARRELL: What

JANE: If I
    treat him like he's really dead then
    that will mean that he's not just Out Of Town

(Jane stares at the paper bag.)

Death has
    got to be stopped Marrell
MARRELL: I know
JANE: I mean
    What are the people left behind supposed to do
    (?) Live

(Jane has opened up the bag and the metal container within it and is staring down at the ashes. She reaches her hand inside the metal container and feels the ashes. Then, she brings a small amount of ashes up to her lips and rubs them against them.)

Down with death

(She reaches her hand into the bag again and rubs some ashes on her face and chest, her arms, etcetera, smoothing them in while repeating:)

Down with death
    Down With Death
    DOWN WITH DEATH
    DOWN WITH DEATH /
    DOWN WITH DEATH *(Etcetera)*

(During the above, Alan has passed the baby to Marrell and moved over to comfort Jane.)

MARRELL *(Quietly)*: Stop Jane
    Stop please
    I'm begging you
    You need to
    stop

(Jane stops. Stillness. Marrell looks at her watch and is shocked.)

TOM: What
MARRELL: It's almost 6:30
    He's been asleep for almost two hours

(Tom and Marrell do a sort of slow-building spontaneous dance of joy together.)

JANE: Oh My God
ALAN *(To Jane)*: What
JANE: I forgot to pick up Maude
    (Crawling toward the door, holding the paper bag to her chest)
Oh My God
    Oh My God
    Oh My God
    Oh My God

(Alan exits with Jane.)

Nighttime. Jane, still slightly disheveled from the events of the after-noon, sits outside Maude's closed bedroom door with a tray of dinner next to her on the floor.

JANE: A person needs to eat Maude
    even when she's angry
    especially when she's angry Anger takes
    a lot of energy so if you want to stay really mad Maude
    You Need To Eat

(Jane sticks her finger on the plate of food.)

It's cold now I'm sorry
    I'm so sorry Maude
    I don't know what else to say
    Mommy screwed up

(Jane knocks on the door.)

Will you let me in

Will you
just let me know that you hear me please
Slam on the wall or
something Maude

(No response. Jane stands up.)

You know what this has gone on long enough
I need to check on you Maude I'm
opening this door Maude Mommy's
coming in

(Jane opens the door to Maude's room.)

Oh are you
asleep

(Jane enters the room.)

You are
asleep

(Pause.)

I'm sorry you went to sleep angry
And hungry
I'm sorry I've been somewhere else for the past year
I'm sorry for all the questions I couldn't answer
About geography and the aurora borealis
I'm sorry for so many things
I'm sorry for
the lullaby I sang to you when you were a baby
You remember
the one entitled
For Fuck's Sake Go To Sleep
I meant it
in a good way

I'm sorry for
the time when you were in second grade and didn't proofread
your homework and I said you hadn't paid attention to capitalization and you said you were done with your homework and done
with capitalization and I said
in this horrible and highly charged
tone of voice I said
WELL IT'S YOUR LIFE
I'm sorry for all the times I used you as an excuse to extract
myself from situations in which I didn't want to participate
I'm sorry for your computational challenges
your flat feet
your future osteoporosis
your propensity toward nail-biting
the strange length of your arms and your irredeemable sweet
tooth
You come by all of it honestly and genetically

(Pause.)

The night your father died I had a fleeting thought
that went something like
Oh Okay Now I'll be allowed to have sex with a couple more
people before I die
but I
didn't mean This

(Pause.)

Why did your father die Maude
Why die
Why die
Don't die Maude
Don't Do It
Ever
Oh that's selfish of me
I don't mean to put that kind of pressure on you I mean
do what you need to do but

try Really Hard not to die Maude
please because
That
I could not bear

(Jane picks up a carrot from Maude's tray. She takes a bite.)

Okay
I'm here now Maude
I'm back

END

suitcase

or,

those that resemble flies from a distance

Production History

Suitcase or, those that resemble flies from a distance was developed as part of the NEA/TCG Theatre Residency Program for Playwrights. The world premiere of *Suitcase* was produced by Soho Rep (Daniel Aukin, Artistic Director; Alexandra Conley, Executive Director), with support from True Love, in New York on January 27, 2004. It was directed by Daniel Aukin; set design was by Louisa Thompson, costume design was by Maiko Matsushima, lighting design was by Matt Frey, sound design was by Shane Rettig, projection design was by Elaine J. McCarthy; the composer was Michael Friedman, the stage manager was Evan Cabnet. The cast included:

LYLE	Thomas Jay Ryan
SALLIE	Christina Kirk
JEN	Colleen Werthmann
KARL	Jeremy Shamos

This production of *Suitcase or, those that resemble flies from a distance* subsequently opened at La Jolla Playhouse (Des McAnuff, Artistic Director; Terrence Dwyer, Managing Director; Shirley Fishman, Associate Artistic Director) in La Jolla, California, on July 6, 2004. All personnel remained the same, with the following exceptions: Jonathan M. Woodward played Karl and the stage manager was Dana Victoria Anderson.

Characters

LYLE, early thirties
SALLIE, early thirties
JEN, early thirties
KARL, early thirties

About the Architecture

Primarily, we see a significant portion of an apartment building's stairwell and two of the apartment doors to which it leads; we also see parts, fractions really, of the interior of two apartments, inside of which should be evidence of Sallie and Jen's dissertations in progress. Perhaps Sallie's apartment also features makeshift furniture fashioned from the arrangement of books. Sallie and Jen live a floor apart, but this doesn't necessarily need to be depicted realistically in the stage space. At times Sallie will gaze out her window into an apartment across the street.

About the Language

The line breaks, internal capitalizations and lack of punctuation in general are intended as guidelines to the characters' thought processes, in terms of emphasis, pattern and rhythm; they should be honored, but should not feel enslaving. The cadence should fluctuate according to circumstance and should avoid falling into repetition. The rhythm of the piece as a whole should reflect the momentum of active thought. (By extension, during the play's many transitions, solutions other than blackouts should at all costs be sought. Moments should not so much cut in and out, as deftly replace one another. The scene titles may or may not be projected or otherwise included in the production.)

When a line is indented, it indicates a line break. When there is no indentation, it indicates a continuation of the previous line. When a forward slash (" / ") appears within the dialogue, it indicates that the next line should begin, creating an overlap with the previous line.

These ambiguities, redundancies, and deficiencies recall those attributed by Dr. Franz Kuhn to a certain Chinese encyclopedia entitled *Celestial Emporium of Benevolent Knowledge*. On those remote pages it is written that animals are divided into (a) those that belong to the Emperor, (b) embalmed ones, (c) those that are trained, (d) suckling pigs, (e) mermaids, (f) fabulous ones, (g) stray dogs, (h) those that are included in this classification, (i) those that tremble as if they were mad, (j) innumerable ones, (k) those drawn with a very fine camel's hair brush, (l) others, (m) those that have just broken a flower vase, (n) those that resemble flies from a distance.

—*Jorge Luis Borges, "The Analytical Language of John Wilkins"*

Exposition

Jen, Karl, Lyle and Sallie sing:

LYLE:
> This funny feeling's really not that funny

SALLIE:
> He says he's never known a nose that's quite as runny

JEN:
> I wonder how we were before we weren't

KARL:
> She says I'm prone to thoughts that are not current

(Chorus:)

SALLIE, JEN, KARL AND LYLE:
> Some words are hard to spell

SALLIE AND JEN *(Said)*: Fahrenheit

SALLIE, JEN, KARL AND LYLE:
  Some words are problematic

KARL AND LYLE *(Said)*: Titular

SALLIE, JEN, KARL AND LYLE:
  Some words sound better in
  Other tongues
  And longing is a seven-letter word

KARL:

  Why do humans feel contempt for human error

LYLE:

  Why is she here while I am always there

JEN:

  Is this house of love just bricks without mortar

SALLIE:

  I should have been a doctor without borders

SALLIE, JEN, KARL AND LYLE:
  Some words are hard to spell

SALLIE AND JEN *(Said)*: Rhythm

SALLIE, JEN, KARL AND LYLE:
  Some words are problematic

KARL AND LYLE *(Said—Karl pronounces it "Yura-nus," Lyle pronounces it "Your anus")*: Uranus

SALLIE, JEN, KARL AND LYLE:
  Some words sound better in
  Other tongues
  And longing is a seven-letter word

What Rhymes with My Girlfriend

In the vestibule. Essentially Karl and Lyle are not welcome in their girlfriends' apartments, an awkward state of affairs that is reflected in the fact that, despite adopting a series of "relaxed" physical behaviors, neither one is able to get truly comfortable during the scene.

LYLE: Won't it be
    Nice
KARL *(It's such an odd word when you think about it)*: Nice
LYLE: When our girlfriends'
    dissertations are
    finished
KARL: My girlfriend's dissertation Is finished Boy
    Is It Finished
LYLE: Oh my
    girlfriend didn't mention that your
    girlfriend's dissertation was
    done
KARL: Oh no
    my girlfriend's dissertation isn't

Done
my girlfriend's dissertation is
Finished

LYLE: My girlfriend said your girlfriend's
dissertation was about garbage

KARL: Garbage Detritus What Is Left My girlfriend
believes what we discard is of much
greater interest than what we keep My girlfriend
went through the garbage of three randomly
selected individuals over a period of
five years My girlfriend
essentially used the garbage as a means by
which to deduce identity or
construct identity depending upon your
point of view What's
your girlfriend's dissertation about

LYLE: My girlfriend's dissertation is an
examination of examples of alternative means of
storytelling by which my girlfriend
means for instance end-beginning-middle or
middle-middle-middle instead
of beginning-middle-end My girlfriend
feels that life actually
actual life feels
an affinity for Other Constructions My girlfriend's
dissertation is called Narrativus
Interruptus but I'm hoping my girlfriend will change it to
something a little

KARL: more catchy

LYLE: less unfortunate

KARL: My girlfriend's dissertation is at
a standstill because of issues of ethics
because my girlfriend received permission from her
adviser to riffle through the garbage of
strangers but not from the strangers
themselves My girlfriend's dissertation has
thus itself become garbage has itself become

a prime artifact of her thesis and of course
though she's angry this also makes my
girlfriend laugh This makes my girlfriend
laugh a lot

LYLE: My girlfriend's dissertation is not
proceeding My girlfriend is in a
rut somewhat My girlfriend says
her adviser is not overly
happy with her My girlfriend is
not overly happy My girlfriend does
not laugh a lot

KARL: I bring my girlfriend
garbage gifts of
garbage The
garbage of three strangers

LYLE: Instead of focusing on her dissertation
my girlfriend focuses on the awkward encounters
she shares with her adviser For
instance she dwells on the time at her department's
holiday party when they were greeting and
misread one another's psychophysical signals
and wound up engaged in what was neither a
hug nor a kiss nor a handshake but some
bungled civilian amalgam

KARL: I enjoy bringing my girlfriend suitcases full of
garbage gifts of
garbage
offerings of unwanted love
unwanted offerings of love I
don't know what I mean

LYLE: My girlfriend has trouble
finishing things

KARL: My girlfriend's dissertation is
Finished
boy is it finished

LYLE: My girlfriend wonders why the world
embraces all things intellectually obvious

KARL: Tell your girlfriend all things intellectually
obvious are deeply lovable and in this age one
cannot argue with even remote lovability
LYLE: I did

Remember Our Cross-Country Trip That Time

Beside Sallie's manuscript sits a lamp without a shade. Sallie picks up her pen, stares at the manuscript, and then puts down her pen. Sallie unscrews the illuminated bulb and inserts another she selects from a pile of bulbs. She is either testing the goodness/burnt-outness of identical-looking bulbs, or trying out a whole array of different styles and colors of bulb at various points during the scene. Meanwhile, Sallie and Jen talk on the phone, while Lyle and Karl loom in the building's vestibule.

SALLIE: What I was saying before it
    depends on your orientation
JEN: Sexually
SALLIE: Directionally
    It depends on which way you're
    facing
    Remember our cross-country trip that
    time
    That was something
    Do you remember our cross-country trip that time Jen

JEN: Why

SALLIE: No reason
I was just thinking about how you
know on our
Cross-Country Trip That Time we were hungry to
See As Much As We Could
That's all I'm sorry I think I'm um feeling
ashamed of my stupid life

JEN: What

SALLIE: Ashamed
Sorry

JEN: Why

SALLIE: Oh
My
Stupid Life I'm
Ashamed of it
It's just that when I was younger I wanted to see everything
Do You Know What I Mean
I wanted to See Everything
But now I find I
basically go through My Stupid Life um
averting my eyes
basically
Do you avert your eyes Jen because
I avert my eyes Jen I
avert my eyes and the
list of things from which I avert my
eyes Jen is um
Big
And getting um
Bigger and that Feels Wrong
Are you there

JEN: I'm here

SALLIE: Oh you're there / good

JEN: Yes

(Karl buzzes Jen's apartment: buzz.)

SALLIE: Do you think that's Wrong

(Buzz.)

JEN *(Speaks into the intercom as she continues to hold the phone)*: Yes
SALLIE: You do

(Buzz, breathing.)

JEN: Yes
SALLIE: See I do too but then I was wondering
    Is that the right word Wrong
    Is Wrong right or um fair to one when one is simply reporting
    one's emotional response—
    (Makes it plural on second thought) —ses

(Buzz.)

JEN: Who is it
SALLIE: Are you / talking to me
KARL: It's me
JEN: Who's me
KARL AND SALLIE: Me
KARL: But um
SALLIE: In any case the list is long
    I mean Big I said Big before I
    Avert My Eyes From A Big Long List Of Things Jen
KARL: But um
SALLIE: That's all I'm basically saying
KARL *(I feel suddenly unsure of your name)*: But um NnnnSsssW-
wwwLllll
LYLE: Lyle
KARL: Lyle's here
JEN: Why
SALLIE: No reason
KARL: He just is
SALLIE: No defensible reason

LYLE: Hi Jen
KARL: He just is
LYLE: Hi Jen
SALLIE: But lots of defensive reasons ha ha
JEN: What
SALLIE: Nothing
KARL: Hi Jen
LYLE: Hi / Jen
KARL: Hi / Jen
LYLE: Hi / Jen
JEN: Right

(Lyle suddenly approaches the intercom.)

LYLE *(To Karl)*: May I
    Super quick thing
    (Cough, into the intercom) Jen
JEN: Pardon
SALLIE: What
    Nothing
LYLE: Sorry
JEN: Why
LYLE: I coughed
SALLIE: Sorry
JEN: Why
LYLE: I / coughed in your ear
KARL: He coughed
SALLIE: Oh
    I don't want to talk about it
LYLE: Okay I have a question / Have you spoken to
    Have you spoken to
JEN: Okay
KARL: I have a question
    I have a question
    I have a question
    (Specifically to Lyle, softly and with a gesture) to pop

LYLE: Oh
   Okay
   Uh okay
   Karl has a Question

(Lyle moves away from the intercom.)

Ask her

(Buzz. Pause.)

KARL: Did we / lose her
SALLIE: I'm sorry
KARL: Did we / lose her
SALLIE: Are you / there
LYLE *(Pronounces the "n" in damn)*: Damn it
JEN: I'm here
KARL: Oh / she's there
SALLIE: Oh you're there / good
LYLE: Good
KARL: She's there
LYLE: Ask her
JEN: What
LYLE *(Pronounces the "n")*: Damn it / man
JEN: WHAT
LYLE: Take charge / of yourself
SALLIE: You mean like what things
LYLE: Karl Jen has a Question
JEN: Uh-huh
   I'm listening
LYLE: I mean I'm
   sorry it's none of my
   (Unfinished sentence) It's your
   (Finished sentence) It's his

(Lyle retreats. There is suddenly nothing between Karl and the intercom except Karl himself.)

JEN: Hello

(Somewhere during Sallie's next lines Karl hiccups.)

SALLIE: Um okay Petitions I avert my eyes from um
    Political Petitions and I avert my eyes from
    Personal Grooming Well
    especially Personal Grooming in Public so uh
    Public Personal Grooming you know
LYLE: What's wrong with you
JEN: Me
SALLIE: Excuse me
LYLE: Him

(Karl hiccups.)

JEN: What's that sound
LYLE: What / sound
SALLIE: It's the sound of me telling you things Jen things /
    from which I Jen avert my eyes

(Karl hiccups.)

JEN: That sound
LYLE: Oh Karl has the hiccups

(Karl nods.)

See he just nodded
JEN: Oh
KARL: Could you

(Karl hiccups.)

LYLE: Could I what
KARL: Could you

(Karl hiccups.)

LYLE: I don't understand
KARL: Could you

(Karl hiccups.)

you know
LYLE: Oh
    please don't tell me you're asking me to ask her You should /
ask her
KARL: Please just

(Karl hiccups.)

LYLE: You / should
KARL: Please /
    Please just

(Karl hiccups.)

Please just

(Karl hiccups.)

LYLE: You should Okay Okay Okay
    (Into the intercom) Will you marry him
SALLIE: I also avert my eyes from um Pain
JEN: What
LYLE: Will you / marry him
SALLIE: Pain

(Karl hiccups.)

JEN: What does that mean
SALLIE: Oh Peoples' Pain
    I guess I'm randomly starting with the P's
LYLE: Can he be your husband
JEN: Oh
LYLE *(?)*: No

JEN: OH
LYLE *(To Karl)*: Oh

(Karl hiccups and indicates through gesture a question:)

Karl is wondering what Oh means
SALLIE: As if anything's random right But
    I avert my eyes from things that start with uh
    tons of different letters Jen Tons of different letters
JEN: Uh-huh
LYLE: Karl wonders is that A Yes
    Will Karl be able to refer to you as wife
JEN: Are you kidding
SALLIE: Well Tons is hyperbole sure but the point is I avert my
eyes from Far Too Many things

(Karl hiccups.)

LYLE: I don't mean Address you as Wife
    I mean in conversation like My
    wife and I just saw this really disappointing uh movie Things
    like that

(Karl gestures and hiccups.)

Oh Karl's trying to say something
SALLIE: Sometimes I stand at my window Jen and I can't tell if
    it's bleak in here or bleak out there or
    both Do you know what I mean

(Pause. We start to see flickers of light emanating from the window across the street. Sallie doesn't notice it yet; instead she puts the phone down and contemplates her stupid life.)

JEN: Are you there
KARL: I'm here I've brought something
JEN: What is it
KARL: I've got Lyle here
JEN: Lyle is someONE

KARL: Yes I know I said the wrong thing I've
  got Lyle here
JEN: Yes I know I didn't know you knew Lyle
KARL: I don't Have you got Sallie there
JEN: What do you mean
  I'm here and Sallie's at Sallie's
  Sallie's there but she's not here Karl
KARL: Lyle's brought her something
JEN: Something for Sallie
KARL: He sends his love
JEN: You're forwarding Lyle's love
KARL: I'm delivering it
JEN: You're working together
KARL: Why not
LYLE: Can he come in
KARL: Can I
LYLE: Can he
KARL: Can / I
LYLE: Can / he
KARL: Can / I
LYLE: Can / he
JEN: Hmm
  hon
  hmm

(Sallie stares out the window.)

SALLIE: All I'm saying is Remember Our Cross-Country Trip
That Time

*(Jen opens a suitcase and pulls out a bag of trash. She opens the bag
of trash and pulls out a late-1960s-era cassette tape player. Then, she
finds several cassette tapes among the garbage in the trash bag. Jen
stares at the cassette tape player while Sallie stares at her dissertation;
a huge stack of paper. Jen picks up one of the tapes and inserts it into
the cassette tape player. She presses the recorder's "play" button: the
tape seems to be blank. She takes the first tape out and inserts another
one. She presses "play" again. This time she hears voices.)*

JEAN: It lights up.
PETER: It does?
JEAN: Doesn't it light up, Gene?
GENE: Yes, it lights up.
PETER: Cool.

(Jen presses "stop," examines the tape and realizes it hasn't been fully rewound; she presses "rewind" and then "play."
Sound of breathing in the forefront, Christmas music and the family unwrapping presents in the background.)

LIZZIE: Okay, so . . .
Daddy.
Daddy.
Daddy.
Daddy.
Daddy.
GENE: What?
LIZZIE: It's not working.
GENE: What?
LIZZIE: My present's broken.

(Slight pause. Breathing again in forefront.)

Daddy.
Daddy.
Daddy.
GENE: What?
LIZZIE: The tape recorder's not working.
GENE: It's not? Yes it is, see? The—what are those knobby things called? / —heads are turning.
PETER: Heads.
LIZZIE: Oh.

(She clears her throat.)

You are my new Sony Series Two tape recorder.

(Sound of breathing.)

I love you.
>   Mommy's opening her present.
>   Everybody's here.
PETER: Can I open one?

(Sound of breathing, unwrapping.)

JEAN: Oh, this is great.
LIZZIE: Mommy got a coat of brown and beige squares and rectangles and she says it's great.

(Sound of unwrapping.)

PETER: Cool.
LIZZIE: Peter got a globe.
PETER: Thanks.
LIZZIE: It lights up.
PETER: It does?
JEAN: Doesn't it light up, Gene?
GENE: Yes, it lights up, Jean.
LIZZIE: Mom's Jean with a J, Dad's Gene with a G.
PETER: Cool.
LIZZIE: Peter got a cool globe that lights up. It's so cool. And now I'm going to open up my puppy!
JEAN: You know it's not a puppy, hon.
>   Daddy's allergic.

(Sound of unwrapping.)

PETER: Dad, I think it needs a special bulb.
JEAN: That wasn't included?
LIZZIE: Oh, look everybody . . .
>   I got a pocketbook.
JEAN: I thought that was supposed to be included. Gene?
LIZZIE: I got a pocketbook.

JEAN: Gene, wasn't that special bulb supposed to be included?
LIZZIE: I got a pocketbook.
GENE: I don't know, Jean. / I suppose it
LIZZIE: I got a pocketbook.
JEAN: I thought you checked / that.
GENE: I didn't.
JEAN: So I guess we won't be able to see it lit up, that's all. I'm sorry your father ruined / Christmas, Peter.
GENE: We can get a / bulb, Jean.
LIZZIE: I got a / pocketbook.
GENE: Jesus.
JEAN: Say sorry, Gene. Peter, your father forgot to check to see if it came with a / special bulb, so we won't be able to see it lit up.
GENE: Oh, for God's sakes, woman, if you say special bulb one more / time.
LIZZIE: I got a pocketbook.
JEAN: Well, you said you'd take care / of it.
GENE: I don't see a piano tied to your ass.
JEAN: WHAT did you say?
LIZZIE: And that's all the presents.
GENE: You heard me. You could've gotten the light bulb your / self.
JEAN: You said you'd do it. / I'll take care of it Jean. I'll take care of it, Jean.
PETER: Are you recording?
LIZZIE: It's mine.
PETER: I'm just looking.
LIZZIE: So, okay,
     That's all for now. Merry Christmas.
     I love you my new Sony Series Two tape recorder.
     I forgot to tell you I'm Lizzie and I'm eight and I LOVE you—
     oh, I did tell you that.
PETER: Say the date.
LIZZIE: December twenty-fifth.
PETER: No, dummy, the year.
LIZZIE: Merry Christmas, 1973.
     Why?
PETER: So you'll know. When you go back to listen to it.

LIZZIE: I wanted a puppy.

JEAN: For chrissakes, Gene, were you too busy to take the time to read the box? This is what I'm talking about. Children get disappointed.

LIZZIE: Did you want a puppy?

GENE: They don't seem disappointed to me.

PETER: I wanted a dog.

LIZZIE: I wanted a puppy to sleep with me in my bed.

(Breathing on tape, over:)

GENE: Only one person seems disappointed to me Jean, that's how it seems to me, Jean. Jesus, Jesus, Jesus, Jean.

(Breathing.

Jen presses "stop." She picks up a Sharpie and writes on a label and affixes the label to the tape. Jen picks up the phone and dials Sallie's number.)

It Is Um Not

Ring ring.

JEN: I forgot to tell you that Lyle sent his
    love
SALLIE: I called you
JEN: So I can't speak first
SALLIE: You saw Lyle
JEN: Karl told me to pass on Lyle's love and then Lyle asked me to
marry him on behalf
    of Karl
SALLIE: Karl proposed
JEN: What a word it's
    absurd don't you / think
SALLIE: Proposed
JEN: Uh-huh
SALLIE: He proposed
JEN: Uh-huh
SALLIE: What did you say

JEN: Nothing

SALLIE: Lyle's passing on his love now

JEN: I guess

SALLIE: Did Karl propose on behalf of Lyle

JEN: No /

    but you know he would

SALLIE: Oh

    Who

JEN: What

SALLIE: He who

    In other words Karl would propose on behalf of Lyle or Lyle
would propose

JEN: Lyle Listen

    were you happy when you were

    little

SALLIE: Little

JEN: Little younger you

    know what little means It's an

    idiom were you /

    happy

SALLIE: I can't remember I don't think

    so but maybe I was Not unhappy I

    was probably neutral Do you want me to say

    no on your behalf

JEN: You had a neutral childhood No

SALLIE: Maybe No

JEN: No no to the proxy no You

    must remember something about your child / hood

SALLIE: Uh I remember playing with my brother in a long hallway
riding a tin car okay I

    remember our first record player You

    don't want me to say yes for you do you

JEN: No So you were happy sometimes

SALLIE: I guess when

    things were involved So

    what should I say for you

JEN: Nothing Things are fraught

SALLIE: Did you say / fraught Nothing
JEN: I did say fraught I did say nothing I
    Don't Want You To Speak For Me
SALLIE: Oh

(Slight pause.)

I don't really like people
    touching my things
    I mean okay

(Slight pause.)

Remember that housesitter I had that time who
    touched some stuff I specifically
    told him not to
JEN: I don't want to talk about / him
SALLIE: It was really Really upsetting
JEN: Maybe he got confused / Anyway
SALLIE: That's not what happened
JEN: you don't know what stuff he touched
SALLIE: Stuff was in different places Jen Stuff
    was all over the wrong place
JEN: I don't understand some
    stuff he Was allowed to touch while other stuff
    he Wasn't
SALLIE: Help yourself to my food I said
    Make yourself Comfy in my bed I said
    Use my towel my soap my chair I said
    Water my plant if you remember I said
    If not it's really okay
    Feel free to read my books I said
    Even the ones with bookmarks in them
    Remember to feed the cat I said
    But anyway the cat will insist
    Basically mi casa es su casa I said in
    you know
    Espanol

except please
Don't Touch This Stuff Here
And
of course /
Guess what he touched
JEN: He touched That Stuff There
He touched it all over the place
He smeared that stuff you told him not to touch
all over his / body I bet
SALLIE: All right Jen all right I
don't need your your My
ability to envision Unpalatable Scenarios is plenty honed Jen
plenty
What I'm saying is I trusted the
housesitter with my Bookmarked Books and
I don't even trust the men I sleep with / with my
JEN *(Did you say)*: men
SALLIE: man
Bookmarked Books No the
housesitter not only Disrupted stuff he Moved stuff to entirely
other places
places where
this stuff
had Never Been People
don't say fraught much anymore you know even
though people's lives continue to be fraught in the um /
extreme
JEN: Maybe you secretly wanted to sleep with
The Housesitter
SALLIE: The cat dish wound up in the cupboard and
my cereal bowl wound up on the
floor full of furry
water
JEN: How did you find him again
SALLIE: He was a stray
JEN: No the housesitter
SALLIE: Oh the housesitter I found the housesitter sitting on that
slippery slope

A Friend of a Friend
JEN: Friends of friends are never friends
    you'd want for yourself
SALLIE: Yes friends of friends should befriend one another and
enjoy one Massive Tenuous Relationship It
    would be easier for the rest of us
JEN: But aren't we someone's friend's friend
SALLIE: I REALLY CAN'T DISCUSS THAT RIGHT NOW
JEN but
    I will say this
    The problem with housesitters is
    they sit all over your house
JEN: And then there are all those friends of
    friends of friends

(Slight pause.)

SALLIE: I didn't Secretly want to sleep with The House / sitter
JEN: I Don't Want To Talk About Him How
    is It going
SALLIE *(Patting her dissertation)*: You mean It
JEN: Um-hmm
SALLIE: It is um not It
    is not going
    It is un-going /
JEN: It is ongoing /
    It is ongoing
SALLIE: It is Un-going
    It is UN-going
    though you might say its un-going
    is ongoing / you might
    say that Jen
JEN: Its un-going is ongoing
SALLIE: What's that / Jen
JEN: You said I might say that
    You said I might say /
    Its un-going is ongoing
SALLIE: Oh

Oh
Haha I see haha so
How is It going for you
JEN: Um it is not as you
    know It is not /
    going
    good
SALLIE: Aargh right
JEN: What oh
    right aargh

(Small silence, in which they both feel silly for using the word "aargh.")

I was listening to a little kid's tape
    before That's
    why I was asking about your
    childhood
SALLIE: What little kid
JEN: I don't know Lizzie
    something
    Lizzie X from the garbage of Subject C
SALLIE: That sounds like a song sort
    of / Anyway
JEN: What
SALLIE: I should
    What
    Oh like

(Singing:)

    Lizzie X from the garbage of Subject C

(Not singing) or something

(Pause.)

Okay I should
    get back to It

JEN: Well okay I should well
   I don't know what I should but
   I'm so confused did you
   want Karl to propose on behalf of Lyle
SALLIE: You're right that word is
   Silly / Do you
JEN: I said Absurd
SALLIE: What
JEN: Nothing
SALLIE: Do you think it's because of the
   proximity of the two P sounds

(Slight pause.)

SALLIE AND JEN *(Hitting the two P sounds)*: Propose

I Said What Rhymes with My Girlfriend

In the vestibule.

LYLE: You said Can he
  (Points at himself) Be Your Husband She said

KARL:	LYLE:
Oh	Oh
You	You
Said	hiccuped
What	What
You	You
said	hiccupped

KARL: Karl Is Wondering What Oh Means
LYLE: She said Uh-huh
KARL: You said Karl Wonders Is That A Yes
LYLE *(Trying to remember)*: She said
KARL: She said Are You Kidding

LYLE: No she said Are You Kidding in response to Will Karl Be
Able To Refer To You As Wife
KARL: Okay right so
    what did she say in response to Karl Wonders Is That A Yes
LYLE: You know what Nothing She didn't have a chance because I
    rephrased Karl Wonders Is That A Yes when I said
    Will Karl Be Able To Refer To You As Wife
KARL: But that's no rephrasing Those questions aren't
    at all the same thing
LYLE: I meant them as the same thing
KARL: You confused her
LYLE: Perhaps
KARL: Jen is so confused that Jen
    is So Confused You Confused Her
LYLE: Sorry
KARL *(?)*: Sorry
LYLE: Sorry

(A genuine silence.)

Did you ever notice Karl how nascent bits of middle of the night
genius vanish without fail with the dawn
KARL: Holy Toledo Lyle and how
    That Woman Is So Confused

Dissertation Shmissertation

Sallie sits in front of her manuscript reading and reordering pages. Eventually, subtly, her revision process seems to border on the random. There is a light flickering in the apartment across the way. Meanwhile, Jen picks up another tape from the stack and presses "play" on the cassette player.

Different Christmas music playing in the background. Unwrapping is going on. Now thirteen, the girl on the tape is chewing gum as she speaks.

LIZZIE: Um, it's Lizzie.

So, so far Peter got a calculator, Jean with a J got a sweater,

Gene with a G got a book and I got a pair of pants with a belt attached.

Uncle Dick and Aunt Helene are here. They live in the Rockies. Aunt Helene says it's God's country.

I've met them before, but it was when I was a baby, so I don't know them from Adam. That's what Aunt Helene said. We don't live in God's country.

SALLIE *(From her apartment, testing the word)*: Propose
Propose
Propose
LIZZIE *(Whispering)*: Uncle Dick gets really drunk by about noon and then starts pronouncing e-ve-ry syl-la-ble he says real-ly care-ful-ly.
JEAN *(From the background)*: Thank you, Helene, I just love it.
LIZZIE: Jean with a J just got another sweater.
She says she just loves it.
HELENE *(From the background)*: Dick picked it out.

(Sallie picks up the phone and dials Jen's number.)

DICK *(From the background)*: We thought it would ac-cen-tu-ate your eyes.

(Ring ring. Jen turns down the volume on the cassette tape player and answers the phone. Pause. Breathing. Sallie is looking out the window.)

SALLIE: I don't think it is because of the proximity of the two P sounds Are
you
there
JEN: I'm here I thought
you might be my adviser
SALLIE: Ew there's a guy outside clipping his
toenails into the sewer Did
you hear from your adviser
JEN: She's trying to
Reach Me

(By now the flickering in the apartment across the way has attracted Sallie's attention. She picks up a pair of binoculars and looks through them as she continues to converse. Via projections, we see what she sees, a section of home movies from circa 1940: a little girl and her parents are sledding. The father wears a suit and overcoat, while the mother wears heels and a fur. They all take a turn on the sled.)

SALLIE: How do you know
JEN: She's left
    Messages
SALLIE: Uh-oh
JEN: And yesterday I received a
    Letter

(Slight pause.)

Are you there
SALLIE: Sorry I got distracted Someone
    across the way is watching some old
    footage What did you receive
JEN: A letter Old
    Footage
SALLIE: Home movies or
    something What
    sort of letter
JEN: She wanted to know where things
    stood dissertation-wise
SALLIE: What did you tell her
JEN: It was a letter Sallie
SALLIE *(Focused on the film)*: Oh right
    Isn't it beautiful Jen I mean is
    there anything more beautiful Jen than
    people who dress in blatant disregard of their
    circumstances
JEN: Oh I don't know blatancy is problematic if you ask me Bla-
tancy makes me nervous She
    said she was going through a messy divorce
SALLIE: Who
JEN: My adviser In her letter
SALLIE: That's too bad
JEN: So she's trying to straighten out her affairs so
    to speak
SALLIE: So she can focus her energy on her messy
    divorce

133

JEN: I guess She said attachment is a
  nasty business

(Slight pause.)

That's a quote from her letter Attachment
  Is A Nasty Business
SALLIE *(Focused on film)*: See I like blatant disregard It's got
  what people used to call spunk
JEN: The rumor is her husband ran off with a grad student
SALLIE: Have you ever noticed how people who run off don't get
any farther than right in front of your face
JEN: I should call her
SALLIE: Do you know her
JEN: My adviser
SALLIE: Oh I thought you meant the grad student
JEN: Maybe a letter would be better Or a tape
SALLIE: A tape A
  tape would be weird
JEN: Okay a letter
SALLIE: A tape would be weird
  (Focusing on the film as the dad is sledding) Whee
JEN: What
SALLIE: Nothing
JEN: I should call her right /
  away
SALLIE: Right
JEN: I'm going to call her Right Away

(Jen and Sallie hang up their phones. Instead of calling her adviser right away, *however, Jen turns up the volume on the tape player.)*

LIZZIE: It's raining. My stomach hurts. I guess that's about it for
now.
  Merry Christmas, 1978.

(Silence, except for the sound of breathing. Jen reaches over to shut off the cassette tape player but then we suddenly hear the girl's voice again, whispering:)

Last night I dreamed I was standing in front of a long clothesline of pieces of toast. All the pieces had a hole punched out of them and when you looked in each slice you saw a different miniature world. That's all I remember.

(Slight pause.)

Please, somebody, get me out of this house.

(The tape continues to play background Christmas noise for a few moments, before Jen presses "stop." Out the window the film is at the end of a reel. Sallie focuses on her work again. She looks up. She sings:)

SALLIE:
>   When I was twenty
>   I got looked at plenty
>   At twenty-nine
>   The world was mostly mine
>   Then the tables turned
>   Now I'm pretty much spurned
>   At thirty-three
>   I'm looked at mostly by me
>   I never knew
>   I'd come to partially miss
>   The looks I once found lascivious

(Jen leans over the cassette tape player and sings:)

JEN:
>   In the back of your photograph
>   See right there
>   I am the one with the
>   Recalcitrant hair
>   You don't know me
>   'Cause we've never met
>   A tragedy for us
>   Both I suspect

If you'd turned around
Maybe you would have found
The one you didn't know you couldn't find
And could you give me directions
To the back of your mind

SALLIE:

I'd like to be the person

JEN:

In the back of your mind

SALLIE AND JEN:

Please keep me in mind

I Saw You Nod Your Head

Ring ring. Jen picks up the phone. Karl, who is at home, has his coat on but takes it off shortly after the scene begins.

JEN: Hello
KARL: It's Karl
JEN: Hi Karl
KARL: Okay I'm going to stop by

(Ring ring. Sallie picks up the phone. Lyle at home.)

JEN: Shoot
KARL: What
JEN: I forgot I'm not answering the phone
LYLE: Sallie
SALLIE: Is this Lyle
LYLE: Yes
    Did you forget to say hello
SALLIE: Yes
    Hi Lyle

LYLE: I'm disturbed

KARL: Why Jen

SALLIE: Why Lyle

JEN: Because anyway
    why Karl

KARL: Why Jen

LYLE: I was thinking about that map

SALLIE: That mat

LYLE: Map

JEN: Why are you stopping by

KARL: Oh because I want to talk to you

SALLIE: What mat

JEN: Oh

LYLE: Mappp

KARL: I want to talk to you about
    you know

SALLIE: Oh map

JEN: Oh

SALLIE: Oh that map of / your father's

KARL: You know

LYLE: My father's map
    you know
    the one from his most recent and possibly fatal trip

KARL: About your thoughts on
    you know

SALLIE: Oh the map you found in your dad's car

JEN: I don't know Karl
    I don't know if it's a good time to talk about

LYLE: that map

JEN: you know

LYLE: Of course That Map

(Pause.)

KARL: Are you there

SALLIE: I'm listening

JEN: I'm here

KARL: My feelings for you are nothing to be afraid of but Jen
   you know I have a policy

JEN: Oh right

LYLE: Of course that map

JEN AND KARL: No feelings over the phone

LYLE: My father took a detour

SALLIE: What do you mean A Detour

LYLE: He'd marked the map with the most direct route

SALLIE: Yes we've been over this and over this
   You think there's something nefarious about that

JEN: Still I don't know if you should come over Karl

KARL: My feelings for you mean you no harm Jen they're as benign
as could be

JEN: Benign feelings are the deadliest kind Karl Besides I'm not in
the mood for feelings Karl

SALLIE: Sometimes a detour is just a detour

LYLE: He'd marked the map Sallie

SALLIE: With the most direct route yes you said

LYLE: But his car was found twenty miles south of
   the most direct route

KARL: I'm re-putting on my coat

JEN: But I don't feel like feelings tonight

LYLE: My father wasn't one to deviate Sallie
   My father didn't Veer Off

JEN: Not just Your feelings Karl
   All feelings Karl All
   Feelings

LYLE *(Pronounces the "n")*: Damn it Sallie that wasn't his nature

JEN: Don't Re-Put On Your Coat Karl

SALLIE: Perhaps something struck his fancy
   Something caught his eye maybe
   Something or Some
   One

KARL: You Never feel like feelings Jen

JEN: That's just not true

KARL: I've zippered up my zipper

LYLE: What's that supposed to mean

SALLIE: What

JEN: What
      Unzipper your zipper Karl

LYLE: My father wasn't one to stray Sallie

SALLIE: Why are you speaking of him in the past tense
      The past tense is so effing boring

KARL: Ew yuck

JEN: What

KARL: There's some old food in my pocket

JEN: Ew
      Is it sticky

KARL: Sticky And wet
      sort of

JEN: Ew

LYLE: The word effing is effing boring
      (Pronounces the "n") Damn it Sallie
      I'm sorry to effing bore you It's just
      my father doesn't disappear

JEN: You can never get sticky stuff out

LYLE: Not every day anyway

KARL: I'd better change coats

SALLIE: It drives me crazy

JEN: You'd better throw out your coat

SALLIE: It drives me crazy that you pronounce the N in
      Damn

LYLE: That's how it's spelt
      (Pronounces the "n") Damn

KARL: Shoot

JEN: What

SALLIE: It's as bad as the effing past tense
      It drives me crazy

LYLE *(Pronounces the "n")*: Damn

KARL: Shoot
      I don't have another coat

JEN: Then that settles it

LYLE: I saw you nod your head

KARL: What

SALLIE: You saw me nod my head

JEN: You can't come over

LYLE: I saw you nod your head

KARL: When

SALLIE: When

JEN: Now

LYLE: Last week

KARL: I can still bundle up

SALLIE: When

JEN: How

LYLE: At the bakery

KARL: I'll wear layers

SALLIE: What bakery

JEN: That doesn't do me any good Karl

LYLE: The new bakery

KARL: What do you mean

SALLIE: Oh the new old bakery

LYLE: Of course the new old bakery

JEN: I mean whether you dress in layers or take off all your clothes
before you come over you'll still want to discuss

    feelings aka you know when you get here

    Won't You

SALLIE: What about the new old bakery

KARL: Nothing's changed if that's what you mean

LYLE: That's where I saw you nod your head

KARL: The fact that my coat has sticky and somewhat wet old
food in the pocket doesn't mean I've lost interest in discussing
you know aka my feelings

    for you

    with you Let's

    stop saying aka okay

SALLIE: So you saw me nod my head so what

JEN: Well as I told you before

    I'm not interested in feelings of any sort this evening

LYLE: The head pastry guy

    was explaining the

    chemistry behind unleavened bread

    and You Nodded Your Head

    When You Didn't Understand

KARL: I've got on three no
   four layers
SALLIE: I don't understand your point but
SALLIE AND JEN: Do me a favor
SALLIE: Don't Explain
JEN: Don't come over
KARL: I'm afraid it's too late
LYLE: I saw you nod your head is all
   When you didn't understand
KARL: I'm on my way
SALLIE: Maybe your father wants to take a break from
   you Lyle did you ever think of that Lyle because
   lately Lyle
   and I've been thinking about this
   lately Lyle
   talking to you is like eating
   a hair omelette
KARL: I'm halfway out the door
JEN AND LYLE: Nice image
JEN: but you're also halfway In the door Karl
SALLIE: When did you start taking emotional messages for Karl
by the way Lyle
KARL: What do you have against Karl's feelings Jen
LYLE: I have no idea what you're saying Sallie but this
   isn't the conversation I pictured before I picked up the phone
JEN: Jen is begging you not to refer to yourself in the third person
Karl
SALLIE: You picture your conversations Lyle
KARL AND LYLE: I do it all the time
SALLIE AND JEN: Let's talk in a little um
   later on okay
KARL AND LYLE: Fine
SALLIE AND JEN *(?)*: Okay
KARL AND LYLE: I said fine

(Everyone hangs up.)

Greek

Jen is sorting through a box of found garbage. Sallie is deeply involved in her dissertation—she's focused and appears to be having a burst of revision success right in front of our eyes. Then, her thought finished, she suddenly puts down her pen and picks up her phone. The phone rings in Jen's apartment. Meanwhile, throughout the scene, Lyle is sitting on the upper steps of the stairwell, visible only from the shins down, his top half in shadow. He might take off his shoe at some point and remove a small rock from his sock and then put his sock and shoe back on. Otherwise, he spends his time debating—from the shins down—his next move.

SALLIE: Tell me if this sounds pretentious but I'm beginning to see my romantic life as alarmingly Aristotelian
JEN: When should I tell you
SALLIE: It's just that Lyle never does anything
    inadvertent Jen He's so
    intentional Jen He just doesn't
    veer Is it too much to ask for
    a partner who's capable of shunning purpose on

occasion I called my
adviser's voice mail
JEN: It's a good word though Aristotelian
SALLIE: and then hung up Sure but
try saying it fast three times
JEN: Why did you do that
SALLIE: Because I can't stop thinking about him
JEN: Aristotle
SALLIE: My adviser / my adviser
JEN: Aristotelian Aristotelian Aristotelian
SALLIE: See
JEN: I thought you said he wasn't attractive
SALLIE: He's not but I Find him attractive
JEN: In what possible context would you find
yourself needing to say Aristotelian three times in a
row
SALLIE: Um say you felt like being
emphatic
JEN: Can you think of even one thing
you would characterize as being super-duper Aristotelian
SALLIE: Okay um
Life is hard for human beings
I am a human being
Life is hard for me
JEN: That was Aristotelian but I wouldn't say
it was super-duper Aristotelian
SALLIE: Okay well what if someone kept calling something
Platonic when it was actually Aristotelian
JEN: Uh-huh and to correct this person you would just
sort of yell Aristotelian in his or her face
three times
SALLIE: Exactly
JEN: It's your adviser's power over you that you find attractive
SALLIE: I find his power over me annoying Actually
I find just about everything he does
annoying If he uses the word moreover in
conversation with me one more time I'll / I don't know
JEN: So you find your adviser annoyingly attractive

SALLIE: I don't know I just want him to think I'm smart AND
    admire my breasts
JEN: Have you ever tried to say Platonic three times fast
SALLIE: Or maybe I just want him to think my breasts are smart
JEN: Yeah but Sallie
    at a certain point a person needs to
    choose between looking good and accomplishing something
because it's just not possible
    to do
    both
SALLIE: Platonic Platonic Platonic
JEN: That sounded much easier
SALLIE: It was

(Longish pause.)

JEN: One time when Karl and I first started
    Ihatethatstupidphrase
    seeing each other he called me up and said
    It's Me before he was a me to me Do you
    understand what I'm saying Sallie He
    prematurely me-ified himself and it pissed me off
SALLIE: Wasn't it sort of flattering that he
    wanted so badly to be a me to you
JEN: Me-ification should be offered not
    taken Sallie
SALLIE: Shouldn't it be pissed off me
JEN: What
SALLIE: Sorry I'm just thinking about the split verbal whatever
JEN: You want me to say Karl's behavior pissed off me
SALLIE: Just if you want your annoyance to be
    correct I mean it's your
    call

(Slight pause.)

JEN: Oh don't worry Sallie my annoyance is correct and
    anyway
    I'm not sure that that is in fact a split verbal whatever

(Karl appears at the intercom and basically buzzes every apartment, in response to which the building's misguided Good Samaritan—every building has one—buzzes the stranger in without so much as a "Who is it?")

SALLIE: Do you think that your adviser could beat up my adviser
JEN: Totally

(They each put down their phones without hanging them up. Sallie gets back to work, Jen gets back to sorting.)

Scene in the Stairway Scene

Karl, appearing as a head, neck and shoulders, begins to ascend the steps as Lyle—feet, shins and knees—is prompted to stand up. Throughout the scene we hear a lot of that sound sandy grit makes when sandwiched between leather soles and faux-marble stairs. For most of the scene Lyle and Karl are unable to see one another. In increments they will advance down and up the steps, respectively, so that by the end of the scene they have entirely reversed positions, with Karl seen only from the shins down and Lyle seen only from the neck up.

LYLE: Is that
    Karl
KARL *(Weird emphasis on "Lyle")*: It's me Lyle
LYLE: I'm Lyle
KARL: I know you're Lyle I
    emphasized the wrong word by
    mistake
LYLE: I used to do that all the time
KARL: You stopped

LYLE: Let's just say I'm more
    careful than I once was It's
    hard to stop entirely How
    is it out there

KARL: It's spitting

LYLE: Is it aggressive

KARL: The spitting

LYLE: Uh-hmm

KARL: So-so

LYLE: Right I guess that's the nature of precipitation-type spitting
as opposed to expectoration-type spitting
    which is almost always um

KARL: aggressive

LYLE: Yeah aggressive Once saliva leaves the mouth its functional
aspect turns ugly Anyway

KARL: It's raining a bit and
    there's a chill in the air

LYLE: Ha in here too

KARL: What's that

LYLE: I said Ha in here too

KARL: But what does that mean

LYLE: It turns out my girlfriend's very anti-sigh We were
    talking through the door and I
    sighed as I stood there

KARL: Sighs have their place

LYLE: Sighs have no place for Sallie It turns out
    she is um aggressively against sighs

KARL: They are funny things sighs Strange
    beasts

LYLE: I don't know I just said what the eff
    and left sort of

KARL: Semiverbal Semiphysical Sometimes signaling
    deflation Sometimes signaling deflation's antithesis Strange
    antithetical beasts sighs are

LYLE: Did I just say what the eff

KARL: Yes

LYLE: I meant fuck

KARL: But I will say this A full-blown sigh is a
corrective thing
LYLE: I just said what the eff Fuck and left
sort of

(As Karl/neck advances one step, Lyle/shins has lifted a shoe off the stair.)

KARL: So you know how when you said
Karl Wonders Is That A Yes
she said
LYLE: She said
nothing Karl
KARL: That's right she said nothing

(Lyle/shins examines the sole of one shoe.)

LYLE: Right

(Lyle/shins thinks "Aha, just as I suspected.")

KARL: and I'm not
saying no means yes Lyle but
LYLE: but
KARL: but
I might be saying nothing means yes

(Lyle/shins thinks "gum.")

LYLE: You think nothing means something Karl

(Pause, during which Karl/neck advances two or three steps while Lyle/shins attempts to scrape the gum off his shoe and onto the step. Perhaps, by the way, Karl had spit out his gum onto the staircase in an earlier scene.)

KARL: I think it's possible

LYLE: That Jen's nothing had content
KARL: That Jen's nothing was half full

(Both men sigh here, Karl's of the elated variety ["things are going good!"], Lyle's of the deflated variety ["you poor sad sack."].)

LYLE: Well that's a really
       gymnastic perspective Karl

(Pause.)

So here I go
KARL: Into the spitting chill
LYLE: I've got a warm coat
KARL: Myself
       I dress in layers
LYLE: You're satisfied with that method
KARL: Ve / ry
LYLE: Really
KARL: Very
       well it's new / so
LYLE: Gotcha
KARL: we'll see

(Lyle exits the building.)

Gesundheit

Sallie and Jen talk on the phone. Sallie sneezes.

SALLIE: So
    How is / It going
JEN: Well /
    It's not
SALLIE: Well
    Well
JEN: Well comma It's not
SALLIE: Oh right
JEN: You
SALLIE: Same here same here Did
    you write that letter to your /
    adviser
JEN: Not yet but guess who I was just thinking about I was just
thinking about that guy Ian
SALLIE: That guy Ian was in my dream
JEN: Really that guy Ian was in my dream
SALLIE: That guy Ian was in my dream

JEN: Really that guy Ian was in my dream
SALLIE: That guy Ian wanted very much to be my
    boyfriend in my dream
JEN: Really that guy Ian Was my boyfriend
    in my dream
SALLIE: Really
    In your dreams
JEN: What
SALLIE *(Hitting the "m")*: In your dreaM
    Anyway I don't know that
    guy Ian thinks he's on film and
    that guy Ian's not on film
JEN: Anyway the pertinent thing is in real life that
    guy Ian doesn't give me the time of day
SALLIE: Because he thinks he's on film
JEN: But in my dreams that guy Ian
    worships me
SALLIE: I'm here to tell you that he's not on film
JEN: And it's Extremely Disconcerting when someone who
    formerly Had No Use For You Suddenly Does
SALLIE: Suddenly Does in your dreams
JEN: Still

(Slight pause.)

SALLIE: Monogamy's a bitch

(Slight pause.)

One time a group of us went to a bar after class and my adviser
was sitting next to me and I suddenly noticed our knees were
touching but I didn't know if he noticed our knees were touching
and I didn't want to make a big deal movement that said Oh Our
Knees Are Touching And That's Socially Inappropriate Given
The Confines Of Our Relationship but in the meantime I had
grown so focused on the contact it felt like my knee was in fact
throbbing so I decided to conduct an experiment in which I would
exert the smallest degree of extra pressure to I suppose make the

contact official but instead I somehow lost control of my leg and basically wound up knocking my adviser's knee with such incredible force that he uttered a sound that can only be characterized as a yelp

JEN: *Gesundheit*

SALLIE: What

JEN: from before when you sneezed I
    gotta go call my adviser

SALLIE: At this hour

JEN: Advisers don't sleep

It's for You

Sallie focuses on her dissertation but then shortly thereafter looks out the window again, while Jen turns up the volume on the cassette tape player.

LIZZIE: Mom, I was listening to that.
JEAN: It's Christmas, Lizzie. At Christmas we listen to Christmas music. That's how you make things Christmassy. What's the point of Christmas if it's not Christmassy?

(Christmas music begins to play. As Jean walks out of the room she says:)

This'll get you in the mood.

(Lizzie issues an ugh-type sound of frustration.)

LIZZIE: FA LA LA LA LA TO YOU, TOO, Jean!

(Slight pause.)

(Whispering into the cassette tape player) Do you see what I mean
About everything?

(Sound of Lizzie breathing and Christmas music.
    Jen presses "stop" on the cassette tape recorder. Meanwhile, Sal-
lie is looking out the window through binoculars at the neighbors'
home movies. She and we see the following as the scene progresses:
in this section of the home movies the family walks around a square,
descends steps, and feeds pigeons. The girl wears a red coat and cow-
boy boots, with which she is obviously quite taken. The phone rings in
Sallie's apartment.)

SALLIE: Hi Jen
LYLE: If we're / speaking
SALLIE: Oh hi Lyle You're up / late
LYLE: If we're speaking I want to say that in one's life there are only
so many significant cusps Sallie
SALLIE: Significant cuffs
LYLE: Significant cusppps
SALLIE: Oh I was trying to figure out what a Significant Cuff would
    Be Maybe like on a bloodstained shirt at a crime scene or
    something
LYLE: If we're speaking that's what I wanted to say
SALLIE: I'm speaking Lyle Aren't you
    speaking
LYLE: I'm speaking
SALLIE: I'm watching a little kid right now
LYLE: You're babysitting
SALLIE: No I'm watching a little kid out the window
    who seems so happy who
    thinks her cowboy boots will guarantee her
    happiness because at this moment anyway they
    define it
    Things can be the authors of a fine albeit temporary happi-
ness and
    fine happiness of any length is hard to
    argue with don't you
    think Lyle

LYLE: Things need to be some other way is what I'm
   saying if we're speaking Sallie
SALLIE: Are you trying to propose Lyle

(Pause.)

LYLE: Uh
   n / o
SALLIE: Oh
LYLE: You mean propose as in / propose propose
SALLIE: No not nothing no

(Slight pause.)

LYLE: Not many people can pull off albeit
SALLIE: What does that / mean
LYLE: You said fine albeit temporary
SALLIE: Did I
LYLE: When you were talking about the intersection of things and
happiness
SALLIE: Oh well I don't like notwithstanding It conjures confus-
ing imagery I don't like it I just
   don't

*(Sallie takes the phone away from her ear without hanging up. She
still watches out the window. Another home movie plays: the little girl
plays a telephone game with her mother. We also see the girl's face
in a sea of her dolls. And then we see her receive instructions from off
camera on how to pray. She prays. She sleeps.)*

LYLE: I'm just saying you pulled off albeit so you know
   Congratulations
   Sallie
   Sallie
   Sallie

*(Sallie hangs up the phone and dials Jen's number. The phone rings
and Jen picks up.)*

SALLIE: Do you ever wonder what
        happens to all those little
        girls at weddings who slide across the
        floor in their stocking feet
JEN: They put their shoes on Sallie

I Have a Policy

Sallie and Jen are still on the phone.

SALLIE: Lyle's dad tried to kiss me once
JEN: In a dream
SALLIE: In real life
JEN: But where is Lyle's dad in real life
SALLIE: Where indeed Lyle
    perceives things selectively
JEN: Well Karl absorbs things slowly
SALLIE: He's not a paper towel Jen
JEN: I wonder
SALLIE: Wow
    that's
    abrasive
JEN: I'm not a cleanser Sallie

(Buzz.)

Hang on someone's at my
    door
SALLIE: All right

(Jen presses "listen.")

JEN: Who is it
LYLE *(Through the intercom)*: Lyle
SALLIE AND JEN: Lyle
SALLIE: What's Lyle doing there
JEN: Hi Lyle what's up
LYLE *(Through the intercom)*: Can I come up
JEN: No I said what's
    up

SALLIE *(Through the phone)*:   LYLE *(Through the intercom)*:
He wants to come up   No can I come up

SALLIE: Why does he want to come up
JEN: Lyle is something up
LYLE: Sort of
SALLIE: What did he say
JEN: He said Sort Of
SALLIE: What does Sort Of mean
JEN: In a way
SALLIE: I Know What It Means

(Buzz, beep.)

Hang on It's my other
    Line
JEN: I'm still here
SALLIE: Hello
KARL: It's Karl
LYLE: What's up
SALLIE: Oh hi Karl
JEN: What
LYLE: Can I come up or
    what

KARL: Can I come over
SALLIE: Can you hang on a sec
JEN: Just a second
SALLIE: Jen it's Karl
JEN: Karl why is Karl calling you
SALLIE: I don't know Where's Lyle
JEN: Lyle's outside He's
    probably getting cold

(Buzz.)

KARL: Sallie
JEN: Hi Lyle
LYLE: I'm getting cold
SALLIE: Sorry Karl
JEN: Sorry Lyle
KARL: I need to talk
SALLIE: Can you hang on a sec
JEN: Crap
SALLIE AND LYLE: What
JEN: I jammed my finger
SALLIE: What if we just spoke on the
    phone Karl
LYLE: Ouch
JEN: I hate that
LYLE: It won't take long
KARL: See I have a policy
SALLIE AND JEN: What's that
LYLE: What I want to talk about
KARL: No feelings over the phone
SALLIE: Wait a minute
    He doesn't want to talk about feelings Jen
LYLE: It's about Sallie
SALLIE AND JEN: What about Sallie
LYLE: It's cold out here
SALLIE: I'm going to ask Karl to break
    his rule
JEN: Karl won't break his rule

SALLIE: Karl could you break your rule Karl
JEN: He won't do that
　　　Sallie
　　　Sallie are you there
KARL: Did you say something
SALLIE: Yes
KARL: I'm sorry
　　　I dropped the phone

(Buzz.)

JEN: I'm here Lyle
LYLE: It's cold out here
JEN: I'm sort of um indisposed Lyle
LYLE: Do people still get indisposed
SALLIE: Do people still drop the phone
JEN AND KARL: I do
SALLIE: Can you hang on a sec
　　　Jen
JEN: I'll be right with you Lyle
SALLIE: What does he want
JEN: I don't know he's cold

(Buzz.)

SALLIE AND JEN: Hang on
JEN: What's the story Lyle
LYLE: I'm looking for your perspective
SALLIE: I'm sort of indisposed Karl can
　　　we do this over the phone
KARL: That's funny I was indisposed
　　　just yesterday
　　　Nevertheless my policy is no feelings
　　　over the phone
JEN: Are you very cold
　　　Tell me you aren't Very cold
LYLE: As much as I'd like to tell you I'm not Very cold Jen
　　　the truth is I'm kinda cold Jen

SALLIE: You see I'm catching a cold Karl

KARL: Sorry to hear that Sallie Still
    my policy stands

JEN: Try imagining you're stuck in an elevator without a fan

SALLIE: Karl could you break your rule Karl

LYLE: Without a Man

KARL: It's actually a policy Sallie it's not a rule

JEN: Without a Fan so that it's you know
    Hot Anyway what is it you
    wanted to talk about

SALLIE: Okay could you amend your policy Karl

LYLE: Sallie said something recently
    something so

SALLIE: Pretty please Karl

JEN: What did Sallie say

SALLIE: Very pretty please Karl

KARL: Are you pressuring me Sallie

SALLIE: For me Karl

LYLE: It was something so

SALLIE: You can do it Karl

JEN: You can tell me Lyle

SALLIE: Come on Karl

LYLE: You know so

KARL: I don't like pressure Sallie
    Pressure makes me FEEL upset oh / MAN

SALLIE: Now that wasn't so hard / was
    it

KARL: That felt like a trick Sallie

SALLIE: Oh I'm not tricky Karl
    Please don't think I'm tricky Karl

KARL: I had been hoping we could speak frankly

SALLIE: Sure thing

KARL: You know best friend's boyfriend to
    girlfriend's best friend

SALLIE: Sure thing

KARL: Or whatever

JEN: Are you there

LYLE: All I can say is Sallie said something
      so uh
      That I guess I was hoping you could shed some light
JEN: I'll do what I can
LYLE: since everything gets filtered through my
      own you know crap
JEN: Your own what
LYLE: My own you know
      crap
KARL: Are you there
SALLIE: If you're asking me for advice Karl my answer is Sure
Thing Karl but keep in mind that whatever I have to say will have
been filtered through my own
        you know crap
LYLE: I'm not like your boyfriend Karl
KARL: Your own what
JEN *(Unwitting weird emphasis on "Lyle")*: I don't have a boy-
friend Lyle
SALLIE: You know crap
JEN: I mean I don't have a boyfriend comma Lyle
LYLE: You don't
KARL: Crap Crap oh sure your crap sure
JEN: In the sense that I hate that stupid word
      All the language of attachment
      I can't make heads or tails of it
      Do you know what I'm saying Lyle
SALLIE: You still feel upset don't you Karl
LYLE: You mean you constantly find yourself deposited
      in Russian novels you haven't read
SALLIE: I can hear it in your voice
LYLE: You mean most days you wake up and say Christ here
      I am again on the train to effing Sverdlosk
      I mean Catherinesburg
JEN: Uh
      nooo not really Lyle
KARL: Of course I still feel upset
      OH MAN I DID IT AGAIN

SALLIE: You're not going to drop the phone again are you

KARL: No but what's the point of a policy if no one
    adheres to it

JEN: I mean I do have a boyfriend Lyle
    I'm just saying I don't like the word boyfriend Lyle
    In other words Karl's my boyfriend in every sense of the
word except the word itself you know what I'm saying Lyle
    What are you saying Lyle

KARL: I mean my policy's not getting a lot of adherence here

LYLE: Wait
    Did I just use the word effing

SALLIE: That's one way of looking at it

JEN: Yes

SALLIE: The other way is to see that you're just filtering through
your own you know crap

LYLE: I meant Fucking

SALLIE: Which is healthy

JEN: You sound upset

KARL: I wanted to get some advice from you Sallie but
    here we are just talking about crap

SALLIE: Well don't take this the wrong way Karl but the
    parameters of your policy kinda kill a phone
    conversation

LYLE: Because it's not even a word

JEN: Effing

LYLE: I hate using words that aren't words

JEN: Well I wouldn't lose sleep over it

SALLIE: But anyway I know where you're coming from Karl I once
had a housesitter who sat all over my house and I'm still not over it
    And speaking of crap try living under the curse of a cute
    name

KARL: What are you talking about

LYLE: I'm sorry I'm a little on edge since my father's
    Disappearance

JEN: That's right Where did he go

SALLIE: I'm
    just trying to think of safe subjects here Karl I mean my
hands are sorta tied

LYLE: Well that's the problem isn't it

KARL: How do you spell it

SALLIE: ie not y

JEN: Oh right

KARL: Oh ie

SALLIE: My parents wanted it to be a little
    Different

KARL: Mine wanted mine to be the same

JEN: So listen Lyle just tell me what Sallie said

LYLE: Right well we were discussing our future
    Essentially

JEN *(Right)*:   SALLIE *(How interesting)*:
Uh-huh   Huh

KARL: I come from a long line of Karlses I mean
    Karls

LYLE: And I was expressing concern about you know the uh
    status quo

SALLIE: How sweet

JEN: Uh-huh

LYLE: Because I love her

SALLIE: I love long lines

LYLE: and because I hate her sometimes too

KARL: My son will be Dave

JEN: That's normal

SALLIE: A break in tradition

LYLE: And she thought I was on the verge of proposing
    and I just find that so

SALLIE: Can you / hang on a sec
    Jen

JEN AND LYLE: What

LYLE: 's the word

KARL: Um sure

LYLE: So

SALLIE: Jen

JEN: What

KARL: Hello

LYLE: What

JEN: So what

KARL: Hello

SALLIE: Jen

JEN: SO WHAT
  SO WHAT

LYLE: Oh uh
  I see

SALLIE: Jen

JEN: WHAT

SALLIE: Karl's son will be Dave

JEN: What

SALLIE: Karl's son he'll
  be Dave

JEN: Lyle

SALLIE: No Dave

JEN: Lyle

SALLIE: Lyle must be freezing

JEN: Are you sure Karl said Dave

SALLIE: Ask Lyle if he's dressed in layers

JEN: Not Dave-id

SALLIE: But don't tell him I asked you to ask

JEN: Lyle what are you wearing

SALLIE: And while you're at it
  askLylewhyhehasn'taskedmetomarryhimbutdon'ttellhimIas
kedyoutoask

JEN: Lyle
  Lyle
  Lyle
  Crap

SALLIE: What

JEN: Lyle left Just
  Plain Dave

SALLIE: Karl definitely didn't say David I wonder
  why Lyle left

JEN: I can't believe Karl's son will be Dave

SALLIE: That's so unlike Lyle to leave

JEN: I can't believe Karl's son will definitely be Dave

SALLIE: Something's up Definitely

(Jen and Sallie put down their phones. Sallie heads over to the window while Jen heads over to the cassette tape player.)

KARL: Um
Sallie

(Sallie picks up her binoculars and again watches the home movies playing in the apartment across the way. Via projections, we see the family and extended family celebrate Christmas. The segment ends with the father writing "Merry Christmas 1940" on the chalkboard the girl has received as a gift. Meanwhile, Jen presses "play" on the cassette tape player. The girl on the tape is now a woman of thirty-seven.)

LIZZIE: Um, hello Sony Series Two. Guess who? It's me, Lizzie. Sorry I lost track of your whereabouts. That was rude.
Um, well it's been an uneventful couple of decades, I guess.
I did just get divorced.
Of course I keep trying to chart the road to my marriage's end.
Jean with a J was sad to hear it, but not surprised.
I was surprised to hear that she was sad and, um, sad to hear she wasn't surprised.
I trace it—the end that is, or the beginning of the end—to the moment when seemingly by accident we switched bedsides. Isn't that funny? He went away for a week and each night I gradually moved my way over a little further and by the time he returned his side was mine. He didn't even mention it. I don't know. It's all the
(Stumbles over the word) insignificancies
(Says it again, still gets it wrong) insignificancies
(Says it again, still gets it wrong) insignificancies. I mean, isn't it?
Dad's mixing up some eggnog in the kitchen right now.
I don't think he knows what he's doing.
GENE *(From off)*: Do you remember where your mother used to keep the baking soda, Liz?
LIZZIE: I guess that's about it. Oh, guess what I did? You'll enjoy this—I bought myself an early Christmas present. Guess what I got?
(Sound of unwrapping) I got . . . a pocketbook.
Merry Christmas, 2002

Bungled Civilian Amalgam

Lyle is on his hands and knees and is peering underneath Sallie's door. We hear the sound of grit meeting shoe as Karl ascends the steps; as he passes by Lyle he says:

KARL: Lyle

(Lyle doesn't move.)

LYLE: Karl

(Karl walks up one more flight.)

Sallie

(Karl knocks on Jen's door.)

KARL: Jen

(Karl knocks on Jen's door.)

LYLE: Sallie

(Karl knocks on Jen's door.)

KARL: Jen

(Karl knocks on Jen's door.)

LYLE: Sallie

(Karl knocks on Jen's door.)

KARL: Jen

(Karl knocks on Jen's door. Rest.)

KARL:	LYLE:
Jen	Sallie
Jen	Sallie
Jen	Sallie

(Jen is by now crouching on her side of the door, mirroring Lyle's position, although they crouch at different doors. In her apartment, Sallie stands facing the closed door with her arms crossed.)

SALLIE: Lyle
JEN: Karl
LYLE: Sallie
KARL: Jen
SALLIE: Lyle
JEN: Karl
LYLE: Sallie
KARL: Jen
SALLIE: Lyle
JEN: Karl
LYLE: Sallie
KARL: Jen

(Etcetera, until the reciting of the four names has accelerated to warp speed. Karl and Lyle suddenly get up and rush past one another on the stairway. As they do so, they say:)

Lyle
LYLE: Karl

(Before heading to the outside of the other's girlfriend's door.)

KARL: Sallie
LYLE: Jen
SALLIE: Karl
JEN: Lyle
KARL: Sallie
LYLE: Jjjjjjennnnn
SALLIE: Karl
JEN: Lyle
KARL: Sallie Sallie
LYLE: Jjjennn Jen Jen Jen
SALLIE: Karl

KARL:	JEN:
Sallie	Lyle

SALLIE	LYLE
(I'm suddenly finding you a wee bit attractive):	*(I'm suddenly finding you a wee bit attractive)*:
Karl	Jen
Karl	Jen
Karl	Jen
Karl	Jen
Karl	Jen
Karl	Jen
Karl	Jen
Karl	Jen
Karl	Jen

(Karl, unnerved, then rushes back to Jen's door and is surprised to find Lyle still there. Karl bends down in an incredibly awkward way— as opposed to just crouching—and whispers to Jen through the space beneath her door.)

KARL: Jen /
LYLE: Jen /
KARL: Jen /
LYLE: Jen /
KARL: Jen /
LYLE: Jenny

(Slight pause.)

KARL: Lyle
LYLE: Jen
KARL: Lyle
LYLE: Jen
KARL: Lyle
LYLE: Jen
JEN: Karl
    Lyle
    Karlyle
KARL AND LYLE: Jen

(Ring ring. Jen picks up the phone.)

SALLIE: Jen
JEN: Sallie
KARL: Lyle
LYLE: Lyle Jen
    Jen Lyle
SALLIE: Jen
LYLE: Jen
KARL: Jen
SALLIE: Jen
LYLE: Jen

KARL: Jen
SALLIE: Jen
LYLE: Jen
KARL: Jen

(Slight pause.)

JEN: Jen

(Slight pause.)

SALLIE: Jen

(Slight pause. Calling through door:)

Kaarll
LYLE: Jen
KARL: Lyle
SALLIE: Kaarll
LYLE: Jen
KARL: Lyle
SALLIE: Kaarll
LYLE: Jen
KARL: Lyle

(Slight pause.)

SALLIE *(Calling through door)*: Lyylle
LYLE: Jen
KARL: Lyle
    Lyle
    Lyle
    Lyle
    Lyle
SALLIE: Lyylle
LYLE: Jen

KARL: Lyle
    Lyle
    Lyle
    Lyle
    Lyle
SALLIE: Lyylle
LYLE: Jen

(Silence. Breathing.)

KARL: Lyle
LYLE: Jen
KARL: Lyle
LYLE: Jen
KARL: Lyle
LYLE: Jen
KARL *(No it's)*: Sallie Lyle
LYLE: Jen
KARL: Sallie Lyle
LYLE: Jen
KARL: Sallie Lyle
LYLE: Jen
KARL *(!)*: Lyle
LYLE *(Exactly)*: Jen Lyle
KARL *(Remember)*: Sallie Sallie
LYLE: Sallie
    (New idea) Karl
    Jen Lyle
    (In other words) Jen Lyle
    Sallie Karl
KARL *(Etcetera)*: Jen Karl Karl Jen Jen Karl / Karl Jen Jen Karl
Karl Jen
LYLE *(Etcetera)*: Jen Lyle Sallie Karl Jen Lyle Sallie Karl Jen Lyle
Sallie Karl

(During the above line, pushing happens. Lyle falls down a flight of stairs.)

SALLIE: Jen
JEN: Sallie
KARL: Lyle
   Lyle
   Lyle
   Lyle
   Lyle

(Lyle stands up and walks halfway up the flight of stairs with some difficulty.)

LYLE: Listen Karl, while I have no wish to add to any man's symphony of sorrows, we must face the facts as they exist

before us: Jen, for whatever reason—there may be one, there may be exponentially more than that—Jen does not find you winsome. Let me say it another way: your longing for Jen, Karl, is not pragmatic. As proof I offer the fact that Jen herself told me, and I quote, that she doesn't Have A Boyfriend Comma Lyle. In closing, I deeply regret that I am the bearer of this unwelcome news, although as such it should not surprise us, as most things that are pleasing are also by definition utterly, maddeningly elusive. If you are so

(Pronounces the "n") damn blind as to be unable to recognize the God's-honest-truth of the situation as I have laid it out before you, all I can say is Jeez Louise. In sum: you are wretched, you are undone, you are not Jen's boyfriend.

(Lyle promptly continues on his way up the stairs and back to Jen's door.
   Karl emits a guttural sound of suffering.
   Karl shoves his way past Lyle and hurls himself at Jen's door, attempting to break it down as he says the following and occasionally clutches his stomach. At the same time, Lyle sort of recoils in embarrassment for Karl and ascends the flight of stairs that takes him back to Sallie's door.)

KARL: I am the boyfriend of Jen
   I am Jen's boyfriend Karl
   I am Karl comma Jen's boyfriend

I Am Karl Comma Jen's Boyfriend
I AM Karl COMMA Jen'S BOYFRIEND
JEN: What are you wearing

(Karl is wretched; Karl rallies.)

KARL: Uh a T-shirt
JEN: And
KARL: A uh shirt
JEN: And
KARL: A uh 'nother shirt
JEN: And
KARL: Yet another one
JEN: No pants
    No socks No
    underwear No
    footwear No
    wristwatch No
    um etcetera
KARL: Of course pants of
    course pants and
    all the rest These are
    givens I thought
    we were talking about
    my top half I brought
    you a suitcasefull of garbage for
    old time's sake of
    course pants I'm a
    fan of pants I'm a
    man of pants
JEN: Let me ask you something
KARL: Shoot
JEN: It's a non sequitur
KARL: Bring it on
JEN: You know that-guy-Ian right
KARL: Ian what's-his-face
JEN: Uh-huh
KARL: Uh-huh

JEN: Does that-guy-Ian-what's-his-face see anybody
KARL: What
JEN: Does that-guy / -Ian-what's-his-face see anybody
KARL: Why are you asking me if that-guy-Ian-what's / -his-face
sees anybody
JEN: For a friend For a friend
KARL: Sal / lie
JEN: No /
KARL: Then / who
JEN: Um that friend of my friend Kate who
only has friends who look just like her
I'm asking for / Kate's friend
KARL: He sees everybody
JEN: What do you / mean
KARL: Tell Kate's friend that that-guy-Ian-what's-his-face sees
everybody
oh and Jen
JEN: Yes
KARL: Eff you
JEN *(?)*: Eff me
KARL: You heard me

(Slight pause.)

JEN: Don't you think love should be more improbable
KARL: I don't know what that means
JEN: We're such a probable Ihatethisstupidword couple Karl
KARL: You think it's a problem that we're probable
JEN: It's a problem if love is supposed to be improbable
KARL: Why are only difficult things admirable to you
JEN: I don't know
KARL: Well I don't want to be forced to use the words juvenile
romantic and vision in close succession but
JEN: I'm complicated You always said you liked complicated women
KARL: Women who are complicated in a FUN way

(Sallie is by now crouching on her side of the door, trying to peer beneath it; Lyle sits on the landing adjacent to Sallie's door.)

SALLIE: You're a causal guy Ly

LYLE: A causal guy

SALLIE: You're such a causal guy Ly

LYLE: As opposed to what

SALLIE: Me

LYLE: You don't believe in cause Sallie

SALLIE: Are you calling me irrational

LYLE: I worry about what's there Sallie

SALLIE: I worry about what's not here Lyle I mean
    there

(Sallie slips her fingers under the door and wiggles them. Lyle turns suddenly and addresses Sallie's fingers.)

LYLE: You know what you do You
    hold forth on subjects Sallie
    you neither fully understand nor
    are completely ignorant of and
    I invest belief in these flambéed theories and
    conclusions this this
    semi-enlightened limbo of yours this this
    no-cigar sagacity only
    to be rudely awakened at
    inopportune social junctures I
    do not like to be awakened rudely at
    inopportune social junctures Sallie I
    do not like it one bit

(Sallie's fingers stop wiggling and start pointing.)

SALLIE: There is little these days Lyle that you
    like one bit In fact I dare
    you Lyle to name one thing these days that you
    like one bit whereas I on the other hand
    like all too many things exactly
    and no more than
    one bit

LYLE: You are cranky Sallie because your
     dissertation has proved a difficult
     birth
     You are a cranky Sallie
SALLIE: Don't apply baby metaphors to artistic
     endeavor Lyle not in my
     building's stairwell
LYLE: Your fear of unfortunate
     phrases is ruining our relationship
     Sallie
SALLIE: What is ruining our
     relationship Lyle is your habit of
     showing up at my door looking
     skinny and appalled
LYLE: I'm not at all
     skinny
SALLIE: You got any gum on ya
LYLE: Yeah

(Lyle slides a piece of gum under the door. Lyle and Sallie chew.)

JEN: What does that mean complicated in a fun way Like
     kooky Like kooky with a C
KARL: I don't want to talk about inane things
JEN: Inanity is plucky honey There's something to be said for that
KARL: I brought you garbage for
     God's sake
JEN: It's too late for
     garbage
KARL: You need to reason with
     those academics
JEN: Ha Anyway
     I've tried
KARL: I doubt it
JEN: Your doubt is simple and idiomatic
     Karl you are lucky
KARL: I have no coat I
     am not lucky

I brought you garbage
and lots
of it
Excellent garbage
I don't deserve this
treatment

JEN: Basically
you have had the misfortune to
fall at the end of a long
line of ill-suitors who
together comprise my relationship history
faulty fellows and handsome
letdowns who were full-fledged
dullards and rascals by turn

KARL: I blame myself

JEN: Self-flagellation is icky and
unresourceful Karl

KARL: All right I blame you

JEN: Oh

(Slight pause.)

KARL: Did you call me honey before

JEN: Um-hmm

(Sallie and Lyle are still chewing.)

SALLIE: I did secretly want to sleep with The Housesitter

LYLE: What

SALLIE: I want to sleep with a lot of people I'll
never sleep with
I mean I
picture myself with one person but then I catch sight of
all the rest of humanity
Sometimes I walk down the street and think
I won't have you and I
won't have you and I
won't have you and

it's a little sad really and it's
strange because sometimes I even mourn that I
won't have the people I'm not even attracted
to Whoever said life is short sure was correct
LYLE: You think Life Is Short is an attributable quote
SALLIE: Everything is attributable Lyle Why do you think I have
such a headache all the
    time
LYLE: Sallie
SALLIE: and when I'm not walking around feeling stupid about my
shameful life and when I'm not walking around averting my eyes
I'm walking around feeling ripped-off Don't you walk around
feeling ripped-off Lyle
LYLE: I feel lucky Sallie
SALLIE: You feel yucky Lyle
LYLE: Lucky
SALLIE: Yucky how
LYLE: Lllucky lllucky
SALLIE: Lucky
    you do
LYLE: I do
SALLIE: You do
LYLE: I do
SALLIE: You do
LYLE: I do
    I do
    I do

(They chew. Pause. Then everybody sings:)

JEN:

    Why not take off your hair shirt
    And stay a while

SALLIE:

    I'd never wake you on purpose

LYLE:

    That would be guile

SALLIE:

> Sleep is sacred

SALLIE AND JEN:

> Sleep is sacred
> Sleep is a sacred thing

KARL:

> My gumption appears

JEN:

> To have been elsewhere shipped

KARL:

> In a world that worships print
> You dream in script

LYLE:

> Script is sacred

JEN AND LYLE:

> Script is sacred

JEN:

> Script is a sacred thing

LYLE:

> Listen to this
> And make it your mantra

KARL AND LYLE:

> Peace will always
> Come back to haunt ya

SALLIE:

> I'd never wake you on purpose
> My vow remains

KARL:
> It is my human nature
> To love what's left

SALLIE:
> If one could only refrain

SALLIE AND JEN:
> From one's refrain

LYLE:
> Sometimes small potatoes

KARL AND LYLE:
> Taste the best

JEN:
> Potatoes are sacred
> Potatoes are sacred

SALLIE:
> Potatoes are a sacred

(And then, after a moment, Jen and Sallie open their doors. And then, after another moment, Lyle enters Sallie's apartment, tentatively, while Karl descends the stairs and exits the building.)

END

$$\left[sic \right]$$

Production History

[*sic*] was commissioned by Steppenwolf Theatre Company in Chicago, Illinois, as part of its New Plays Lab during the 1997–1998 season. It was then workshopped at Soho Rep's Summer Camp in 1999, and subsequently received a production at Roadworks in Chicago in June 2000, both productions under the direction of Melissa Kievman. [*sic*] received its New York premiere at Soho Rep (Daniel Aukin, Artistic Director; Alexandra Conley, Executive Director) on November 21, 2001. It was directed by Daniel Aukin; set design was by Louisa Thompson, costume design was by Kim Gill, lighting design was by Matt Frey, sound design was by Robert Murphy; the stage manager was Mandy Sayle. The cast included:

THEO	Dominic Fumusa
BABETTE	Christina Kirk
FRANK	James Urbaniak
WOMAN	Jennifer Morris
MAN	Trevor A. Williams

Who

THEO, in his thirties

BABETTE, his neighbor, in her thirties

FRANK, their neighbor, in his thirties

THE AIRSHAFT COUPLE, somewhere nearby, in their thirties, in dispute

VOICE OF MRS. JORGENSON

VOICE OF DELIVERY PERSON

VOICE OF DR. GREENSPAN

Where and When

New York City, in a prewar apartment building, now-ish.

How

The play's language: please see the Playwright's Note.

Also, please note, in terms of the pronunciation of Mrs. Jorgenson's name: Frank pronounces it "Geor-genson"; Babette pronounces it "Your-genson"; and Theo pronounces it "Your-GEN-son," stressing the middle syllable.

Playwright's Note

[*sic*] takes place primarily in the doorways and shared hallway of three neighboring apartments; periodically within the apartments; and ultimately on the building's rooftop. "The Airshaft Couple" was originally imagined as a pair of voices that, in every sense, speak to the main characters from an offstage source, presumably another part of the building. It is possible, though, to bring The Airshaft Couple onstage in some partially visible way. Either way, it's important that the concept of an obstructed view be explored in some tangible sense within the production as a whole. Instead of having the actors in full and presentational sight at every moment, I imagine a scenario in which the visual story is as occasionally fragmentary as the verbal one; wherein, for instance, during selected parts of scenes we watch the action unfold through a half-closed door or a partially open window blind. In this way, the visual perspective of the audience is at times as limited as the outlook of the main characters, whose self-absorption makes them prone to misinterpretation and paranoia at every turn.

Which brings me to the title. *Sic*, of course, is a Latin term that appears in writing, as a signal to the reader that an apparent mistake is in fact an accurate citation. This notion of distancing oneself from responsibility informs the three main characters of the play, who exist at arm's length from their own situations, as if their real lives are yet to be inhabited. (A recipe for dissatisfaction, but there you go.) The main characters are all in their thirties, well past the point at which being a wunderkind is a viable option, a fact whose repercussions are very present.

Which brings me to the line breaks, internal capitalizations and lack of punctuation in general. These are intended as guidelines to the characters' thought processes, in terms of emphasis, pattern and rhythm; they should be honored, but should not feel enslaving.

When a line is indented, it indicates a line break. When there is no indentation, it indicates a continuation of the previous line. When a forward slash (" / ") appears within the dialogue, it indicates that the next line should begin, creating an overlap with the previous line.

The cadence should fluctuate according to circumstance and should avoid falling into repetition. The rhythm of the piece as a whole should reflect the momentum of active thought. By extension, during the play's many transitions, solutions other than blackouts should be at all costs sought. Moments should not so much cut in and out, as deftly replace one another.

NOTE: All quotations from Frank's Very Important Cassette Tape are excerpted from a training tape of the Missouri Auction School, Kansas City, Missouri.

Part One

From the virtual darkness we hear the sound of a very old woman singing in the shower. She has a throaty voice and sings with gusto:

MRS. JORGENSON'S VOICE:
    Oh I once loved Dick
    But Dick he loved Tom
    Butterflies were worms
    I don't love Dick no more

(We hear the sound of a synthesizer played very slowly; the first couple of bars of a song are played over and over with increasing speed and then with decreasing speed. It sounds like music from an amusement park ride. A phone rings a couple of times. We hear the sound of someone fumbling to pick it up.)

THEO: Are you awake
BABETTE: I was dreaming
THEO: But look outside

(As we see the shadow of a woman approaching a window blind we hear:)

191

FRANK: And when the winter will withdraw the weather won't be
wild
    And when the winter will withdraw the weather won't be wild
    And when the winter will withdraw the weather won't be wild

*(As the lights rise, we see portions of a prewar apartment building,
primarily four apartment doors that occupy the same floor, a hallway, a flight of the building's stairs and part of the building's rooftop.
Babette stands outside of Theo's apartment door and knocks. Theo
answers the door. They stare at one another for a period of time.)*

THEO: Ten
BABETTE: Twenty
THEO: Ten
BABETTE: Eighteen
THEO: Ten
BABETTE: Twelve
THEO: Ten
BABETTE: Fifteen
THEO: Ten
BABETTE: Fourteen
THEO: Ten
BABETTE: Twenty
THEO: Ten
BABETTE: Eighteen
THEO: Ten
BABETTE: Twelve
THEO: Ten
BABETTE: Fifteen
THEO: Ten
BABETTE: Fourteen
THEO: Five
BABETTE *(Did she hear correctly)*: Fine
THEO *(No)*: Fivvveh
BABETTE *(Without pause)*: Ten Great Theo Ten Okay Theo Ten
Okay Great

*(Theo opens his wallet, pulls out a ten-dollar bill and hands it to
Babette.)*

I'll be able to get
    this ten back to you
    well Not This Ten
    obviously Theo obviously but
    A Ten Plus Interest
    sometime uh
THEO: No interest necessary
BABETTE: No it's
    Something I'm Doing
    to clear my Slates
    Debt and Conscience
    Thanks Theo
    Theo thanks

(Babette retreats from Theo's door and enters her apartment just as Frank emerges from his apartment and knocks on Theo's door. Theo answers it.)

FRANK: I was wondering if I could borrow your
    Cassette Tape Player
THEO: IIII don't have one
FRANK: I wonder who has a
    Cassette Tape Player
THEO: III don't know
FRANK: Does Babette have a
    Cassette Tape Player
THEO: II don't know
FRANK *(As he walks away)*: I don't know
    I don't know I don't
    Know how I'm going to listen to My Very Important
    Cassette Tape

(Theo closes his door as Frank knocks on Babette's door. She answers it.)

BABETTE: Hi Frank
FRANK: Could I borrow hi Babette your
    Cassette Tape Player
BABETTE: I don't have one

FRANK: But what has become of all of the
   Cassette Tape Players

(Frank retreats from Babette's door. Babette closes her door and then suddenly reopens it as she calls down the hall.)

BABETTE: Why not ask Mrs. Jorgenson

(There is the sound of the same short piece of synthesizer music. Pause. And again. Perhaps Babette is visible in silhouette behind her blind. She is searching through the pockets of clothes that are lying around her apartment.)

FRANK *(From his apartment)*: Sally sought some seeds to sow but sadly soon it snowed
   Sally sought some seeds to sow but sadly soon it snowed
   Sally sought some seeds to sow but sadly soon it snowed

(Babette knocks on Theo's door. Theo answers it.)

BABETTE: I'm going to the store downstairs Do you need anything from The Store Downstairs
THEO: No Uh Yes I need candy bars Could you pick me up some Candy Bars
BABETTE: How many candy bars
THEO: Six or seven Candy Bars
BABETTE: Six
   Or Seven candy bars
THEO: Seven Candy Bars
BABETTE: Do you have Uh money
THEO: I just lent you ten dollars
BABETTE: I'm not in a position
   Uh
   Theo think about it
   to antilend
   Just Now
THEO: Antilend
BABETTE: I mean I'd have to be a fool

(Theo hands Babette a couple of dollars and starts to close his door but then stops as he watches Babette knock on Frank's door. Frank opens his door just barely.)

Do you need anything from the store Frank
FRANK: I need a Cassette Babette Tape Player
BABETTE: The store downstairs Frank
FRANK: Something with Babette which to
    Gargle
BABETTE: Mouthwash Frank
FRANK: For my Babette
    Throat
BABETTE: I'll need the money up front Frank

(Frank hands Babette some money.)

FRANK: But Babette
    nothing too Harsh
BABETTE: Your throat didn't sound sore last night
FRANK: My throat's not sore
THEO: Last night
BABETTE AND FRANK *(Didn't realize he was there)*: Hi Theo what's uh shaking
THEO: Not much By the way did I hear your doors shutting at almost the same instant last night
BABETTE AND FRANK: Last night
THEO: I think I did
BABETTE AND FRANK: Last night
THEO: The one that's two nights before tomorrow
    night I think I did
BABETTE AND FRANK *(Each says one)*: You did/Did you
THEO: I'm pretty sure I did and then I happened actually to be over by the window and I think I saw you guys cross the street together
BABETTE AND FRANK *(Each says the other one)*: Did you/You did
THEO: Yeah and then if I'm not mistaken I saw Frank look up at my window and Babette covering the side of her face as you both rushed out of view

195

BABETTE AND FRANK: Oh Theo please we were Here we were Here
BABETTE *(Continues without a break)*: I fell asleep in the middle of
a poorly edited epic
FRANK: And I stopped off at Mrs. Jorgenson's
THEO: Funny you should mention Mrs. Jorgenson because I ran
into Mrs. Jorgenson and Mrs. Jorgenson said that you said that
you and Babette were going out for dinner Mrs. Jorgenson also
said that you said that you might try to see a movie Mrs. Jorgenson also said that you said not to mention any of that to me if Mrs.
Jorgenson happened to see me Mrs. Jorgenson did happen to see
me but Mrs. Jorgenson didn't happen to remember your request
not to mention anything to me until the details of your evening's
plans had fallen unfortunately from Mrs. Jorgenson's mouth

(Pause, then:)

BABETTE AND FRANK: It's true we did Socialize without you last
night but only because we were meeting to plan an impromptu surprise party for you having nothing to do with your birthday and
having everything to do with your being You Theo You
BABETTE *(Continuing on without a break, irrationally annoyed)*:
Now if you'll excuse me I need to pick up some things at
    The Store Downstairs

(Babette storms off down the hall. Slight pause.)

THEO: When's the surprise party
FRANK *(Irrationally annoyed, too)*: I don't know Theo We didn't
get that far but frankly I suspect the party's off

*(We hear the sound of the same few bars of synthesizer music. It stops.
Theo gets up, crosses to a window and opens it.*
    *From The Airshaft Couple's apartment, from their kitchen, we
hear the sound of a bowl falling to the floor and then spinning: wah,
wah, wah. Throughout the scene, shadows are thrown of bodies moving in their kitchen but we can't actually see the bodies themselves.)*

MAN'S VOICE: Did you throw that

WOMAN'S VOICE: No
MAN'S VOICE: Oh I thought you threw it
WOMAN'S VOICE: It dropped
MAN'S VOICE: Is it broken
WOMAN'S VOICE: No
MAN'S VOICE: Oh

(The man walks away and then returns.)

Is this yours
WOMAN'S VOICE: Where did you find that
MAN'S VOICE: On the bottom shelf
WOMAN'S VOICE: Which bottom shelf
MAN'S VOICE: The bottom shelf of the gray thing
WOMAN'S VOICE: Oh
MAN'S VOICE: I've never seen it before
WOMAN'S VOICE: Someone gave it to me
    I forget who
MAN'S VOICE: Do you want it
WOMAN'S VOICE: I forgot I had it
MAN'S VOICE: Should I get rid of it
WOMAN'S VOICE: No
MAN'S VOICE: You forgot you had it
WOMAN'S VOICE: I might want it
MAN'S VOICE: You forgot you had it but now you want it
WOMAN'S VOICE: I forgot I might want it
MAN'S VOICE: Do you forget what you might want a lot
WOMAN'S VOICE: Constantly

(Frank knocks on Theo's door and Theo closes the window before answering the door.)

FRANK: What rhymes with
    Letter of Eviction

(Frank hands Theo a letter.)

THEO *(Reading)*: Uh-oh

(Slight pause.)

FRANK: Is that all you have to

(Slight pause.)

THEO: say

(Apparently. Babette appears from the stairwell. As she distributes the candy bars and the mouthwash it turns into a mutual exchange as together Theo and Frank hand Babette the letter.)

BABETTE *(Reading)*: Uh-oh

(Frank looks at her expectantly.)

(That's genuine tough luck) Say

(Pause.)

THEO: Let Her Love The Kitchen

(Rhymes with Letter of Eviction. Slight pause.)

BABETTE AND THEO *(Each saying the other's name at the end of the line, with emphasis)*: I guess if you're stuck you could stay with me
    or
    Theo/Babette

(Pause.)

FRANK: I can't think about it right now
BABETTE AND THEO *(Relieved, each picking two out of three words)*:
Okay/Say/Boy

(Babette unlocks her door.)

THEO: Babette was there any change
    from the Candy Bars
BABETTE: Oh yes I forgot

(Babette hands Theo his change.)

THEO *(Selective memory is a fascinating thing)*: Oh yes I forgot
I need to get back to work
BABETTE: Thrill-o-rama still
THEO: It's a complicated piece
BABETTE: The first two bars Still sound really good
THEO: Did she just Hit that adverb with something akin to
    Mockery or was that Merely my iMagination
BABETTE: I just said that Thrill-o-rama's first two
    bars Still sound really good

*(Babette and Theo enter their apartments and close the door. Frank
lingers in the hallway, Little Boy Lost, holding his Letter of Eviction.
We hear a couple of loud meows.*

*Theo sits at his synthesizer. He stares at the keyboard. He is seen
in shadow behind his blind. In compositional hell, Theo will punctu-
ate the following section with abortive and puny attempts to further
his score.*

*Babette is standing next to a table on which rests a jar filled with
coins; Babette makes rolls of quarters, dimes, nickels and pennies
throughout the section. Or perhaps she has one of those plastic coin
organizer things into which one can insert a bunch of coins and it sorts
them by denomination. We should have noticed, incidentally, that her
apartment is appointed with few things.*

*Frank sits in a schoolhouse-type chair in his apartment; he has
an instructional pamphlet open on his lap. A tape recorder sits nearby.
Throughout this section he is flipping through the pamphlet, practicing different exercises and listening to his Very Important Cassette
Tape. Frank presses "play" on his tape recorder.)*

VERY IMPORTANT CASSETTE TAPE: This training record is a part of
the home study course of the Missouri Auction School, Kansas
City, Missouri. Its purpose is to assist you with the various meth-
ods of bid calling, filler words and general auction salesmanship.
Auctioneering offers you a pleasant and honorable profession.
The well-trained auctioneer is always in demand. You may be
self-employed. Your life is enjoyable. You meet fine people. The
hours are short, the pay sure.

(Frank stops the tape and practices a lip trill as Babette speaks into the phone.)

BABETTE: Larry it's me
No Me
No Me

(Larry tries to escape.)

I'm willing to call-wait

(Babette waits as Theo makes a puny attempt to further his score. Frank presses "play" again.)

VERY IMPORTANT CASSETTE TAPE: Most auctioneers use two different chants. One is what we call a talking-type chant that sounds like this. *(He demonstrates)* The other is what we call more of a rhythm chant. *(He demonstrates)*

(Frank stops the tape and rolls his R's. Larry has flashed back from call-waiting and voices his dubiousness about the ingenuousness of Babette's call during her line.)

BABETTE: Hi
I was calling to ask
I was calling to ask
No I Was Not Calling To Ask You To Lend Me

(Frank presses "play" on his tape recorder, so that "Let's drill" comes in on top of Babette's "To Ask," and "One dollar" comes in right after Babette's "Lend Me.")

VERY IMPORTANT CASSETTE TAPE AND FRANK: Let's drill
One dollar one dollar two dollar two dollar
three dollar three dollar four dollar four dollar
five dollar five dollar.

(Frank stops the tape in order to study a passage in the manual as Larry abruptly puts Babette on hold again.)

BABETTE: I'm still willing to call-wait

(Frank attempts an exercise from his manual.)

FRANK: 'Course your cousin couldn't kiss you 'cause you can't
kiss kin
      'Course your cousin couldn't kiss you 'cause you can't kiss kin

*(Frank repeats this exercise, faster, but at a lower volume. Larry
has flashed back from call-waiting, although his commitment to the
conversation is truly waning. Meanwhile, during the following Theo
makes more puny compositional attempts.)*

BABETTE: Hi
      I Was Calling To See
THEO: *(Plink)*
BABETTE: To See
THEO: *(Plink)*
BABETTE: To Find Out
THEO: *(Plink, plink)*
BABETTE: if any of the Stuff I
      brought in last week has Sold

(Frank fantasizes about a sale, perfecting his technique.)

FRANK *(Says first "Sold" with Babette's "Sold")*: Sold *(Gavel sound)*
Sold *(Gavel sound)* Sold *(Gavel sound)*
BABETTE: that's all
      since
      my book is This Close To Completion
      My book
      My book
      Larry you can't tell me in all seriousness that I haven't told
you about
      My Book

*(Barely concealed laughter coupled with an attempt to extricate him-
self from conversation on Larry's part.)*

Uh-huh well you're in luck as
    I'm more than willing to call-wait
THEO: *(Thinks he's inspired but is sadly mistaken)*

(Frank presses "play.")

VERY IMPORTANT CASSETTE TAPE: Back to the business of polishing up that all-important chant, the sound that moves millions—I mean people and dollars. And it's a curious fact that auctioneers bear the honorary title of colonel. It dates back to the days just after the Civil War when army colonels handled the job of disposing of cannons, guns, mules and other military equipment, all at public auction.

(Frank presses "stop" as Larry oh-so-reluctantly returns.)

BABETTE: Hi
    So I'm trying to Buy Some Time
    so
    Well has the fur vase sold I know there was
    water damage but
    and the glow-in-the-dark telephone table
    What about the lamp covered with those
    charming depictions of mid-century coal mining
    agitation Well
    are you sure you've displayed it Prominently Enough
    oh can you call-wait a second
THEO: *(Makes yet another pathetically puny attempt)*

(Babette flashes to call-waiting.)

BABETTE: Hello
    Who's calling
    No Babette moved
    No far
    I'm pretty sure she died actually and
    her debts died with her
    That's what I heard anyway Sorry

(Babette flashes back to Larry.)

Sorry so
    Larry
    Larry
    Larry

(Babette paces a little and then redials as:)

THEO: *('s plinks become plonks)*
BABETTE: Larry Me

(Frank presses "play" once again, as, throughout the following, Babette listens to Larry's unbridled outburst, the content of which we cannot make out, the volume of which perhaps we can.)

VERY IMPORTANT CASSETTE TAPE: For well over half a century many of America's foremost auctioneers have obtained their initial training in Kansas City. A sincere welcome awaits you here in Kansas City, and every effort will be made to make this the most pleasant and profitable two weeks of your lifetime.

(Frank stops the tape as Babette hangs up the phone in frustration and then yells in its direction, in response to Larry:)

BABETTE: Phone calls are Self-Serving by DEFINITION
    and BEsides
    It's All For The Sake Of MY BOOK
THEO: *(Accuses his synthesizer with Germanic non-words of disgust)*

(Frank crosses to his window and opens it.
*   In The Airshaft Couple's apartment the woman, who's in the kitchen, calls to the man, who's in the bedroom.)*

WOMAN'S VOICE: I'm making toast

(No response.)

I'm making toast

(No response.)

I'm making toast

(No response. A set of keys is thrown into the kitchen from the bed-room. It hits the floor.)

MAN'S VOICE: Before I forget

(Sound of the woman stepping down off a stool and picking up the set of keys from the floor. The woman clears her throat. The following is overlapped conversation. Each new line begins at the " / " of the previous line.)

WOMAN'S VOICE: Did you call the bank guy / about the account
MAN'S VOICE: He says we have to go / in
WOMAN'S VOICE: Why do we have / to go in
MAN'S VOICE: To sign / something
WOMAN'S VOICE: We can't just do it over / the phone
MAN'S VOICE: I said we have to sign / something
WOMAN'S VOICE: When should we / go in
MAN'S VOICE: We don't have to go in / together
WOMAN'S VOICE: We / don't Oh Okay Well that's different
MAN'S VOICE: We just have to sign it You can sign it and I'll sign it We don't have to sign it together we just both have to sign it We can't just do it over the phone

(Sound of the woman buttering toast.)

WOMAN'S VOICE: You must be hungry

(Toast is thrown from the kitchen into the bedroom.)

The Exposition Scene

Babette, Frank and Theo.

BABETTE: Before I knew Frank Larry told me he was saving up
money to be Frozen
THEO: I'd heard from Larry that this girl
    Babette this woman was an editor who specialized in
    incredibly obscure subject matter which I understood to
    mean that she was mostly out of work
BABETTE: It took a month or two before I understood that it was
some guy Theo who was saving up to be Frozen not
    some guy Frank
FRANK: Larry said something about some guy
    having lost his wife
    literally
THEO: Larry told me that he'd been seeing some guy named Frank
for a while but that things were going Disastrously
FRANK: I asked Larry what do you mean he lost his wife Did she
die Did he leave her somewhere Were they at a
    Mall
THEO: Larry's pretty unlucky in love but
    This Guy Frank sounded particularly awful
FRANK: Larry and I were doing Really Well at that point except
    I wondered about his friends who to a
    one sounded like a bunch of Losers
BABETTE: I was worried about Larry seeing a guy who sounded
like such a Loser I mean a Profound
    Loser Profoundly Depressed
    and in Profound Denial
    Larry also told me that the guy who was saving up to be Fro-
zen also lost his wife
    What do you mean Lost His Wife
    At the Mall or something
THEO: I started to get this paranoid
    feeling that Larry was telling everybody my
    personal business

FRANK: Besides the guy who Lost His Wife At The Mall Larry
   also talked about this woman named Babette this
   unemployed faux-literary person who was always borrowing
money from him and
   never repaying him and how he found it impossible to say no
   to her even though he had absolutely no desire to sleep with
her which was good because he was sleeping with me but
   it became a point of curiosity for me because Why Lend
Money To Someone You Aren't Interested In Sleeping With
BABETTE: Then one day I bumped into Theo at Larry's Shop and
Larry introduced us
   I asked him if it was true that he was saving up to be
   frozen and with bug-esque eyes full of accusation and hurt
   he looked
   over at Larry and then back at me and hissed None Of Your
   Beeswax
   He also said he was saving up to buy a really ancient bonsai
plant
THEO: Tree
BABETTE: but I could tell that part was a lie an arcane and
   fictitious addition to his autobiography designed to deflect
attention from the Truly Strange Fact
   that He Was Actually Saving Up To Be Frozen
THEO: One day when Larry had invited me over to the store he
   suddenly ran into the back and said to say that he
   Wasn't In this Woman came in and started to waltz
   into the back and I said Excuse Me
   Larry's
   Not
   In and she
   said Who Might You Be and I said I'm Theo I'm Sure and she
   asked me Rather Aggressively if I was the one who was saving
   up to be Frozen
   and she hit that word Frozen with an industrial mallet full of
judgment and preconception
   and I tried to pretend I hadn't heard the question but
   she said No Really Are You and I said very calmly you know
and with a smile in my voice I said None Of Your Beeswax

BABETTE: Just hissed it None Of Your Beeswax
THEO: And are You The One Who's Sending Larry To The Poor
House
    You Must Be Babette Yes He's Told Me About You
FRANK: Finally I ran into Both Of Them One
    day when I
    stopped by the store as a Special Surprise
    For Larry and there
    They Both Were sharing what seemed to be a rather
    Charged Silence and I started
    to walk into the back and they said in unison
    Larry's Not In
    and I kept walking because Larry Was Always In For
    Me
BABETTE: Larry called out to me from the back suddenly
THEO: Larry dropped something in the back suddenly
FRANK: Larry emerged from the back suddenly and put his arm
around me and said
    Frank this is Theo this is Babette I've
    So Longed For Them To Meet You
BABETTE: and said Babette These Are The Two I've
    Been Telling You About
THEO: and said Theo I Asked You To Do One Thing
BABETTE: They weren't at all what I expected
THEO: They weren't at all what I expected
FRANK: They were exactly what I expected

(Slight pause.)

I don't exactly know how we became friends but it was some time
after
    Larry told me I wasn't the guy for him
THEO: I didn't like either one of them at first but then one of them
sublet their way into my building and then
    the other got the other an
    apartment and somehow we were all
    neighbors and when you share a landlord with people you
have of course a

Built-In Common Enemy and there's just about nothing
more bond-inducing than Sharply Focused Ill Will
BABETTE: Basically I think we all felt a little
   sorry for each other Isn't that how most friendships start
I mean when
      choosing friends you're either drawn to people You
      Wish You Were or you're drawn to
      people You're Afraid You Are

(Theo sits at his synthesizer, while Babette and Frank stand in his open doorway.)

THEO: It's not finished but its main themes are in place

(Theo prepares to play as if he were giving a concert at Carnegie Hall. He plays for a very short time, then looks expectantly toward the door, toward his friends. The development in the piece of music is virtually indiscernible.

We hear the sound of the throaty-voiced very old woman having a good laugh.)

MRS. JORGENSON'S VOICE: Alas Alas

Part Two

Babette, Theo and Frank stand in the hallway.

THEO: That's so odd
FRANK: You never know
BABETTE: It makes me want to move
THEO: Everything makes you want to move
BABETTE: Maybe because I want to move Is she still there
THEO: Of course not
FRANK: Yes
BABETTE AND THEO: Ew
BABETTE: When did it happen
THEO: Frank said Weren't you listening Late last night
FRANK: Early this morning
BABETTE: Exactly I mean
    I wonder if I had a parallel dream
FRANK: No one knows I found her at ten by which point she
seemed let's say deeply invested in her death
BABETTE AND THEO: Wow
THEO: I'm glad it was you I wouldn't have known who to call
FRANK: I haven't called anyone
BABETTE AND THEO: You haven't

FRANK: What's the rush
THEO: I guess you're right
BABETTE: Does she have family
FRANK: She never mentioned family to me
BABETTE: She never mentioned family to me
THEO: She mentioned family to me
BABETTE AND FRANK: Like what
THEO: Children but I think they were estranged
BABETTE: Oh yeah the estranged children that's right
FRANK: Oh yeah well I knew about the estranged children
      I thought we were talking about active familial relations
THEO: I think we should call someone
FRANK: But I've been thinking
BABETTE: I've had parallel dreams before you know I've been known to be uncannily in tune with calamitous events
THEO: I'll say Jane
BABETTE *(To Theo)*: What was that
THEO: I didn't hear anything
FRANK: I found a note
BABETTE: You kept it
THEO: Shouldn't you have
FRANK: Do you want to see it
BABETTE AND THEO: Yes

(Frank pulls a piece of paper out of his pocket. Theo and Babette try to read it for themselves, but Frank holds the note close to his chest and reads out loud:)

FRANK: See ya
BABETTE AND THEO: Wow
BABETTE: Concise
FRANK: Mm-hmm
THEO: Do we know anyone who needs an apartment

(Theo and Babette put their fingers on their chins for a moment and shift their eyes in unison. Frank regards them expectantly.)

BABETTE: What's the exact layout again

THEO: Is it nicer than mine

BABETTE: I think it's bigger than mine but I think it's
    darker than mine

THEO: And no doubt cheaper than mine

BABETTE: And no doubt quieter than mine

FRANK: Uh I need an apartment

BABETTE AND THEO *(Each pick two out of three)*: Oh that's right/
Of course/Yes you do

FRANK: They'll do a cosmetic fix-up and jack up the rent They
    can do that

BABETTE AND THEO: You're right they can

FRANK: That's what they do

BABETTE AND THEO: You're right it is

(Slight pause.)

BABETTE: Hey listen do you want to see the snapshots from that
trip I took last year

*(Frank and Theo eye each other as Babette pulls them out of her coat
pocket.)*

THEO AND FRANK *(Unsure)*: Sure

FRANK: I thought they were holding those hostage

BABETTE: They were but they finally threw them out today and my
    little friend at the Quick Clicks tipped me off

THEO: What exactly is a little friend

(Babette opens the packet.)

BABETTE: Wait a minute This
    isn't my trip They must've mixed up names at the Quick Clicks

THEO AND FRANK *(Suddenly more interested)*: Let's see

(All three crowd around the photos.)

BABETTE, THEO AND FRANK: Wow it's
    Mrs. Jorgenson

FRANK: Who's the guy

THEO: What are they

(Babette and Frank look at Theo in unison, then turn back to the photograph.)

BABETTE: He looks young In terms of what we can see

FRANK: I should probably hold on to these They should probably stay with the note

THEO: Or I could keep them since I have better locks

BABETTE: They're mine you perverts they're mine

but

I wonder who's flipping through my trip

FRANK: It looks like Mrs. Jorgenson's trip was more eventful

BABETTE: How do you know

THEO: What do you mean by that Babette

BABETTE: My life is full of

events

THEO AND FRANK *(Hurt/surprised, i.e., Theo is hurt, Frank surprised)*: Really

THEO: You don't think this guy did something to Mrs.

Jorgenson

BABETTE AND FRANK *(Annoyed/philosophical)*: You saw the pictures Theo he obviously did something to Mrs. Jorgenson

THEO: No I mean in terms of foul play

BABETTE AND FRANK *(Annoyed/philosophical)*: Depends on your definition

THEO: In terms of her death did it look like she met with foul

play

FRANK: It looked like she was sleeping It probably still does

BABETTE: Why are you using that language Met With Foul Play What is that exactly

THEO: An uh expression

BABETTE *(Everything about him is annoying)*: How do you do that with your eyebrow

THEO: It's involuntary but I'm glad you find it compelling

BABETTE: I didn't say that

FRANK: What's wrong with you

BABETTE AND THEO: Nothing

FRANK: I meant Babette

THEO: Oh
    Listen I have to make a call

BABETTE: See ya
    I mean

FRANK: Bye Theo

THEO: Are you two staying out here

FRANK: I don't know

BABETTE: Why Theo

THEO: Maybe I'll wait to make that call

BABETTE: Actually I have to clean my apartment

FRANK: My cats are probably hungry

(Frank and Babette unlock their doors. Theo follows suit. As soon as Frank enters his apartment and the door starts to close Theo addresses Babette just before her door shuts.)

THEO: Can I talk to you Babette

BABETTE: Is it about Mrs. Jorgenson

THEO: As a matter of fact it's not about Mrs. Jorgenson It's about what happened between us last week

BABETTE: I thought

THEO: We did I just had One More Quick Question

BABETTE: It's not that much fun to talk
    about this

THEO: When I started doing that thing you
    know right before you

(Frank's door opens.)

FRANK: I thought I heard voices

BABETTE: Theo can't stop thinking about
    Mrs. Jorgenson

FRANK: Who can

(Slight pause.)

THEO: Okay

BABETTE, THEO AND FRANK: See ya
    Around

(All three enter their respective apartments and almost close their doors.)

FRANK: Has anyone heard from Larry
BABETTE AND THEO: Depends on your definition of heard
FRANK: Uh Have either of you spoken to him
BABETTE AND THEO *(Each picking two out of three)*: Briefly/In
passing/Just hi bye
FRANK: Is he okay
BABETTE AND THEO *(Each picking two out of three)*: Seems it/Fine/
Far as I can tell
BABETTE: Oh boy Look at the time You have to run Theo
FRANK: Say hi to Dr. Greenspan
THEO: Okay will do When do you see her next Babette
BABETTE: I can't afford mental illness right now
FRANK: You'd better hurry Theo Otherwise you'll have to waste
precious time talking about why you Chose To Be Late
THEO: I guess you're right I'll see you guys later
    Right
BABETTE AND FRANK *(Each says one)*: Bye/Right

(Theo exits down the stairs.)

BABETTE: Frank I need to talk to you
FRANK: Is it about the annoying manner in which Theo's approach-
ing life these days
BABETTE: As a matter of fact it's not about the annoying manner
in which Theo's approaching life these days It's about
BABETTE AND FRANK: Mrs. Jorgenson
BABETTE: She pulled me aside recently
    and mentioned something that I find
    in retrospect quite disturbing
FRANK: I think I know what you're
    going to say That you think that
    I had something against Mrs.
    Jorgenson

BABETTE: She did say something to that
     effect I brushed it off Frank
     I assure you at the time
FRANK: She played loud music Babette
     At all hours She was constantly
     reciting poetry in that remarkable late octogenarian chain-
smoking tenor voice of hers But she didn't
     recite the good modern ones she Nooooooo
     she didn't have the decency Mostly
     she picked that old windbag Whitman
     I'm sorry I know it's sacrilege to say but
BABETTE: Frank you misunderstand Mrs. Jorgenson told me she
was in love with you I guess the Whitman was just an attention-
getting ploy
FRANK: Oh brother
BABETTE: Did you and Mrs. Jorgenson
     How should I put this
FRANK: She wasn't my gender as you know
     although she had great ankles and wrists They usually are
     attractive in sync I find Anyway I had a thought that
     happens to involve
BABETTE AND FRANK *(Statement/question)*: Mrs. Jorgenson

(Theo appears in the hallway.)

THEO: I
     forgot something
FRANK: We were just talking about how great it would be if we all
went to the beach
THEO: A day at the beach Great idea
BABETTE: I HATE THE BEACH

(Babette slams her door.)

THEO: What's eating her
FRANK: I didn't say anything to upset her if that's what you mean
THEO: Did you just hit that personal pronoun or was that my
     imagination

FRANK: I just said that I didn't say anything to upset her
THEO: There You did it again
FRANK: Did you really forget something
    Theo or were you just inventing an
    excuse to return to see if Babette and
    I were having a private conversation
THEO: Do you think it's possible that Babette's out of love with love
FRANK: Anything's possible

(We hear a couple of loud meows.)

I still haven't fed them

(Frank turns to enter his apartment.)

THEO: Frank I think you should know
    that something's going on between
    Babette and me although we would
    never let that come between our
    friendship with you

(Babette's door flings open.)

BABETTE: What are you saying lunatic There's
    nothing going on Frank

(Babette's door slams shut.)

THEO: Frank
FRANK: I'VE GOT TO BE A RESPONSIBLE PET
    OWNER THEO PLEASE

(Frank enters his apartment. Babette's door opens a crack.)

BABETTE: How dare you Theo
THEO: We're close friends He has a right
    to know if you and I are seeing each other

BABETTE: I don't even remember the incident Theo
    Recall that I was drunk
    Go get graced by the gift of retrospect

(Babette's door starts to close but Theo jams his foot in it to prevent it from closing all the way.)

THEO: You'll see
BABETTE: LISTEN I'm not going to be pushed into a situation with you where every time I see you the embrace is awkward and
    neither Fish Nor
    Fowl It's hard enough to hug as it is

(Babette slams her door. Theo walks toward the stairwell.

    Babette is standing in her apartment. She is situated behind her window blind, so that all we see of her is her shadow. She is on the phone.)

(A torrent of words with line breaks) It was on a subway train I was
    headed uptown and I
    sat down next to a Strange Old Lady who was reading a book
the
    title of which I couldn't see I happened to
    sit down right at the beginning of a
    chapter She was roughly a third of the way through the book
Anyway
    I of course having forgotten to bring reading
    material of my own started
    reading the book over her Strange Old Lady Shoulder and
became immediately absorbed in the story Each
    time we reached a station I
    tensed in fear that the Strange
    Old Lady would get off the train and leave me
    hanging but she didn't get off the train She didn't
    leave me We
    seemed to read at exactly the same speed She
    turned the pages with an uncanny timing that seemed
    based purely on the speed with which I was reading until at

some point I'd reached the end of the
page and the page didn't
turn I
waited for Several Seconds Then a minute Then two full
minutes Then finally I looked over at the
Strange Old Lady and saw that she'd
fallen asleep This was very distressing because I was very
absorbed and I really wanted to know what happened
next so I turned the page I turned the page and read the next
two pages and then turned the page again and again until I'd read
another
oh
ten pages and then the Strange Old Lady woke up and she
started to read again and she
paused and she
turned back to the page before and then she
turned back to the page before that and so on until without
looking up she said
Can you hang on a second

(Babette has raised her blind and has been struggling to open her window during the last part of her speech. She places the receiver on her windowsill and expends a considerable amount of energy forcing her window open. Finally she succeeds, but before she reengages in her telephone conversation she becomes distracted by the conversation occurring between The Airshaft Couple, who are in offstage, but separate, rooms. As they speak, they each sort through a pile of books and place them just inside the stage area, so that only their hands, parts of their arms and the books themselves are visible to the audience. The sound of books stacked upon one another adds a percussive note to the scene.)

MAN'S VOICE: Yours
WOMAN'S VOICE: Yours
MAN'S VOICE: Yours
WOMAN'S VOICE: Yours
MAN'S VOICE: Mine
WOMAN'S VOICE: Yours

MAN'S VOICE: Mine

WOMAN'S VOICE: Yours

MAN'S VOICE: Mine

WOMAN'S VOICE: Mine

MAN'S VOICE: Mine

WOMAN'S VOICE: Mine

MAN'S VOICE: Mine

WOMAN'S VOICE: Mine

MAN'S VOICE: Mine

WOMAN'S VOICE: Mine

MAN'S VOICE: Yours

WOMAN'S VOICE: Yours

MAN'S VOICE: Mine

WOMAN'S VOICE: Mine

MAN'S VOICE: Are you saying you no longer like the way I look

WOMAN'S VOICE: I'm saying I no longer like the way I look at you

MAN'S VOICE: Yours

WOMAN'S VOICE: Mine

MAN'S VOICE: Yours

WOMAN'S VOICE: Mine

MAN'S VOICE: Yours

(Babette remembers her telephone conversation and picks up the receiver from the sill. Perhaps the rest of Babette's monologue is scored by a slightly muted continuation of The Airshaft Couple's book-sorting dialogue: "Yours," "Mine," but mostly, "Mine.")

BABETTE: Sorry so the Strange Old Lady turned those
    military-blue eyes on me and said
    So What's The Story
    and I mumbled something about having turned
    several pages and the Strange Old Lady cut me off and said
    No Whadd'I Miss
    And I said Oh In The Story
    And I said Annabelle
    And the Strange Old Lady corrected me and said Isabelle
    And I said sorry Isabelle made it to the other side
    And the Strange Old Lady said that's impossible

And I said it's not impossible if Isabelle fashioned some kind
of raft
And she said
Out of what
And I said
Out of wood
And she said
There are no trees on the island We learned that chapters
ago And I said
I came in late
And she said
Isabelle must've hitched a ride on someone else's raft
And I said
Whose raft
And she said
A native must've been passing by
And I said
Native of where
And she said
Oh spare me your Knee-jerk Literal-minded Bourgeois
Worldview would ya It's a Gee Dee romance novel For Crying
Out Loud
And I said
Aren't you being literal-minded about the trees
And she said
That's different That's internal logic
And I said
I am not bourgeois
And she said
Did Isabelle reach Karl with the antidote
And I said
Not yet and the vial is leaking and
I am not bourgeois
And she said
If you can spell bourgeois you're bourgeois
And then the Strange Old Lady grabbed me by the arm and
whispered in my ear in that
oddly elegant Bronx-soaked Camel Light croak of hers

Meet Me At Three On The Downtown Train
and she was gone
and I did
and we read until Karl uttered his Last Words
which were
Alas Alas

(On second thought:)

Actually that's not
    true Karl said
    Alack Alack
    Alas implies pity whereas Alack says regret
    Karl said Alack and that's
    the first memory I have of Mrs. Jorgenson Llllisten
    My Book is This Close To Completion and
    I was wondering if by any chance you
    could ssssspare
    Okay Okay Understood
    Okay
    'kay
    'kay
    'kay

(Babette hangs up the phone.)

I am not bourgeois

(Momentary silence that is broken by The Airshaft Couple:)

MAN'S VOICE: I'm still hungry
WOMAN'S VOICE: Call for something
MAN'S VOICE: What do you feel like
WOMAN'S VOICE: I don't care
MAN'S VOICE: You don't care what you feel like
    or you don't
    care what I call for
WOMAN'S VOICE: Both no
    the last thing

MAN'S VOICE: In other words you don't want to make
WOMAN'S VOICE: Right right
MAN'S VOICE: So what
   Chinese
WOMAN'S VOICE: But
   nothing too eggy
MAN'S VOICE: Eggy
WOMAN'S VOICE: Eggy Eggy Eggy Eggy Eggy

(Theo is sitting in a chair that is suspended in the air.)

THEO: She has a tendency to deny what is right
   in front of her I try to point out to her what's going on
   the reality of the case but I suppose certain of her
   defense mechanisms kick in and do her a disservice
   I've tried to be patient I've waited it out all these
   years now you know but just as I get a little satisfaction
   in terms of physical contact not that other types of contact
aren't important I value our friendship of course she pulls away
and as I said tries to deny what we both know to be
   true that we have fallen deeply in love with one another and
   should probably marry the sooner the better
VOICE OF DR. GREENSPAN: Is it possible that you've
   misread the situation
THEO: No absolutely not No it's not possible The facts have been
   staring both of us all of us right in the face No No No
VOICE OF DR. GREENSPAN: Go on
THEO: No
VOICE OF DR. GREENSPAN: We're running out of time Theo
THEO: You'll see

(We hear the sound of the same piece of synthesizer music. Babette emerges from her apartment and knocks on Frank's door. He answers it.)

BABETTE: Hungry
FRANK: I guess
BABETTE: Why not order something
FRANK: All right Any ideas

BABETTE: Moo Shoo Easy on the egg tell them

FRANK: Anything else

BABETTE: Anything preceded by General That's always
    good And egg rolls And whatever You want

FRANK: Okay

*(Frank closes his door as Theo appears in the hallway. Babette sees
him and starts to enter her apartment.)*

THEO: You can run

BABETTE: I'm not hiding Theo

THEO: Why don't you come over I'll give you a
    massage and we'll talk this Thing through

BABETTE: You say Thing Theo like it has a capital letter and it
    doesn't have a capital letter Theo There's no thing in the
    Thing Theo and Theo I think you need to give Susan what's-
her-name with the hair a call

THEO: You're lying that's not
    what you really
    think

BABETTE: Oh really Tell me what I
    Really Think

THEO: You wish external circumstances would mirror internal circumstances
    You wonder why our fateful encounter did not occur sooner
    You want me

BABETTE: I wish you'd recall that I was

BABETTE AND THEO: drunk

BABETTE: I wonder when you became this tiresome
    I want you
    to leave me the four letters sounds like duck alone

THEO: Poor deluded Babette

(Frank's door opens.)

FRANK: They didn't have anything General so I
    ordered something Chairman

BABETTE: As long as the chicken's authoritative

223

FRANK: Are you joining us for dinner
THEO: Okay

(Babette enters her apartment and slams the door.)

Several Pseudo Scenes of Love
Thwarted at Every Turn

Frank and Theo in the hallway.

FRANK: Listen Theo do you have a minute
THEO: Is it about Babette
FRANK: As a matter of fact it's not about Babette It's about the
erotic dreams I've recently been having
    in which you figure prominently
THEO: I'm flattered Frank but I'm afraid
    your dreams won't do me any good
    I'd better check my machine before
    dinner She's probably called

(Theo enters his apartment as Babette emerges from hers.)

BABETTE: Whatever he said he's lying
FRANK: Is that what you think
BABETTE: Recall that I was
FRANK: Oddly we weren't discussing you
BABETTE: Oh
    Listen Frank I don't know why this image has floated into
my mind but do you remember that time during the snowstorm
when you
    and I were forced to

(The buzzer sounds in Frank's apartment. He leans inside.)

FRANK: Yes
VOICE OF DELIVERY PERSON: Chinese food

FRANK: Third floor
    I have to get my wallet Do You need to get Your wallet Babette

(Frank enters his apartment as Theo exits his.)

THEO: Was that Frank's buzzer
BABETTE: The food's arrived I'd
    better get my wallet
THEO: I'll spring for you
BABETTE: We're not a couple Theo
THEO: You'll see

(Babette enters her apartment as Frank exits from his. Frank approaches the stairwell and meets the delivery person out of sight.)

FRANK: How much do We owe you
VOICE OF DELIVERY PERSON: Twenty-five fifty-nine
FRANK: Tweny-five twenty-five twenty-five
    twenty-five fitty fitty fitty fitty fitty
VOICE OF DELIVERY PERSON: Nine
FRANK: Here you are my good man

(Frank carries the food down the hall.)

THEO: I'll pay for Babette and me

(Babette emerges from her apartment.)

BABETTE: No you won't but I can't find my
    wallet Frank Could you cover my part
FRANK: Sure Babette But
BABETTE: I know Frank that I owe you from not too long ago
FRANK: And not too long Babette before that
BABETTE: I don't know where Frank I left my
    wallet Maybe at Larry's Shop I'm not sure
THEO: I'm buying you dinner Babette
FRANK: I hope Babette you didn't leave your wallet at Larry's Store
    If you did you'll probably never see it again Still you
    should probably call Or I will If You Want

THEO: I'm paying for your dinner Babette That's
   final
BABETTE: Frank please lend me the money It
   won't happen again I'll call Larry right
   after dinner
FRANK: Or I mean I'll Call If You Insist

*(Frank has reached into the delivery bag and begun eating an egg roll.
Theo also helps himself to one.)*

THEO: I SAID IT'S MY GODDAMN TREAT
   I just need to get my wallet

(Theo enters his apartment.)

FRANK: Good egg rolls
BABETTE: Were they
FRANK: Oh didn't you get one
BABETTE: That's okay

(Theo emerges from his apartment.)

THEO: Here you are my good man
BABETTE: When did you start saying my good man
THEO: I heard Frank say it to the delivery person
BABETTE: When did you start saying my good man
FRANK: I never stopped

(Theo has opened up one of the main dishes and is digging in.)

THEO: Chairman Cho's chicken I love
   Chairman Cho's chicken
   I love all communist chicken
FRANK: Larry loves communist chicken
BABETTE AND THEO *(Oh no/not again)*: Does he/Really
FRANK: I ran into someone who saw him the other day who said
he looked tired
BABETTE: Hey did I tell you that he's got one of Mrs. Jorgenson's
paintings on the wall

FRANK: Mrs. Jorgenson couldn't paint to save her life

BABETTE AND THEO: Guess not

BABETTE, THEO AND FRANK: Mrs. Jorgenson

BABETTE: I think we should call someone

FRANK: I've been thinking you know

THEO: The police I guess or at least the operator

FRANK: that Mrs. Jorgenson's lease hasn't lapsed and I've been thinking

BABETTE AND THEO: What are you suggesting Not what I think you're suggesting I hope Illegally appropriating Mrs. J's apartment because you've been evicted from yours Frank how could you

(By now the Chinese food is almost gone. Theo and Frank are eating with their hands. Slightest pause.)

FRANK *(You both misunderstand)*: I've been thinking Great moo shoo

BABETTE: Was it

THEO AND FRANK: Oh didn't you get any

BABETTE *(It's not fine)*: It's fine

FRANK: I was also thinking about going out for a beer tonight Want to come along Theo

THEO: I don't think so

BABETTE: Why didn't you ask me

FRANK: Are you sure

THEO: I'm kind of tired

BABETTE: I'm not I'm not tired

FRANK: You can't find your wallet

THEO: Would you like me to take you
        out for a drink tonight Babette

BABETTE: No

FRANK: Why do you want to go all of a sudden

THEO: I'm trying to learn to respond to
        Babette's needs

BABETTE: An interesting development

FRANK: I have needs too Theo

THEO: No one's denying that I just feel tonight
        a need to be with the one I

FRANK: When did I turn into the third wheel
BABETTE: I have needs too Frank
FRANK: I think I hear my phone ringing

(Frank enters his apartment suddenly.)

BABETTE: I think I hear my phone ringing
THEO: Your phone's not ringing Babette
BABETTE: Oh but it is

(Babette rushes into her apartment and Theo is left with the take-out food remains, which he carries into his apartment.)

. . .

(Theo, Babette and Frank are lying in bed in their respective apartments. Theo and Frank are asleep. Babette is making animal and other shadows with her hands—rather elaborate and impressive.)

BABETTE: I once met a man at a party as we were both going
    for the same Potato Chip
    Our respective hands halted
    their downward descent and instead
    gestured for the other to Dig In
    to said Potato Chip
    It became a showdown of manners We
    held our hands like that for
    nineteen full minutes until
    finally he lifted the Potato Chip
    and placed it gently on my
    tongue

(Babette falls asleep as Theo begins making interesting animal and other shadows.)

THEO: I worked at a skating rink as a teenager
    I got to skate for free all through high school
    My life pretty much continued on that rhapsodic trajectory
right up until The Mysterious Disappearance Of My Wife

(Theo goes back to sleep and Frank begins to make shadows.)

FRANK: Be on the lookout for strange spots in
     otherwise uniformly colored food That's
     my best advice

(Frank goes back to sleep and Babette makes shadows again.)

BABETTE: I once spilled red wine on a dear friend's white
     carpet and nothing was ever the same

(Babette goes back to sleep as Theo makes shadows again.)

THEO: Maybe I never gave her my last piece of gum

(Theo goes back to sleep as Frank makes shadows again.)

FRANK: People talk about things they know nothing about all the
time
     and with confidence
     and with nerve

(Frank goes back to sleep as Babette makes shadows again.)

BABETTE: If someone asks you if you're free on the weekend they
Might want to take you to brunch but they Probably want you to
help them move

(Babette continues to make shadows as Theo wakes up and also makes shadows.)

THEO: And though good things have happened and though I've
assembled some very complicated model airplanes over the years
my disappearing wife will not reappear I
     know that for a strong feeling

(Frank wakes up and joins the other two in making shadows. He practices lip trills briefly.)

FRANK: The question is why must I
spend my life assessing the
pregnancy of any given
pause
BABETTE: Who are these people who come unexpectedly into small
fortunes That's what I'd like to know
THEO: In lieu of living life with my wife
I suppose I would like to end up with
someone with a fondness for remaining
FRANK: Please pardon my partially purple paisley pants
Please pardon my partially purple paisley pants
Please pardon my partially purple paisley pants

(Slight pause.)

Basically I guess I'd just like to
wind up with someone who'd say after
I'd walked through the front door
boy am I glad to see you
THEO *(Starts speaking after Frank says "after")*: Basically I guess
I'd just like to
wind up with someone who'd say after
I'd walked through the front door
boy am I glad to see you
BABETTE *(Starts speaking after Theo says "after")*: Basically I guess
I'd just like to
wind up with someone who'd say after
I'd walked through the front door
boy am I glad to see you

*(The hallway, a few moments later. Frank has his hand on the door-
knob of Mrs. Jorgenson's door as Babette and Theo emerge from their
apartments.)*

(Are you doing) What
THEO *('s going on)*: What
FRANK *(Did I do)*: What

Part Three

Frank, Babette and Theo are in their own apartments. Theo is seated at his synthesizer, which, according to him, is clearly malfunctioning; he spends the scene attempting to repair it. Babette is on the phone, and Frank is standing, holding his tape recorder in the palms of his hands at chest level. Frank presses "play."

VERY IMPORTANT CASSETTE TAPE: You practice it when you're driving down the road, you practice it when you're going in the shower, this morning, in the morning, tonight, wherever you are I want you to practice it and practice breathin' right.

(Frank stops the tape.)

BABETTE *(On the phone)*: It's actually a compendium of mostly twentieth century outburst

(Frank presses "play.")

VERY IMPORTANT CASSETTE TAPE: Eight hundred dollar bid and now fifty
　　Now go on! You didn't take that big deep breath to start with! Before you start it, get a good deep breath and then go!

BABETTE: Twentieth
Century
Outburst

VERY IMPORTANT CASSETTE TAPE: Eight hundred dollar bid and
now fifty now fifty
Bid
Eight fifty bid and now nine now nine nine bid will you give
me nine
Bid nine
Nine hundred dollar bid and now fifty
Bid
Nine hundred dollar bid and now fifty now fifty will you give
me fifty

(Frank stops the tape.)

BABETTE: Little-known stuff
Outbursts by Unknowns
that had repercussions of a uh
Global Nature

*(Frank presses "play" on the tape recorder. Note: as Frank attempts
to practice the drill that appears below, he manages only to hit in sync
the words that appear in **bold**.)*

VERY IMPORTANT CASSETTE TAPE AND FRANK: Here we go. Betty
Botter bought some **butter** but she said this butter's **bitter** if I put
it in my batter it will make my batter bitter so she bought a bit of
better **butter** put it in her bitter batter made her **bitter batter better** so it's better Betty **Botter** bought a bit of better butter
     Ten ten twenty **twenty** thirty thirty forty forty fifty fifty sixty
sixty seventy seventy **eighty eighty** ninety ninety ninety ninety
eighty **eighty** seventy seventy sixty sixty fifty fifty forty forty
thirty thirty twenty twenty ten ten
     Betty Botter bought some **butter** but she said this butter's **bit-
ter** if I put it in my batter it will make my batter bitter so she bought
a bit of better **butter** put it in her bitter batter made her **bitter batter better** so it's better Betty **Botter** bought a bit of better butter

One one **one** and a quarter one and quarter one and a half one and a half seventy-five **seventy-five** Two two two and a quarter two and a quarter two and a half two and a half seventy-five **seventy-five** Three three three and a quarter three and a quarter three and a half three and a half seventy-five **seventy-five** Four four four and a quarter four and a quarter four and a half four and a half seventy-five **seventy-five** Five five five and a quarter five and a quarter five and a half five and a half seventy-five **seventy-five** Six six six and a quarter six and a quarter six and a half six and a half seventy-five **seventy-five** Seven seven seven and a quarter seven and a quarter seven and a half seven and a half seventy-five **seventy-five** Eight eight eight and a quarter eight and a quarter eight and a half eight and a half seventy-five **seventy-five** Nine nine nine and a quarter nine and a quarter nine and a half nine and a half seventy-five **seventy-five** Ten ten ten and a quarter ten and a quarter ten and a half ten and a half seventy-five **seventy-five**

Betty Botter bought some **butter** but she said this butter's **bitter** if I put it in my batter it will make my batter bitter so she bought a bit of better **butter** put it in her bitter batter made her **bitter batter better** so it's better Betty **Botter** bought a bit of better butter

Take a big hand for yourself and have a seat.

(Babette is still on the phone.)

BABETTE: It's it's
 what it Is
 is
 a collection of Modern Era Outbursts It'll be a book of
 of
 Seminal Outbursts you know Outbursts that really Went
Somewhere Got Something
 Done
 And and I mean it's a very exciting project because
 I mean if I do say so myself
 a deconstruction of the Outburst could do a lot to
 illuminate evolution itself
 I mean

In My View
In My Book
The History Of The World
IS
The History Of The Outburst
Hang on Someone's at my door

(Theo has abandoned his synthesizer, emerged from his apartment and knocked on Babette's door. Babette opens her door.)

THEO: I need to talk
BABETTE: I'm on the phone
THEO: Good that's a start but I need you to talk to me
BABETTE *(Into the phone)*: Can I call you back Theo's here m-hm mm-hmm
    mmm-hmmm zzactly bye Hi How's Thrill-o-rama
THEO: Boring I'm feeling very
    Well am
    I correct in understanding
    that you're rejecting me

(Babette has immediately shifted her focus to her rolls of coins, and is offering Theo but a portion of her attention.)

BABETTE: Just sexually
THEO: Oh phew
BABETTE: How foolish of me to assume that you value our friendship
THEO: I value it so much that I want to enhance it
BABETTE: With sex
THEO: Intimacy in general
BABETTE: Intimacy is never general Theo

(Theo mimics her, mouthing the words, "Intimacy is never general Theo." Babette doesn't notice.)

THEO: Am I that repulsive

(Babette actually considers this question for a moment and then proceeds to think aloud:)

BABETTE: It's Physics not Physical Theo by which I mean
      you don't Disgust Me
      you just exert a Repulsive Force for me on a
      what
      Molecular Level
THEO: Oh
      So it's nothing personal
BABETTE *(Sincere)*: Not
      At
      All

(Theo starts to leave.)

Oh hey Theo
      any spare quarters on ya I'm this close to a roll

(Frank practices.)

FRANK: Belligerent Beulah bellowed bloody bombast
      Belligerent Beulah bellowed bloody bombast
      Belligerent Beulah bellowed bloody bombast

(Theo plays around on the synthesizer. Eventually he begins to croon:)

THEO *(Singing)*:
      Babette Babette you put
      a hex on me
      Babette Babette why not
      have sex with me

(Babette, pencil in hand, hovers over the manuscript of her "Outbursts Text," and reads aloud:)

BABETTE: 1457 A cell full of monks hunched over myriad ecclesiastical texts they are diligently recopying
      Brother Theodore Klotz stands suddenly as he hurtles his quill to the stone floor and shouts
      I'll Be Fucked If I'm Transcribing One More Word
      The next day Brother Klotz visits his friend Johann Fust

son-in-law of Johann Gutenberg
They share a bottle of claret
Movable Metal Type is born

. . .

*(Three bathrooms. Babette is perched on the side of her bathtub. She
is shaving her legs. Frank and Theo are shaving their faces in their
respective bathrooms. We see all three of them through the reflections
of their mirrors.)*

FRANK: Why auctioneering I want my words to
    Succeed
BABETTE: When I went to work in an office I spent my day
    negotiating my way
    through a sea of people who kept
    repeating and repeating
    in one way or another
    the same five words
    The Mistake Is Not Mine
THEO: And I mean the whole experience of dissolution
    of dissolving leads one inevitably to try to
    identify The The
    Dissolvent because
    I thought we were profoundly happy Beth and I
FRANK: It's not that I plan to start using words like Humdinger or
anything
THEO: I learned sadly enough that profound happiness is itself a
    Dissolvent
BABETTE: The Mistake Is Not Mine
FRANK: It's not like I'll start walking around saying
    Mighty to modify Fine
THEO: I guess I just wish I was back at the skating rink
BABETTE: What I was never able to express
    much to my regret is that the mistake
    is precisely what is of Interest

(Babette, Frank and Theo all cut themselves shaving.)

. . .

(Theo is procrastinating. Frank knocks on his door. Theo opens his door and Frank enters Theo's apartment.)

THEO: I'm composing what's up

(Frank sits down and plays a tune on Theo's synthesizer.)

FRANK: What if it went something like that
THEO: Have you been thinking about this
FRANK: It just came to me
THEO: I don't think it's right It's not
    bad it's good but it's not
    Thrill-o-rama
FRANK: Okay
THEO: I appreciate the thought
FRANK: Okay
THEO: I'll know Thrill-o-rama when I
    hear it in my head
FRANK: Okay
THEO: It's not that I haven't been thinking
    about it It's all that I think about when
    I'm not thinking about having sex with Babette
FRANK: Okay
THEO: I appreciate the gesture but you see
    Thrill-o-rama the Gestalt of
    Thrill-o-rama is not reducible to
    some formula some expected formula
    I'm operating under the assumption that
    Thrill-o-rama the ride is thrilling
    because it's thrilling in an unexpected
    way and does not simply rehash a
    familiarly thrilling type ride experience
    The music needs to reflect this Frank
FRANK: Okay
THEO: Thrill-o-rama the melody can't be
    obviously thrilling In fact I'm coming
    to believe that it should be in fact

seemingly boring so as to enhance the
    rush of the thrill experience when
    it is finally manifest I'm not
    criticizing but your Little Tune does
    not adequately subvert the thrill
    expectation
FRANK: Okay
THEO: And that is after all what we're
    doing here I mean I'm doing here I'm
    subverting the thrill expectation in order to
    intensify the rush of the ride Thrill-o-rama's
    not a simple thrill Frank
FRANK: Okay
THEO: It's a complex thrill It's a layered
    thrill It's as enigmatic as well as
    can be
FRANK: Okay
THEO: Okay so I appreciate as I said the
    effort on your part I'm flattered
    that Thrill-o-rama and my
    opus even appear as a Blip On Your
    Screen but Frank I'm sorry Frank
    Thrill-o-rama is something you Just
    Don't Grasp
FRANK: Okay
THEO: Okay
FRANK: Okay may I

(Frank crosses to the synthesizer and plays another catchy tune—even catchier, of course, than the last.)

I mean that was the other one I was
    wondering about I don't know I mean
    obviously you're the composer and I
    hardly play
THEO: Frank Frank Frank uh how did you I
    mean when did you come up with these
    little little ditties

FRANK: I don't know I guess I was in the
    checkout line flipping through a
    magazine wondering what I was
    forgetting to buy having forgotten my list at home
    trying to recall the subject of my thesis paper in college
    while trying also to pinpoint the precise
    moment when my relationship with my father
    went Sour when they just uh
    Popped Into My Head

THEO: Exactly Frank exactly They just Popped
    Into Your Head Is that how you think
    this works Is that what you think
    composing's all about

FRANK: No I

THEO: Do you think I don't think of phrases
    all day as I'm working That's what
    they're called by the way Frank phrases musical
    phrases Do you think musical phrases
    and I mean Super Involved Really Complex
    musical phrases aren't Popping as you
    say into my head all the time

FRANK: No I

THEO: Because they are Frank They are but
    I don't even let myself actually play these
    Trifles on the keyboard because
    I don't want to Violate the keyboard's
    Integrity If it's not right it's not
    right Why waste time Do you think I'm
    interested in wasting time

FRANK: No I

THEO: That's right I'm not and I'll tell you
    why Frank Because these people
    these Amusement Park People are
    Professionals okay These Amusement Park People
    mean Serious Business okay and that means they're
    not interested in messing around with
    Amateurs and that's why they hired me
    a Professional to lovingly sculpt an

appropriately Weighty not to mention
Mysterious score for Thrill-o-rama Sure
they could have hired Some Hack but they
wanted the job Done Right They wanted
a classically trained composer who attended a genuine School
of Music
or or Conservatory as we say in the field to
craft a melody as memorable as Thrill-
o-rama is sure to be for the average pimply prepubescent who
rides it
Are you saying the average pimply prepubescent
doesn't deserve a real musical score
for his Amusement Park Ride Experience

FRANK: No I

THEO: Of course the average pimply prepubescent
deserves a real musical score and I
know you don't mean disrespect

FRANK: No I

THEO: There's no shame in what you've done

FRANK: No I

THEO: I forgive you Frank

FRANK: Okay

THEO: I forgive you but if you ever ever approach
my keyboard again without an express
invitation from me to do so I will be
forced to Kick Your Ass No No I won't
kick your ass I'll Break Your Fingers
That would be more appropriate don't
you think

FRANK: Okay

THEO: I don't mean to be insulting

FRANK: Okay

THEO: No hard feelings

FRANK: No

THEO: Okay

FRANK: Okay so you don't want to hear the third tune I thought
up right

(Babette is on the phone.)

BABETTE *(Into the phone, fluid)*: Well I like her
    Or I want to like her
    Because other people I like like her
    But the truth is
    I don't like her

(There is a knock at Babette's door.)

(Into the phone) Just a second there's someone at my door

(Babette answers the door; Frank is standing outside of it.)

I'm on the phone Frank
FRANK: Can I sit in your apartment Babette
BABETTE: Why
FRANK: My cats need some space

(Babette opens the door wide so that Frank can enter and then immediately returns to her phone conversation.)

BABETTE *(Into the phone)*: But then I think Why don't I like her
    Do I not like her because I think she doesn't like me
    which I do think
    or do I not like her because I can't relate to her intellectually
    But if I can't relate to her intellectually is that because
    she's smarter or Stupider OR are we in fact such
    intellectual equals
    that we can't recognize the intelligence of the other so blinded
are we by the reflection of comparable thought
    But frankly
FRANK *(Did you say my name)*: Yes
BABETTE *(Continuing into the phone)*: I don't think that's it
    and anyway the larger question is

BABETTE *(Into the phone)*:	FRANK:
Why Do I Want To Like Her	Why Do You Want To Like Her

BABETTE *(Into the phone)*: and I have to say that I don't think I actually have Any Interest in liking her

BABETTE *(Into the phone)*:	FRANK:
I Just Want Her To Like Me	You Just Want Her To Like You

BABETTE *(Into the phone)*: and and
    of course the truly haunting aspect of all of this is that

BABETTE *(Into the phone)*:	FRANK:
All Of The People I Like	All Of The People You Like
Like Her	Like Her

BABETTE *(Still into the phone)*: At The Same Time As They Like Me
    so so
    Where does the true affection lie and
    well okay I guess I do recall ONE MOMENT when
    I Thought I Liked Her when we happened to be in a bathroom at
    the same time and of course there was no toilet paper in the stall to which I had gravitated and she somehow psychically sensed my predicament and passed some toilet paper to me under the stall and in that moment
    okay
    I actually Loved Her but
FRANK: WHAT ABOUT MY DESIRES

(Slight pause.)

BABETTE: Frank I'm on the phone *(Into the phone)* Oh you do Okay Okay Talk to you soon

(Babette hangs up the phone.)

Shoot
    I forgot to ask her something
FRANK: The thing is Babette that it's not a matter
    of talking fast it's a matter of
    fast talkin' It's a different thing entirely

(Slight pause.)

Is it okay if I vacuum
BABETTE: Feel free Frank Nice shirt
FRANK: Thanks

(Frank crosses to a closet and pulls out an old pink vacuum cleaner.)

BABETTE: Where'd you get it
FRANK: I don't
    know I picked it up somewhere

(Frank plugs in the vacuum and begins vacuuming. He makes a long horizontal across the room. He is a graceful vacuumer. He makes another long horizontal cross and then pauses to pick up a piece of paper from the carpet. He turns the vacuum off as he reads.)

When um did you receive This
BABETTE: What
FRANK: This um this invitation to Larry's
    Party
BABETTE: I don't know Recently
FRANK: I wasn't invited
BABETTE: Really
FRANK: You know I wasn't invited
BABETTE: I've seen that shirt before
FRANK: Larry thinks I'm not handling this breakup well
    He thinks I can't handle seeing him
    Is Theo invited
BABETTE: I don't know

(Frank moves toward the door.)

Yes
FRANK: Did you know I wasn't invited
BABETTE: Where have I seen that shirt before
FRANK: Are you going to go
BABETTE: Possibly

FRANK: Is Theo going
BABETTE: How should I know
FRANK: All he thinks about is having sex with you
BABETTE: I thought you were here to vacuum

(Frank begins vacuuming again. Babette continues to watch Frank. Frank stops vacuuming in order to move something out of the way.)

FRANK: Boy when was the last time you vacuumcd
BABETTE: Boy I don't remember

(The phone rings.)

(Into the phone) Hello Hi I didn't forget What would
     you like me to bring Okay Great but
     I'm Kind Of In The Middle Of Something
     Okay I'll talk to you later when I'm less
     Right

(Babette hangs up the phone.)

FRANK: Was that Larry Babette

(Slight pause.)

Please just answer my question Babette
BABETTE: And then will you
FRANK *(Cutting her off)*: Yes Babette
BABETTE *(Cutting him off)*: Yes Frank

(Frank begins to vacuum again as Babette continues to watch him. After a few moments of vigorous vacuuming in a corner, Frank turns off the vacuum.)

FRANK: Did Larry tell you not to tell me about
     The Party
BABETTE: You just
FRANK *(Cutting her off)*: Did he

BABETTE: No
FRANK: Did he
BABETTE: Yes

(Frank begins vacuuming again. There is a knock at Babette's door. Neither Babette nor Frank hears the knock, so there is a bang on Babette's door. Frank turns off the vacuum.)

FRANK: I'll get it Babette
BABETTE: Super Frank

(Frank opens the door. It's Theo.)

THEO: Oh I was looking for Babette
FRANK: She's right over there
THEO: What are you doing here
FRANK: Vacuuming
THEO: Oh Have you been talking about me
BABETTE AND FRANK: No/Yes
THEO: I wanted to ask Babette something
    but I'll come back later
FRANK: Yes
THEO: What
FRANK: She's going to Larry's Party to which everyone in the world was invited except me
THEO: Great I'll see you there Babette

(The scene is over, but then suddenly it isn't as Babette realizes:)

BABETTE: I know where I've seen that shirt
    On Mrs. Jorgenson

(The scene is over. Frank practices.)

FRANK: At least leave the lederhosen
    At least leave the lederhosen
    At least leave the lederhosen

The Interrogation Scene

Babette, Theo and Frank are in Frank's apartment.

FRANK: Who else was there

THEO: Peter

FRANK: Peter Larry hates Peter

BABETTE: Not that Peter another Peter you don't know

FRANK: A Peter I don't know Does
    Larry like Peter-I-don't-know

THEO: He likes him but he doesn't like-like him

BABETTE: It wouldn't matter This Peter this other Peter doesn't like-like boys

FRANK: Oh so Larry found him captivating no doubt Was Clarissa there

BABETTE: No

THEO: Yes she was She just didn't stay long because Joseph was there with his new girlfriend

BABETTE: I didn't talk to her Did you talk to her

THEO: Clarissa or the new girlfriend

FRANK: WAS IT FUN

THEO: No

BABETTE: No

FRANK: Are you lying

BABETTE: Yes

THEO: Yes

FRANK: Was it Very fun

BABETTE: Yes

THEO: Yes

FRANK: Was it the best party you've ever been to

THEO: The best

BABETTE: Yes

FRANK: Are you lying

BABETTE AND THEO *(Face the truth, damn it/unable to lie)*: No

BABETTE: I don't like this game

THEO: Me neither

FRANK: In my sandbox I make the rules Did my name
    cross Larry's lips

THEO: We weren't standing beside him all night Frank

BABETTE: We also weren't standing beside each other

THEO: Much to my chagrin

FRANK: Meanwhile back to Larry's lips

BABETTE: Well I did hear him say Frank as I was on my way to the
bathroom once but he might've just been saying frank-ly

THEO: He does say that word a lot

BABETTE: For emphasis It's true

FRANK: How many people were there total

BABETTE: Ooh I don't know Two fifty

FRANK: Two hunderd n fitty

THEO: Two fifty
    Three

FRANK: Half the city in other words

BABETTE: Not half

THEO: It was pretty intimate actually I
    mean the conversations were intimate

BABETTE: That's true but there was a sort of
    expansiveness to people's talk that
    gave you that Anything's Possible feeling

THEO: I know what you mean The chitchat had a
    weight to it that somehow managed to avoid pretension

BABETTE: I didn't encounter one especially obnoxious person

THEO: And I was impressed with the array of people's accom-
plishments I mean that was one diverse group of people

BABETTE: But still there wasn't a single conversation that made me
feel hopeless in terms of my own achievements or goals and
    actually I witnessed several people receive quality job
    offers from partygoers they'd just met

THEO: Oh yes people were supportive

BABETTE: And fun

THEO: It was the most supportive and fun party No question

BABETTE: No question

THEO: In every case as far as I'm aware the conversation
    transcended what people had in common

BABETTE: Definitely
    And there was none of the usual Floating Party Anxiety
THEO: God no
BABETTE: It was a peaceful party
THEO: And never a line for the bathroom
BABETTE: And never a shortage of food
THEO: or drink
BABETTE: And not too smoky
THEO: And not too hot
BABETTE: And not too crowded
THEO: And no trouble locating one's belongings when it was time to go
BABETTE: My coat was on the top of the pile
THEO: Mine too And someone had stuck twenty bucks in my pocket

(Slight pause. The hint of a sigh.)

BABETTE AND THEO *(There will never be another like it)*: It was the most supportive and fun party ever No question

. . .

(Babette, Theo and Frank are situated at their respective windows listening to The Airshaft Couple, from whose apartment we hear the sound of shower water running. The man calls to the woman from outside of the bathroom.)

MAN'S VOICE: Why am I leaving again
WOMAN'S VOICE: What
MAN'S VOICE: Why am I leaving again

(The water is turned off.)

WOMAN'S VOICE: Pass me

(She cuts herself off as the man has thrown the woman her towel.)

Thanks
MAN'S VOICE: Why am I leaving again

WOMAN'S VOICE: You're not leaving again you're
    leaving for the first time
MAN'S VOICE: Tell me again why I'm leaving
WOMAN'S VOICE: Because
    your strange isn't my strange
MAN'S VOICE: I would hope not
WOMAN'S VOICE: Oh
MAN'S VOICE *(What I mean is)*: I would hope not
WOMAN'S VOICE: Oh

· · ·

(Babette, pencil in hand, is poring over her "Outbursts Text.")

BABETTE: 6 28 1914 the wife of Archduke Francis Ferdinand sug-
gests a Sunday drive in Sarajevo
    Suddenly the duchess begins to feel faint and Ferdinand
instructs their driver to run into a Slavic shop to purchase an ice
cold beverage
    Several seconds after a young Bosnian nationalist emerges
from the store sipping a drink the driver returns to the vehicle
to explain that the young Bosnian nationalist got the last ice cold
beverage in town
    The outraged Archduke cries out after the young Bosnian
nationalist
    The Duchess Had Dibs On That Ice Cold Balkan Beverage
    The young Bosnian nationalist pauses to take a long sip
before he fires fatal shots into both Ferdinand and his thirsty wife
    World War I begins

(There is a knock at Babette's door. She opens it.)

THEO: Could you come over for a few minutes It
    won't take long I promise not to beg you to
    be my girlfriend

*(Theo leaves. Babette exits her apartment immediately thereafter and
knocks on Theo's door. He opens it.)*

What brings you here Kidding Why don't you have a seat

BABETTE: To keep Really

THEO: Ha ha So uh as you know it's been a while since since

BABETTE: Recall

THEO: Since the uh mysterious disappearance of my
    Beth

BABETTE: Uh-huh

THEO: And uh and uh well I'm beginning to
    think her departure is going to stick
    That is I'm beginning to believe that
    she's not coming back

BABETTE: Yeah she's not

THEO: Beth's not coming back and so I've
    decided that I'd like you to have
    her things

BABETTE: What do you mean by that exactly

THEO: She left most of her things here I want you to have them

BABETTE: Why

THEO: It seems silly for them to go unused

BABETTE: Give them away

THEO: That's what I'm attempting to do

BABETTE: Why me

THEO: You're my
    friend

BABETTE: Have you ever seen *Rebecca*

THEO: Yes

BABETTE: Is this a *Rebecca* thing

THEO: Beth had some nice things clothes
    and I thought since money's tight you
    might want to take a look at them and
    see if there's anything that you would
    enjoy having that's all

BABETTE: Is that the pile over there Did you
    make that pile

THEO: I gathered a few of her
    things together

BABETTE: I don't know that I want her things

THEO: She was nice You would have liked her

BABETTE: She abandoned you

THEO: Something must've been afoot I
    should've known when she lost her wedding
    ring
BABETTE: When did you start saying afoot
THEO: Just now I think
BABETTE: What do you mean she lost her wedding
    ring
THEO: I thought she'd use the insurance
    money to have another one made but
    she spent it otherwise it turns out
BABETTE: On what
THEO: Luggage I later discovered Pick out some stuff

(Babette starts to go through the pile of Beth's belongings.)

BABETTE: This is a nice coat
THEO: Try it on

(Babette tries on the coat.)

It looks good on you
BABETTE: It doesn't make me look short bulky or pale

(Theo shakes his head twice in response to the first two but admits, through subtle facial expression, that the coat MIGHT make her look pale.)

You aren't getting rid of that couch are you
THEO: No
BABETTE: You shouldn't it looks really good in there
    This is a pretty dress
THEO: She was wearing that when I proposed
    the first time Try this on over it That's
    the way she always wore it
BABETTE: There's a piece of paper in the pocket
THEO: What is it
BABETTE: It's a To Do list
THEO: What does it say

BABETTE: Pick up dry cleaning
 Return library books
 Leave The
THEO: Leave The
BABETTE: Leave the O
 Oh Leave Theo
 I couldn't read the O at first
THEO: Um will you be my girlfriend

. . .

(Frank practices.)

FRANK: Mother made me mysterious meat at mealtime mostly
 Mother made me mysterious meat at mealtime mostly
 Mother made me mysterious meat at mealtime mostly

(In the hallway. Frank and Theo stand near Frank's door.)

THEO: Two weeks in Kansas City
FRANK: Plus the countless hours with the at-home training tape
and manual
THEO: Oh that's what that noise was
FRANK: Noise
THEO: Sound

(Babette appears from the stairwell.)

BABETTE: Hi guys I just picked up the photos from my trip The
real photos this time My little friend at the Quick Clicks found
them Wanna see
THEO AND FRANK: Sure but maybe later I have to go take care of
 something

. . .

(Frank stands in between the doorways of Theo and Babette's apart-
ments. When he speaks, Frank adopts a bad Southern accent, or maybe
several. Throughout the auction Babette will continue to attempt to work
on her "Outbursts Text" and Theo will continue to attempt to compose
on his synthesizer.)

FRANK: All right we're gonna open the bidding at one fifty

BABETTE: What's for sale Frank

FRANK: Colonel

    A fact

BABETTE AND THEO: Like what

FRANK: A Fact each of you would like to know and Don't

THEO: The same Fact Frank

FRANK: Colonel A different Fact One each

BABETTE AND THEO: You've been keeping Facts from us Frank

FRANK: New Facts

    Colonel

    Brand spanking new Facts

BABETTE: How do you determine a winner

FRANK: The bidding will stop when this piece of gum I will now place on the ceiling loses its stickiness and falls to the floor All right we're gonna open the bidding at one fitty

BABETTE: One fifty

FRANK: One fitty one fitty over here it's one fitty

THEO: One seventy-five

FRANK: Senty-five senty-five

    do I hear

    two hunderd two hunderd

BABETTE: Two hundred

FRANK: Two hunderd two hunderd

THEO: Two twenty-five

FRANK: Tweny-five tweny-five ana quarter ana quarter

BABETTE: Fifty

FRANK: Two naf two naf

THEO: Seventy-five

FRANK: Three quarter three quarter

    senty-five senty-five

THEO:	BABETTE:
Three	Three three

FRANK: And the lady three hunderd three hunderd

THEO: FOUR HUNDRED

FRANK: Four hunderd four hunderd
  Do I hear
  OH
  The gum has fallen and the bidding has closed at
  Four Hunderd Dollars
  Sold to the Man At The Synthesizer
BABETTE: What about my Fact
THEO *(This is old news)*: The gum has fallen Babette
FRANK: There'll be other auctions Little Lady
THEO: Forget about her Fact Colonel What's my Fact
FRANK: All right well your Fact
  your Brand Spanking New Fact is this
  I saw Beth on the street yesterday
THEO: My
  Beth reappeared
  Did you speak to her
FRANK: Yes I spoke to her but that's not all
  There's more
THEO: A lot more
FRANK: She was with Larry
BABETTE AND THEO: Larry
FRANK: They've been in touch and strange as this will sound
  I suspect they've been touching
BABETTE AND THEO: Larry and Beth have been touching
  Ew
THEO: What did my
  Beth say
FRANK: She lives here She never left town
BABETTE AND THEO: Wow
FRANK: She had a message for you
THEO: What
FRANK: She wants to come by and
  pick up her things

. . .

(Babette, Frank and Theo lie in their respective beds. Frank and Theo are asleep. With hand gestures, Babette makes elaborate shadows on the ceiling.)

BABETTE: As children my brothers and I had a toboggan we called Jeremiah
Last night as I was sledding down a sand dune in my dream Jeremiah told me to Get The Hell Off

(Babette turns to go to sleep as Frank wakes up and begins to make shadows.)

FRANK: I was born on the third story of a
hospital and grew up on the third story of a
house and today live on the third story of an
apartment building
I've always inhabited the third story

(Frank turns to go to sleep as Theo wakes up and begins to make shadows.)

THEO: When I met her I told Beth I want to be the one you'd sleep with if you didn't have a girlfriend already I want to be first in line I couldn't find the line I thought Ah I must create the line I didn't know where to stand I picked a spot and waited for a long long time We kept in touch at a safe distance and then Beth finally gave up and let me step out of
line

(Theo turns to go to sleep as Babette wakes up and begins to make shadows.)

BABETTE: In other words I had a dream Theo didn't want to be my friend anymore

(Frank wakes up and joins Babette in making shadows.)

FRANK: Don't use other words

(Theo wakes up and joins Babette and Frank in making shadows.)

THEO: Pick the right ones

(Frank suddenly sits up in his bed and makes a very speedy, greatly enunciated speech.)

FRANK: Cut the cake cut the crap the cardinal can't come over
    Cut the cake cut the crap the cardinal can't come over
    Cut the cake cut the crap the cardinal can't come over
    Peachy keen Peach pit
    Peachy keen Peach pit
    Peachy keen Peach pit
    Theda thought the thigh was thawed but it was thoroughly
tholid
    Theda thought the thigh was thawed but it was thoroughly
tholid
    Theda thought the thigh was thawed but it was thoroughly
tholid
    Romance is really rather a riddle
    Romance is really rather a riddle
    Romance is really rather a riddle

. . .

(Babette knocks on Frank's door. He answers it.)

BABETTE: I've come for my Fact
FRANK: You can't have your Fact
    Not just like that
BABETTE: I'm not bidding for it
FRANK: Suit yourself
BABETTE: Who else would I suit

(Frank's door closes.)

Fine I have a Fact too
    About You

(Frank's door opens.)

FRANK: What Fact

BABETTE: It's not a Fact exactly
      It's an opinion
      but it's Deeply Held
FRANK: By whom
BABETTE: By Larry
FRANK: What's Larry's opinion
BABETTE: What's your Fact
FRANK: You first
BABETTE: Same time
FRANK: Fine
BABETTE: On the count of three
FRANK: One
BABETTE: After three or On three
FRANK: After One
BABETTE: Two
FRANK: Three

BABETTE:	FRANK:
Larry says you've gone off the deep end	Larry feels sorry for you

BABETTE AND FRANK: Pardon

BABETTE:	FRANK:
Larry says your dreams of auctioneering are ridiculous	Larry says you can't keep your word

BABETTE AND FRANK: What

BABETTE:	FRANK:
Larry thinks you're a fool	Larry thinks you're a fool

(Slight pause.)

BABETTE AND FRANK: Oh

.   .   .

(Babette, Frank and Theo sit in their apartments next to their phones. At once the three of them pick up the phone, dial a number—we should hear the sound of the individual number tones—and hang up in frustration, the number they have dialed apparently busy. After a moment, simultaneously inspired, the three of them dial another number, only to find that number busy as well. All three hang up the phone in frustration.

In the hallway. Ideally, the following is scored by Fats Domino's version of "Kansas City." Theo and Babette stand in their doorways. Frank, dressed in an old-fashioned suit and bow tie, walks down the hall, suitcase in hand, offering a small wave.)

BABETTE: You don't just leave without saying good-bye Frank
FRANK: Good-bye Frank
BABETTE: Good-bye Frank
THEO: Good-bye Colonel

(Theo enters his apartment and Babette remains where she is as Frank descends the stairs and then ascends them a VERY short while later, during which time the music should have faded somewhat and then increased in volume again, according to Frank's whereabouts. The music stops abruptly.)

BABETTE: Hi Frank
   How was it
FRANK: I don't wish to discuss it
BABETTE: Why
FRANK *(Isn't it obvious)*: My talkin' doesn't have any legs all right
BABETTE: Oh

(Theo emerges from his apartment.)

THEO: Hi Frank
BABETTE: He's not discussing it
THEO: Why Frank
BABETTE *(Isn't it obvious)*: His talkin' doesn't have any legs all right
THEO: Wow

. . .

(Frank is hanging outside of Babette's window. He wears a window washing harness and is cleaning her window. Babette opens her window and leans outside. Theo stands next to her. Throughout the scene, all we hear is the text that appears in **bold.***)*

BABETTE: **Would you care for something to drink Frank**
THEO: **Babette I need**—to talk to you about a rather delicate matter

(Theo closes the window so that we miss the rest of his line. Babette starts to speak before she reopens the window so that we miss the first part of her line.)

BABETTE: Listen Theo whatever you have—**to say you can say in front of Frank**
THEO: **Frank doesn't**—want to hear the content of this rather delicate matter

(Once again Theo closes the window so that we miss the second half of his line, and once again Babette starts to speak before she reopens the window, so that we miss the first part of her line.)

BABETTE: Frank does—**too want to hear it**

(Theo immediately closes the window; we miss the first part of his line but then hear the rest after Babette reopens the window. The pattern continues.)

THEO: Listen Babette the fact of the matter is—**I need those things I gave you back You know the coat the dress and the thing that goes over the dress that makes it an outfit**

(Theo closes the window; Babette claps during the first part of her line. By the end of her line Babette reopens the window. Theo closes the window by the end of his line.)

BABETTE: Oh that is great just great I'm so proud of you but you know what the answer is Theo the answer is—**Forget it**
FRANK: **Could you**

THEO: **Please she asked about those items speci**—fically

(Babette opens the window by the end of her line.)

BABETTE: How many times can one person be taken Answer me that You—**owe her nothing**

(Theo closes the window and Babette reopens it shortly thereafter.)

THEO: **Look Listen**—there's something you need to understand Beth's a truly dan—**gerous woman She's got a really bad temper**

(Theo closes, Babette opens, Theo almost closes, Babette reopens the window.)

BABETTE: **You are so pre**—dictable just so utterly fu—**cking**—pre—**dictable**
FRANK: **Um could you**
THEO: **Frank do you think I should call someone**
BABETTE: **Frank do you think he should call his mommy**

(Again, a struggle at the window ensues.)

THEO: **I am asking you for the**—last time as a—**gentleman**—would ask a lady if you would please—**gimme back**—my ex-wife's personal be—**longings**
BABETTE: **N-o The-o**
FRANK: **It would actually help if the window remained closed**
BABETTE: **You want the coat**

(Theo nods and closes the window. Babette finds the coat and opens the window halfway into her line.)

Here's—**the coat**

(Babette throws the coat out the window. Frank catches it. Theo closes the window, Babette opens it, Theo closes it, and Babette opens it again.)

Oh and here's—you know lady to gentleman—**Beth's dress**

(Babette unzips the dress she is wearing. She steps out of it and throws it out the window.)

Would you mind not staring at my breasts Theo when I'm try-ing to make an interpersonal point

(Frank is deeply philosophical.)

FRANK: They'd have us believe that a certain Betty Botter Just Happened to buy a bit of bitter butter that she was foolish enough to add to her batter and that then this Betty this same Betty Botter attempted to rectify the situation by buying better butter to add to her already ruined batter
    Frankly
    I'm coming to suspect Betty's motives were purely alliterative

. . .

(Theo dramatically lifts a hand and almost plays a note. He holds his finger above the key for an extended period of time before, after deep thought, he reconsiders and quite definitely almost plays another note. He then, slowly at first and eventually in a mad frenzy, reaches the cusp of playing a dozen notes only to change his mind each time at the last possible moment. Finally, Theo plays the same few bars of his composition but then miraculously continues to play, only to realize, as should we, that he is playing a familiar tune not of his composition, perhaps Kurt Weill's "Mack the Knife." An extended and strange outburst, a sound of unique anguish and frustration, emerges from Theo. Silence.
    Theo knocks on Babette's door. She opens it.)

THEO: Hi
    FYI
    I don't want you to be my girlfriend anymore

. . .

(Night. Frank, Babette and Theo are lying on their backs on the roof of their building. They are staring at the sky.)

THEO: Do you wanna play Choose Your Parents
BABETTE AND FRANK: Nah
BABETTE: Anyway Theo it's called Choose Your Ancestry It's
    about Deep Lineage
    not just one generation

(Slight pause.)

FRANK: Actually Babette I made up the game
    It is called Choose Your Parents

(Slight pause.)

BABETTE: Do you wanna play All The Conversations I Don't Want
To Have
THEO AND FRANK: Nah
THEO: All The Conversations I Don't Want To Have takes for-
ever and Besides
    I'd rather not discuss that game
FRANK: Do you wanna play Do You Smell Something Burning
BABETTE AND THEO: Nah
FRANK: What about I Either Left The Iron Plugged In Or The
Door Unlocked I Just Know It
BABETTE: I Either Left The Iron Plugged In Or The Door Unlocked
I Just Know It gets too personal
THEO AND FRANK: It does
THEO: What about My Favorite People Should Be Your Favorite
People
FRANK: No
    Way
    My Favorite People Should Be Your Favorite People is inher-
ently homophobic and I'm not sorry if I'm offending whoever
thought of it
BABETTE AND THEO: You thought of it Frank

(Slight pause.)

THEO: How about a round of Landlord Go Home or a little Landlord Gimme Back My Rent

FRANK: Or Excuse Me You Annoy Me

BABETTE: Or Mi Casa Is Not Su Casa

THEO: Or Teacher's Doubts Panned Out

BABETTE: I told you I wasn't playing Teacher's Doubts Panned
Out anymore

THEO: Shitty prescient bastards

FRANK: What about Where Were You Really

THEO: What about I Saw You Go Into A Restaurant After You
Said You Weren't Hungry

BABETTE: You always want to play that game

FRANK: What about The People With Whom I've Blown It

BABETTE AND THEO: Oh please Frank We don't have all night

BABETTE: What about The People I Meant To Sleep With

THEO AND FRANK: Oh please Babette We don't have all night

FRANK: What about The People Who Never Got Back To Me

THEO: What about Could You Cloak Your Animosity A Little I
Just Woke Up

FRANK: What about I'm Lousy With Unrequited Love, i.e., I Have
Utterly No One To Kiss

BABETTE AND THEO: How do you play that

FRANK: Oh I thought for sure you could tell me

THEO: How about Stop Saying Cinema When You Know You Mean
Movie and Other Pretentious Words

FRANK: What about Larry's game

BABETTE AND THEO: You mean Grand Rationalization

FRANK: I mean Larry's Other Game

BABETTE AND THEO: You Mean Best Friend

(Slight pause.)

BABETTE *(How could you)*: I'm sorry but I can't believe you sug-
gested that Frank

THEO *(Yeah how could you)*: I really can't either

(Slight pause.)

FRANK: I'm sorry I
    momentarily forgot what happened last time
THEO: Some of my hair still hasn't grown back
FRANK: Mine neither
BABETTE: Whose has

(Pause.

    They are quiet and stare some more at the sky; the silence is inter-
rupted by The Airshaft Couple, who are standing in awkward relation
to each other—visible only in shadow—in the front doorway of their
apartment.)

WOMAN'S VOICE: So do you
MAN'S VOICE: Why does it matter
WOMAN'S VOICE: I need to know Do you
MAN'S VOICE: Maybe
WOMAN'S VOICE: Maybe
MAN'S VOICE: Yes
WOMAN'S VOICE: You Maybe forgive me

(Pause.)

MAN'S VOICE: Hon it's the best I can do

(Pause.

    Theo, Frank and Babette suddenly sit up as they share a simul-
taneous recollection.)

BABETTE, THEO AND FRANK: MRS. JORGENSON

(A sneeze from the airshaft. Babette, Theo and Frank wait. Then:)

Bless you

(Blackout.)

END

brooklyn bridge

including

"Wire Wings," a song by Barbara Brousal

Production History

Brooklyn Bridge was developed through Playground, a joint commissioning program of Children's Theatre Company and New Dramatists, funded by the Jerome Foundation. The world premiere of *Brooklyn Bridge* was produced by Children's Theatre Company (Peter C. Brosius, Artistic Director; Teresa Eyring, Managing Director) in Minneapolis, Minnesota, on January 21, 2005. It was directed by Daniel Aukin; set design was by Louisa Thompson, costume design was by Maiko Matsushima, lighting design was by Matt Frey, sound design was by Victor Zupanc and Chris Heagle; the dramaturg was Elissa Adams, the stage manager was Kathryn Sam Loftin. The cast included:

SASHA	Emily Zimmer
SAM	Neil Dawson
TRUDI	Angela Timberman
JOHN	Steve Hendrickson
TALIDIA	Susanna Guzmán
THE SINGER/SONGWRITER	Barbara Brousal

Ensemble roles were played by Robert Beahan, Hillary Bertran-Harris, Celeste J. Busa, Erin Nicole Hampe, Benjamin Hanna, Theo Langason, Rebecca Lord, Jessica Miano, Anna Reichert, Damian Robinson, Jen Scott, Jessie Slagle, Emily Van Siclen and Katie Weber.

Who

SASHA, a ten-year-old with a deadline, child of Russian immigrants

SAM, a cab driver/student of dentistry, West Indian, twenties

TRUDI, a businesswoman with time-management issues, forties

JOHN, a wheelchair-bound Brooklyn Bridge buff, nineties

TALIDIA, a mother with a lot of laundry, Puerto Rican, forties

THE SINGER/SONGWRITER, a woman stuck on a song

ENSEMBLE ROLES: two musicians, two Shadowy Figures, Bridge workers, civilians, Washington Roebling, Emily Roebling, a letter carrier and a pizza deliveryman

Where

A Brooklyn apartment building, the Brooklyn Bridge, the imaginative space between.

As their elements are gradually introduced, the building and Bridge should be represented through architectural bare bones: steel pipes and cables and frameworks.

How

The line breaks, internal capitalizations and lack of punctuation in general are intended as guidelines to the characters' thought processes, in terms of emphasis, pattern and rhythm; they should be honored, but should not feel enslaving.

When a line is indented, it indicates a line break. When there is no indentation, it indicates a continuation of the previous line. When a forward slash (" / ") appears within the dialogue, it indicates that the next line should begin, creating an overlap with the previous line.

One

The Brooklyn Bridge, floating in space. Then, hallways, apartment doors, stairs, windows, a front stoop, a fire escape, a roof, and an elevator stuck between floors become visible in the foreground, thereby placing the Bridge in perspective. As with an advent calendar, five tenants of the building are suddenly visible standing in their respective windows. Just as suddenly, the tenants and the Bridge are gone.

Two

The sound of a bell ringing at the end of class and of kids leaving the classroom. Heard, but not seen:

TEACHER *(Voice-over, over the noise)*: Don't forget
 your New York City research papers are due
 TOMORROW
 No excuses
 No twenty-four-hour flus No
 dogs ingesting homework

(The noise starts to die down as most of the kids have left the classroom.)

(Voice-over) Sasha
   I WILL have a completed New York City research paper from
you tomorrow
   riiiiiight

(Slight pause.)

Does that noncommittal movement of the head mean yes
SASHA *(Tiny voice-over)*: Mm-hmm
TEACHER *(Voice-over)*: Good

(Sasha starts to leave.)

Oh and
   Sasha
   Remind me of the subject of your New York City research
paper
SASHA *(Tiny voice-over)*: The Brooklyn Bridge
TEACHER *(Voice-over)*: Pardon
SASHA *(Slightly less tiny voice-over)*: The Brooklyn Bridge
TEACHER *(Voice-over)*: Pardon
SASHA *(Slightly too loud voice-over)*: THE BROOKLYN BRIDGE

Three

Sasha, a girl of ten, appears. She walks in a tilted-forward fashion, propelled by the weight of the ENORMOUS book bag she carries on her back. Throughout the following, as Sasha moves through the building, its sounds are amplified (not in a fee-fi-fo-fum way; rather, the amplification should reflect what happens when one focuses on the sounds that surround us at all times). We watch as she ascends the steps to her apartment building's stoop. She inserts one of the keys hanging from her neck into the outside door's lock, checks the mail—it hasn't arrived—and trudges to the elevator. She presses the button, realizes the elevator is out of order AGAIN, and trudges up two flights of stairs. She walks to her apartment door, inserts another of the keys hanging from her neck into the lock, and then another and another into the other two locks, and enters her apartment. After she's crossed the threshold she turns around three times and then falls backward onto the floor from the weight of her book bag. The phone rings. Sasha checks the clock. Sasha extricates herself from the clutches of her book bag and picks up the phone; she speaks into it immediately, without waiting to hear the caller identify herself, as she knows who's calling. During the above, the Singer/Songwriter begins to work on a song in her apartment. During the following Sasha looks around for a writing implement.

SASHA: Hi Mom
    Sorry
    Hi *Mamochka*
    Yes
    I came straight home
    Yes
    I turned three times
    Yes
    I locked the door
    No
    I won't go out
    Yes
    I'll eat what's there
    No
    there wasn't mail
    Yes
    I spent it all
    Yes
    of course it's done
    Yes
    I'm sure I'm sure I'm sure I'm sure I'm sure I'm sure Do you know what happened to all our pens
    Pens
    Pens as in
    No I looked there

No I looked there
No I looked there
Never mind
I'll talk to you later
Bye Mamochka

(Sasha hangs up the phone. Slight pause.)

Uh-oh

(Sasha goes to her book bag and begins to look for a pen. As she does so, she removes book after book after book after book after book. Finally, she reaches the bottom of her book bag and comes up with a . . . fuchsia crayon, which she casts aside. She turns over her book bag and shakes it. Nothing. She riffles through various as yet unchecked piles in her disorganized foyer—clearly, both she and her mother are bibliophiles, as their apartment is jammed with books and newspapers in both English and Russian. Underneath a particularly thick volume she comes up with a . . . huge thick permanent green marker. She tosses the marker aside, too. Then, from across the room she spies, resting on a shelf—could it be?—a pen! She rushes over and grabs the pen, tests it on a nearby newspaper and discovers that it is out of ink. She throws the pen over her shoulder.)

Uh-oh

(For this next section, Sasha engages in a dance of sorts, that is comprised of the actions listed below, but whose engine is a deep ambivalence made up of equal parts of fear of the unknown and fear of the known—Mom. Sasha thinks, Sasha paces, Sasha thinks and paces. Sasha moves to the door, Sasha moves away from the door. Sasha unlocks all the locks. Sasha opens the door, Sasha closes the door. Sasha opens the door, steps into the hall, and then runs back into her apartment and locks all the locks. Sasha unlocks the door again, moves into the hall, walks up to a neighbor's door and raises her hand to knock. Sasha moves her hand away and then up again, away and then up again, away and then up again. The above is unwittingly scored by another section of the Singer/Songwriter's song in progress.)

Sasha knocks on the neighbor's door and all sound stops. Silence. Then we hear footsteps approach the door. The door opens quickly and all the way. Standing in the doorway is Sam, who speaks with a thick Caribbean accent.)

Hi

SAM: Hi

SASHA: Hi

SAM: Hi

SASHA: Hi

SAM: Hi

SASHA: Hi

SAM: Are we going to be doing this for a long time because I could get us some chairs

SASHA: I'm Sasha I
    live over there

SAM: I'm Sam I live here

SASHA: Hi

SAM: Hi

SASHA: Hi

SAM: Hi

SASHA: Hi

SAM: Is this a local custom I'm just now finding out about

SASHA: I'm looking for a
    pen but
    I'm not supposed to

SAM: You're not supposed to look for a pen

SASHA: I'm not supposed to
    leave the apartment

SAM *(Hmmm)*: Hmmm

SASHA *(What does hmmm mean?)*: Hmmm

SAM *(Hmmm)*: Hmmm

SASHA *(Uh-oh)*: Hmmm

SAM: This is what's known as a predicament

SASHA *(Is it?)*: It is

SAM *(It is)*: It is

SASHA *(I knew it!)*: It is
    (But wait) What's a predicament

SAM: Well
    You're not supposed to leave your apartment
SASHA: No
SAM: But you did leave your apartment
SASHA: Yes
SAM: And you do need a pen
SASHA: Yes
SAM: And if you were to turn around right now
    and go back into your apartment you will have
    both broken a rule AND failed to find a pen
SASHA: Yes
SAM: So I think the only way for us to address this predicament
    is to make your behavior
    Bad But Successful
SASHA *(A new thought)*: Bad But Successful
SAM: So
    let me go see if I have a
    pen
SASHA: Okay

(As Sam goes off in search of a pen Sasha holds the door open with her foot. Suddenly a cat escapes from Sam's apartment.)

Uh-oh
    (To Sam) uh Sam

(Sasha follows the cat down the hall, and tries to capture it. Sam reappears in the door.)

SAM: She's Red
SASHA: Excuse me
SAM: My cat's name is Red
SASHA: She's gray

(Sam retrieves the cat and pets her for a moment before putting her down inside the apartment.)

SAM: She wishes she were red

SASHA: Oh
    Did you find a pen
SAM: I had a pen
SASHA: Had
SAM: Last night at school
SASHA: You go to school
SAM: I'm studying to be a dentist

(Sasha instinctively recoils.)

Don't worry I'm not a dentist YET I drive a cab
SASHA: I never get to take cabs
SAM: The subway's significantly safer believe me

(Sam's cat escapes from the apartment again. Sam retrieves her and pets her for a moment before putting her down inside the apartment.)

SASHA: Why do you want to be a
    Dentist
SAM: Ah
    I can tell you view dentistry in a negative light
    and you are not alone
    There's no question the profession has a PR problem of
major proportions
    Major proportions
    I keep trying to enlist my classmates in my cause
    I want to change people's philosophy and get them to view
the dentist/patient relationship this way
    (Gestures as if reading a large sign) Together We Are Building
A Smile
SASHA *(Together We Are Building A What)*: Together We Are
Building A Smile
SAM: I'm having T-shirts made up
SASHA: So Sam it seems you're saying that you
    don't have a pen
SAM: Last night I was taking a test on the typical progression of
molar decay
SASHA: What's that

SAM: Do you like horror stories

SASHA: No

SAM: Then you don't want to know

It was a hard test and I chewed on the end of my pen until it began to leak

and I was forced to throw it out

SASHA: Oh

SAM: And of course at my school they knock off a whole letter grade if they catch you chewing on your pen

SASHA: That's terrible

SAM: Not as terrible as the damage chewing on your pen does to your

upper central cuspids

SASHA: Upper central cuspids

SAM: Your front teeth

(Sam's cat escapes again, only this time Sasha is the one who goes down the hall to retrieve her. Sasha holds her and pets her for a moment before returning her to Sam and turning to reenter her apartment, utterly defeated.)

Sasha

SASHA: Yes

SAM: Why do you need a pen

SASHA: My fifth grade research paper is due

tomorrow

SAM: What's a fifth grade research paper

SASHA: It's a lower middle school assignment of

milestone proportions

SAM: So it's like a comprehensive exam on periodontal tissue graft

SASHA: I guess

SAM: That's major What's the subject of your research paper

SASHA: The Brooklyn Bridge

SAM: That one over there

SASHA: There's only one as far as

I know

SAM: Someone tried to sell it to me when I first came to this country

SASHA: For how much

SAM: Three million

SASHA: That's a lot of money

SAM: On the contrary in my country three million is equivalent to roughly ninety-five dollars so I thought it was a pretty good deal

(Sam's cat jumps out of Sam's arms and scurries down the hall. Sasha and Sam spend the next several lines working as a team trying to catch her.)

What have you written about the Brooklyn Bridge

SASHA: You mean so far

SAM: Yes

SASHA: Nothing

SAM: Nothing

SASHA: Nothing

SAM: But I thought you said your middle school assignment of milestone proportions was due tomorrow

SASHA: I HAVEN'T BEEN ABLE TO FIND A PEN

HAVE I

I'm sorry I yelled I don't yell

(Unfortunately, Sasha stood still during the above outburst, providing Sam's cat with the means of escape she was looking for.)

SAM: This subject seems to be for you what we call in my profession a tender region

SASHA: It's not that I haven't done research

I've read every book there is

I know everything there is to know about the Brooklyn Bridge

(Sam succeeds at last in capturing his cat.)

SAM: So

what's the problem

SASHA: I don't know where to begin

I don't know where to end

I don't know where to middle

(Sam puts his cat down inside his apartment. Sasha looks as if she is about to cry. At this moment the woman we will later know as Trudi opens her door, starts to leave her apartment, checks her watch and then reenters her apartment and closes the door. At the same time the Singer/Songwriter composes the first two lines of her song, writing down the lyrics after she sings each line.)

SINGER/SONGWRITER *(Sung)*:
Sheltered by its wire wings
They come with offerings

(Said) Hmmm

SAM *(Please don't cry)*: I bet I know something you don't know about the Brooklyn Bridge

SASHA *(It's not as if I want to cry)*: Well excuse me if this sounds egotistical Sam
but I very much doubt that

SAM: Okay
What's the best way to drive across the Brooklyn Bridge

SASHA: In a car of course

SAM: Yes but how

SASHA: I don't understand the question

(Sam acts out the following as the Singer/Songwriter tries to make compositional headway:)

SAM: At the bottom of the ramp on the Manhattan side there's a pothole the size of Montana so you need to stay Left but then you immediately encounter a buckling steel road cable that necessitates a veer to the Right which brings you to the Center lane which is fine for all of three seconds when you hit a pavement dip that makes you have to swerve Left again and then without even time to remove a hand from the steering wheel you encounter some deadly serious roadway rutting so that you're forced to go Left Right Left Right Center Left Right Left which brings you to the Brooklyn ramp where you are greeted with no option but to take the first exit if you want to avoid replacing your shock absorbers directly after driving off the Bridge
Did you know that Sasha

SASHA: No
SAM: Maybe you could put that in your research paper
SASHA: I don't think it would go
SAM: What's the paper about
SASHA: I told you
    the Brooklyn Bridge
SAM: Yes but what ABOUT the Brooklyn Bridge
SASHA: Just stuff
SAM: Stuff
SASHA: THINGS
    DETAILS
    STUFF LIKE THAT
    JUST STUFF
    I'm sorry I yelled I don't yell
SAM: So you said
    Can your parents help you with your paper
SASHA: My mother works nights

(Slight pause in which Sasha regards Sam regarding her with compassion.)

I can take care of myself
    I can take care of myself
SAM: Okay
    Okay

(Slight pause.)

How long have you lived here
SASHA: In New York or this building
SAM: Both
SASHA: All my life
SAM: How long is all your life
SASHA: Ten years seven months six days and seventeen hours

(A plaintive meow.)

SAM: I'm coming Red
    She's hungry

SASHA: How long is all your life
SAM: I've stopped counting in hours put it that way
SASHA: Wow
SAM: How long has it been since you've seen a dentist

(Sasha covers her teeth tightly with her lips.)

I was only going to offer to clean your teeth
SASHA: Thanks
 but my mom would notice right away if my teeth looked cleaner
and I'm pretty sure I'm not allowed to get my teeth cleaned when
she's not at home

(An impatient meow.)

SAM: Good luck with your pen
 and paper
SASHA: Enjoy your dinner Red
SAM: Bye
SASHA: Bye
SAM: Bye

(Sam starts to close his door.)

SASHA: Bye
SAM: Bye

(A ciao meow.
 *Sam's door is closed. Sasha stands there for a moment looking at
it, looking very alone.)*

SASHA: Bye

*(After several seconds, very quietly at first but then with increasing
volume, she emits a sound of panic. She raises her hand to knock on
Sam's door once more, but then stops, as she reminds herself that:)*

I can take care of myself

(She heads back toward her door just as the silence is filled once more with the sound of the Singer/Songwriter working on her song. Sasha listens.)

SINGER/SONGWRITER *(Sung)*:
   A long list of wishes and dreams
   Is left here by the sea

(The Singer/Songwriter writes down these new lyrics.
   Sasha, somewhat mesmerized, tries to identify where the music is coming from. She starts to move along the hallway toward the stairway, when suddenly a giant crash is heard from within an apartment two doors down. Sasha rushes back into her apartment, turns around three times and then opens the door just a crack. She peers into the hallway. A Shadowy Figure emerges from an apartment down the hall carrying a large bag of trash. The Shadowy Figure walks toward the garbage chute, grumbling.)

SHADOWY FIGURE: Gagruhiuolfmelnetcgndkeffrdetcetckecfeffder

(The Shadowy Figure opens the door to the garbage chute room so that all we can see is the open door, held so by a slippered foot. As the Shadowy Figure attempts to shove the large bag of trash into the garbage chute, it grumbles some more as it struggles, for the bag is too large for the chute, and the Shadowy Figure must employ its entire body in the act of making it go.)

Frefereaftafddetcgbzlkgadfsdetcserrrerearsars

(Finally the Shadowy Figure emerges from the garbage chute room, having succeeded in shoving the trash down the chute. The Shadowy Figure starts to return to its apartment, and then suddenly veers the other way, instead, and walks down the hall. The Shadowy Figure stops at a very sad-looking but large potted plant. The Shadowy Figure, expending considerable energy, and of course, grunting—)

Grrgwerwthketcfjatiuypsgnetckgjklgldfkljrtgf

(—drags the plant about six inches to the left, so that it covers a spot in the carpet just as it reveals another spot on the carpet from where it was moved. The Shadowy Figure then moves to return to its apartment, but just as it passes Sasha's door, from a crack through which she is still peering, it hears:)

SASHA: Ah-chew
    (In spite of herself) Oops

(The Shadowy Figure stops for a second and regards Sasha's door, deciding what to make of the sneeze. Finally, the Shadowy Figure moves on, enters its apartment and closes the door. After a few moments Sasha quietly emerges from her apartment and approaches the potted plant, eager to understand the import of its placement, but a few seconds later there is the sound of another apartment's door unlocking. Sasha rushes back inside her own apartment and again watches through the tiniest crack. From this other apartment emerges the Other Shadowy Figure, who goes directly to the sad and large potted plant, also grumbling—)

OTHER SHADOWY FIGURE: Bleredgbbfktlktbetcbeltrjtgetc blejtwelktjal

(—and moves it six inches to the right, so that it is restored to its former position and once again covers the other spot on the carpet. The Other Shadowy Figure heads back to its apartment, still grumbling—)

Gyhkjgdfkjtjlktketcaslkjdflgketcasklgjafd

(—but just as it passes Sasha's door, it hears:)

SASHA: Ah-chew
    (In spite of herself again) Oops

(The Other Shadowy Figure stops and regards Sasha's door.)

OTHER SHADOWY FIGURE *(?)*: Jklftjltjetcasldkjfselk;retcdfjklejd

(Sasha is paralyzed, and then, at last, improvises a response:)

SASHA: Ferehjteffhhrerllkkfkje

(The Other Shadowy Figure accepts this response—)

OTHER SHADOWY FIGURE: Ssdfkjsltjlgjkfghtjdffdfa

(—and moves on down the hall. The Other Shadowy Figure reenters its apartment and locks the locks. Once again, there is the sound of the Singer/Songwriter working on her song—she la la la's to a variation on the song's melody. And once again Sasha, entranced by the music, is drawn slowly down the hall toward the stairway, in search of the singer's whereabouts.

Meanwhile, the doors to the elevator—which has been stuck between the basement and first floor—suddenly open, and inside we see the interior of a caisson, an airtight chamber employed in the construction of the underwater portions of the Bridge's towers. Several men dig with shovels and pickaxes. The mud on the bottom is thick and the rock beneath it hard. The only light source is a calcium lamp. The only sounds are of the implements in use and the men's exertion.

By the time Sasha has reached the stairway and is about to put her foot on the first step, the music stops suddenly, the elevator's doors close and Sasha's trance is broken. Sasha regards her foot, which is still hanging midair. Just then, Sam walks past her on his way down the stairs.)

SAM: Going upstairs to look for a pen
SASHA *(Putting her foot down)*: I don't go upstairs
SAM: Why not
SASHA: I don't wish to discuss it
SAM: Why not
SASHA: Where are you going
SAM: Red is blue
SASHA: Red is gray actually
SAM: No Red is blue
    by which I mean
    she's sad

(Meow of sorrow.)

We've run out of cat food so
    I'm going to get more
    Are you afraid to go upstairs
SASHA: I told you
    I don't discuss it
SAM: Red's afraid to go up those stairs
SASHA *(Great relief)*: She is
    (Amended to) I mean
    (Clinical interest) She is
SAM: Makes it easier to catch her when she slips out the door
    (Loud whisper) Don't tell her I told you but she's an archetypal fraidy cat

(Meow of protest.)

SASHA *(Guard down)*: Maybe there's something scary on the fourth floor
    (Guard up) to her
SAM: The fourth floor is exactly like the third floor is exactly like the second floor
SASHA: The tenants aren't all the same
    Maybe a larger-than-fairy-tale-giant lives on the fourth floor
SAM: You think a larger-than-fairy-tale-giant lives on the fourth floor
SASHA: I DON'T BUT IT SOUNDS LIKE YOUR CAT DOES
    I'm sorry I yelled I never used to yell
SAM: You think a giant lives up there
SASHA: Ten-year-seven-month-six-day-seventeen-and-a-half-hour-year-olds do not believe in giants
SAM: But cats do
SASHA: Red probably hears footsteps
    Early in the morning and late at night Red probably hears
    footsteps that are SO incredibly heavy SO incredibly textbook mythical they could
    ONLY be the footsteps of a fourth floor larger-than-fairy-tale-giant

SAM: Do you hear footsteps like that Sasha
SASHA: That's a second thing I don't discuss

(Mournful meow.)

SAM: I'd better get to the store
     Need anything
SASHA *(Rote)*: I'm fine

(Sasha walks into her apartment and turns three times as Sam walks down the stairs. A few seconds after Sasha closes her door, she reopens it, runs to the stairway and yells:)

I mean YES
     I NEED A PEN

(Alas, we are watching Sam exit the building as Sasha calls; he doesn't hear. Sasha turns to reenter her apartment just as the music starts once more, the Singer/Songwriter trying another variation. Sasha is again entranced, and this time slowly walks up the flight of stairs to the floor above. She follows the sound down the hall, trying to figure out from which specific apartment the music is emanating. After approaching several doors, Sasha finally identifies the right one.)

SINGER/SONGWRITER *(Sung)*:
     Take a moment

(The Singer/Songwriter writes down this new lyric, taking a moment to figure out the rest of it.)

     (Sung) There's a perfect view
     (A different note) View
     (A third note—the right one) View

(Just then, thunderous footsteps are heard approaching the door next to where Sasha stands. Sasha gasps, as she realizes she has unwittingly brought herself to the floor on which the giant resides. Sasha starts to take a step in the direction of the stairway, but suddenly the

giant's apartment door swings open, and standing in the doorway is, in fact, the giant, except the giant is a VERY tiny and impeccably dressed businesswoman. Any time Trudi, the tiny giant woman, takes a step in the following scene, it should be accompanied by a disproportionately loud footstep sound effect. Trudi herself is oblivious, however, to the force of her gait.)

SASHA: *(Gasp)*

(Trudi assumes, from Sasha's reaction, that an ax murderer is standing behind her so she, too, elicits a:)

TRUDI: *(Gasp)*

(Which causes Sasha to run partway down the hall only to stop in a there's-nowhere-to-run pose, punctuated by another:)

SASHA: *(Gasp)*

(Which causes Trudi to do the same, also punctuated by a:)

TRUDI: *(Gasp)*

(Which causes Sasha to make yet another dramatic movement accompanied by a:)

SASHA: *(Gasp)*

(Which causes Trudi to once again do what Sasha did, accompanied by a:)

TRUDI: *(Gasp)*

(Only to recall her identity as the grown-up of the situation, which inspires her to ask a grown-up question:)

Wait
    Why are we doing this
SASHA: You're not a giant
TRUDI: You're not so tall yourself

SASHA: I meant it as a compliment

TRUDI: I'll take you at your word for you are young

> Why are you staring at my
> feet

SASHA: No reason

> Do you um live alone

TRUDI: Yes why do you ask

SASHA: No reason

(Sasha looks up suddenly.)

Do you um have a pen

TRUDI *(Makes a writing gesture)*: A pen

SASHA: Yes

TRUDI: I'm in a hurry

SASHA: You don't carry pens when you're in a hurry

TRUDI: Is that slightly veiled sarcasm

SASHA: What's slightly veiled sarcasm

TRUDI: It's when you say something snotty while

> pretending it's the farthest thing from snotty

SASHA: You mean like teenager language

TRUDI: Grown-ups speak it fluently too

SASHA *(Trying not to get upset again)*: I wasn't trying to be unsnottily snotty I just

> really Really REALLY need a pen and anyway I shouldn't even be

> asking you because I'm not supposed to have any strange talk

(Trudi immediately searches through her purse since making the neighbor kid cry is the last thing she needs right now.)

TRUDI *(What the heck is)*: Strange Talk

SASHA: My mother's English isn't so great That's how she

> says

SASHA AND TRUDI: Don't Talk to Strangers

TRUDI: Well I'm sorry about your troubles but

> I have troubles of my own
> For instance I can't be late
> I'm on probation as it is

SASHA: Late for what

(Trudi suddenly makes another there-must-be-an-ax-murderer-standing-right-behind-me gesture.)

TRUDI: OH-NO-AM-I-LATE

(Sasha responds with an in-kind gesture.)

SASHA: I don't know
    When are you supposed to be where you're supposed to be

(Trudi consults her wristwatch.)

TRUDI: I have a board meeting
    and I purposely walked out my door forty-five minutes early
    because of my recently diagnosed condition
SASHA: What's your recently diagnosed condition
TRUDI: It's called *Sensus Lackus Ofus Timus*
    which means I have a tendency to lose track of time
SASHA: But we've only been standing here for a minute or two

(Trudi consults the wristwatch on her other arm.)

TRUDI: Of course we have
    That's QUITE RIGHT
    You needed a pen

(Trudi returns to looking through her purse.)

SASHA: What's your job
TRUDI: I move money
SASHA: You mean with a van or something
TRUDI: Oh no I don't TOUCH the money
    I just move it

(Trudi empties out her purse onto the floor, still looking for a pen. We should notice several timepieces among her purse's contents.)

SASHA: Sounds confusing
TRUDI: No
     boring
SASHA: Is that why they call it a board meeting
     No wonder you're running late

(Trudi is once again terribly alarmed. She lifts up her pant's leg to check her ankle watch.)

TRUDI: WHAT TIME IS IT
SASHA: About a minute after the last time you checked
TRUDI: That's right, and I left my apartment seventeen minutes early so
     let's all just try to stay calm shall we
     Why do you need a pen
SASHA: I have a research paper due
TRUDI: What's it about
SASHA: Do you really want to know or are you
     just making conversation
TRUDI: Both
     I'm a New Yorker
SASHA: The Brooklyn Bridge

(Trudi takes a step—which makes an enormous sound—and then bends down to replace her things in her purse.)

TRUDI: The Brooklyn Bridge
     I love the Brooklyn Bridge
     I jog across it every morning
SASHA: Do you um wear wooden clogs when you're at home
TRUDI: No why
SASHA: No reason
TRUDI: So you're writing a paper about the Brooklyn Bridge
     What ABOUT the Brooklyn Bridge
SASHA: I
     DON'T
     KNOW
     I'm sorry I yelled I've recently turned into a yeller

For me this is what's known among students of dentistry as
a tender region
TRUDI: Oh
Well
is your paper about the Brooklyn Bridge's construction
SASHA: Sort of
TRUDI: Is it about that father/son team who designed and
built it What was their name
SASHA AND TRUDI: Roebling
SASHA: Kind of
TRUDI: Is it about how it forever changed the lives of the inhabit-
ants of
the boroughs of Manhattan and Brooklyn
SASHA: In a way
TRUDI: You haven't started have you
SASHA *(Suddenly upset)*: No
TRUDI *(You mean)*: Nothing nada nyet zippo
SASHA: Well I've done the research part
I just need to do the paper part
TRUDI: When's it due
SASHA: Soonish
TRUDI: Tomorrowish
SASHA: Yesish
TRUDI: We've got to find you a pen before it's too late

(Trudi suffers another panic attack.)

WAIT A SECOND

(Sasha is drawn into Trudi's panic attack.)

SASHA: What
TRUDI: It's not tomorrow yet is it

(Trudi pulls a timepiece out of her hairdo and checks it.)

SASHA: No and as long as it's today I'm quite sure it will not be
tomorrow

TRUDI: Right you are So
    tell me about the Brooklyn Bridge
SASHA: Why
TRUDI: Practice
    It'll be like a verbal rough draft
SASHA: Aren't you in a hurry
TRUDI: Yes but I left my house an hour and a half early so
    I still have time to hear you speak about the Brooklyn Bridge
    AND make it to my board meeting on time

(Sasha clears her throat. She opens her mouth as if to speak but nothing comes out. She paces. She stops.)

SASHA *(A very long sentence for four words)*: The Brooklyn Bridge is

(Sasha paces some more. She stops.)

(A very short sentence for six words) a third thing I don't discuss
    plus
    my mother would be very upset is she knew we were having
this
    strange talk
    plus
    I'm not allowed to leave the apartment this late

(Trudi has fallen asleep; Trudi snores loudly and wakes herself up.)

TRUDI: UH-OH-WHAT-TIME-IS-IT-AM-I-LATE
SASHA: I'm not wearing a watch

(Trudi pulls timepieces from several surprising places in her clothing and observes that:)

TRUDI: And all of mine seem to have stopped
    What's your name
SASHA: Sasha
TRUDI: That's Russian
SASHA: That's right

TRUDI: Sasha

SASHA: Yes

TRUDI: We need to go up to the roof

SASHA: We do

TRUDI: We do

We need to check the time on the clock of the Williamsburgh Savings Bank

SASHA: We do

TRUDI: I have to be on time for my board meeting Sasha

Did I mention that I'm already on

SASHA AND TRUDI: Probation

(Sasha and Trudi climb the two flights of stairs to the roof; the sound of Trudi's footsteps is, again, extremely pronounced. They converse as they climb:)

TRUDI: And after we check the time on the clock of the Williamsburgh Savings Bank

you need to go buy yourself a pen

SASHA: I can't

TRUDI: Why not

SASHA: My mother doesn't give me Leeway Money

TRUDI: Leeway Money

SASHA: Just In Case Money

TRUDI: Oh Just In Case Money

SASHA: Every spare cent goes to my college fund

TRUDI: But what if something comes up

SASHA: You mean like an Unforeseen Crisis

TRUDI: Yes

SASHA: I'm not allowed to have Unforeseen Crises

TRUDI: Zowie

I wish I weren't

(At the same time, Sam reenters the building and climbs the stairs to the third floor. At the same time, the man we will come to know as John begins to clean his window, inside and out, with a clever device that allows him to do so, as he is wheelchair-bound. At the same time, the Singer/Songwriter da-da-da's to an upbeat riff on her theme. As

Trudi and Sasha unlock the door to the roof, a symphony of what-took-you-so-long meows scores Sam's entrance into his apartment. Trudi takes Sasha's arm and leads her over to the side of the building from which the Williamsburgh Savings Bank building is visible.)

What time is it
    in your opinion
SASHA: It's five after six
TRUDI: In your opinion
SASHA: I would say it's five after six
    in most people's opinion
    unless you live in Australia or something
TRUDI: Okay
    Phew
SASHA *(You're going to be late, aren't you)*: You'll still be on time
TRUDI: I have Lots and Lots of time
SASHA: Would you like to say hi to my mom
TRUDI: Does she live on the roof
SASHA: Of course not
    She lives with me in an apartment below a fourth floor larger-than-fairy-tale-gian
    (But that would be impolite) below
    You
TRUDI: In that case I'll meet her when she gets home
SASHA: She works very hard and very
    (Starts to say) la(te)
    (Amends it to) long hours
TRUDI: What about your father
SASHA: My mom says he's out of town
TRUDI *(On business)*: Oh
SASHA: permanently
TRUDI *(Uh—)*: Oh
SASHA: But we can say hi to my mom right now
TRUDI: Are you asking to borrow my cell phone
SASHA: We don't need a cell phone
    See that building two buildings east of the one with the flashing red light on top
TRUDI: No

SASHA: Squint
TRUDI: Okay I see it
SASHA: Start on the right hand side
TRUDI: Okay
SASHA: Count seventeen windows down from the top
TRUDI: Okay
SASHA: Count three over
TRUDI: Okay

(Sasha waves.)

SASHA: Hi Mom

(The mom in her head corrects her.)

Sorry
       Hi *Mamochka*

(Sasha nudges Trudi.)

Say hi

(Trudi waves.)

TRUDI: Hi Sasha's mother
SASHA: Mi mamochka says
       hi yourself
       Mom's always trying to use American ideams
TRUDI: You mean idioms
SASHA: No kidding
TRUDI: Who takes care of you at night
SASHA: What do you mean
TRUDI: Who makes your dinner
SASHA: Lots of people
TRUDI: Like who
SASHA: Aunt Jemima Chef Boyardee and the Swanson family
       pretty much
TRUDI: You eat dinner alone every night

SASHA: No

    My mom and I eat dinner together every night

TRUDI: I'm confused

SASHA: My mom goes on break at eight

    I bring my dinner up here at eight

    We have dinner together every night at eight

TRUDI: Does your mother know you have dinner together every night at eight

SASHA: How could she not know We have

    long conversations

TRUDI: When will your mother be home

(Sasha squints at her mother's building.)

SASHA: Mi mamochka says what's it to you

(Trudi addresses Sasha's mother's building.)

TRUDI: I'm worried about your daughter's research paper

SASHA: Mi mamochka says don't be

    Mi mamochka says she calls me every three hours to check in

    and besides

    Mom's not there

TRUDI: Excuse me

SASHA: You're looking in the wrong office

TRUDI: You said seventeen windows down and three over

SASHA: That was several minutes ago

TRUDI: Your mother has more than one office

SASHA: My mom has between twenty-one and twenty-three offices

    depending upon the day

TRUDI: I don't understand

SASHA: My mom cleans

TRUDI: Offices

SASHA: My mom's four windows over now

    My mom's got to work fast

    No more than nineteen minutes per office

TRUDI: Oh

SASHA: And my mom's supervisor really watches the clock

    None of the maintenance crew is allowed to run late

(Trudi gasps.)

TRUDI: WHAT TIME IS IT
SASHA: In my opinion it's 6:15
TRUDI: Oh no
SASHA: What
TRUDI: I'm late for my board meeting

(Trudi rushes to exit from the roof and Sasha follows. They continue to converse as they rush. At the same time, the Singer/Songwriter takes another stab at the upbeat music, her da-da-da's punctuating the dialogue between Sasha and Trudi.)

SASHA: What time did it start
TRUDI: It started at six
SASHA: In your opinion
TRUDI: In fact
SASHA: But at five after six you said you had plenty of time
TRUDI: My *Sensus Lackus Ofus Timus* must've been in an acute phase

(When she reaches the first landing Trudi rushes over to the elevator and presses the button, but then remembers that:)

TRUDI AND SASHA: It's out of order
    again

(Trudi returns to the stairs and continues to rush down them, Sasha following behind. The earth shakes with each step Trudi takes, so much so that as she and Sasha converse they are forced to yell. When Sasha reaches the third floor she stops and simply leans over the banister to continue the conversation.)

TRUDI *(Calling up the stairs)*: Tell your mamochka it was nice to meet her
    but not to be offended if I don't recognize her in a crowd
SASHA *(Calling down the stairs)*: Are you going to take a cab
TRUDI *(Calling up the stairs)*: Of course
SASHA *(Calling down the stairs)*: Lucky

(Sasha starts to straighten up and then suddenly leans over the banister once again.)

(Calling down the stairs) Do you um wear steel-toed slippers around the apartment
TRUDI *(Calling up the stairs)*: No why do you ask
SASHA *(Calling down the stairs)*: No reason

(Trudi exits the building; Sasha hears the sound of the front door closing.)

Bye

(At the same time, Talidia opens her window and shakes out a rug.
    At the same time, two clever, sculptural representations of the Brooklyn Bridge's towers will become visible far downstage left and far upstage right, so that they are situated on a diagonal in relation to the building.
    At the same time, the Singer/Songwriter tries to work out the song's third verse—)

SINGER/SONGWRITER *(Sung)*:
    da da da
    Here's the water
    da da da

(—but her efforts end in a decidedly vocalized frustration.
    At the same time, a sense of the direness of her straits returns to Sasha; she stands in the hall and covers her face with her hands, utterly paralyzed. Then, the phone begins to ring in her apartment. Sasha enters her apartment, turns around three times and rushes to the phone.)

SASHA: Hi Mamochka
    No
    I was in the other room
    (Crosses her fingers) Yes
    the door's still locked

Yes
I ate what's there
Yes
of course it's done
Yes
I'll tuck myself in
Yes
I'll give myself a good night *poʒeluy*
Yes
I'm sure I'm sure I'm sure I'm sure I'm sure I'm sure
(Help, please) Mamochka
Could You Come Home Early
(Okay, forget it) Uh-huh
Uh-huh
Uh-huh
I know
Never mind Mom
I'll see you later
Bye Mom

(Sasha hangs up the phone and lets out a half-plaintive, half-angry sound of distress. She heads out into the hallway once more; the potted plant catches her attention. She crosses over to it and picks off a dead leaf. The door right next to the plant is suddenly unlocked, and, feeling somehow that she's been caught doing something wrong, Sasha instinctively hides behind the potted plant. The door is pushed open slowly, and an old, but not frail, man in a wheelchair emerges—John. He closes his door, reaches up to lock it and wheels himself over to the elevator. He presses the button. Sasha speaks before she thinks:)

(From behind the potted plant) It's out of order
SASHA AND JOHN: again

(The old man spins his wheelchair around.)

JOHN: Who's there
SASHA *(From behind the potted plant)*: Nobody
JOHN: Nobody who

SASHA *(From behind the potted plant)*: Just plain nobody

JOHN: Do you make a habit of hiding behind potted plants and informing tenants as to the status of the elevator Just Plain Nobody

SASHA *(From behind the potted plant)*: This is my first time

JOHN: I'm honored

SASHA *(From behind the potted plant)*: I'm Sasha

JOHN: No
>   I'm not
>   honored

SASHA *(From behind the potted plant)*: You said you were

JOHN: It's an expression It means
>   Lucky Me

SASHA *(From behind the potted plant)*: Then why didn't you say Lucky Me

JOHN: It wasn't what came to mind
>   and that's all one has at one's disposal
>   after all

SASHA *(From behind the potted plant)*: Oh

JOHN: I'm John

SASHA *(From behind the potted plant)*: I'm in trouble

JOHN: I thought you were Sasha

SASHA *(From behind the potted plant)*: I'm both

JOHN: If I were you I'd keep the former and drop the latter When
>   did the elevator break down

SASHA *(From behind the potted plant)*: It was working this morning

JOHN: Drat

SASHA *(Giggling from behind the potted plant)*: Did you say drat

JOHN: Did I say something amusing

SASHA *(From behind the potted plant)*: My father used to say drat
>   My mom told me it was the first word of English he learned

JOHN: It's a handy one all right

SASHA *(From behind the potted plant)*: My mom says it's out-of-date

JOHN: Each generation has a right to its own words of frustration It's how we tell each other
>   apart

SASHA *(From behind the potted plant)*: What's a generation again

JOHN: People of your grandparents' age make up one generation
    People of your parents' age make up another
    People of your age make up another
SASHA *(From behind the potted plant)*: I don't know what my generation's words of frustration are
JOHN: That's because you're too young to feel frustration
SASHA *(From behind the potted plant)*: HOW WOULD YOU KNOW WHAT I FEEL

(John is taken aback.)

JOHN: You're right that was presumptuous of me
SASHA *(From behind the potted plant)*: Is presumptuous another one of your generation's words
JOHN: It means I thought I knew more about you than I do
    Would you mind coming out from behind there
    It's a bit disconcerting
SASHA *(From behind the potted plant)*: I'm not supposed to have strange talk
JOHN: Excuse me
SASHA *(From behind the potted plant)*: I'm not supposed to talk to strangers
JOHN: Well I'm not supposed to talk to plants

(Sasha emerges from behind the potted plant.)

SASHA: We've never met have we
JOHN: No
SASHA: That's what I thought
    But you never know when some adult is going to tell you they've known you all your life when as far as you know you've never seen them before
JOHN: Ah yes My mother used to make me kiss all sorts of strangers who claimed to be close relations
SASHA: Ugh
JOHN: There you go
    That's a good one
SASHA: Good what

JOHN: Expression of frustration

SASHA: Ugh

JOHN: Ugh is simply a modern translation of drat

Could I ask a favor of you

SASHA: Does it involve breaking the rules

JOHN: It involves going to the mailboxes

I'm expecting an important piece of mail and

it doesn't look as though I'll be getting downstairs today

SASHA: I'm not even supposed to be outside of my apartment this late

JOHN: In that case never mind

Rules are rules

SASHA: But you need a favor

JOHN: Rules overrule needs

(John turns to wheel himself into his apartment.)

SASHA *(A genuine question)*: They do

JOHN *(A genuine realization)*: Truthfully I'm not sure

I just said that

SASHA *(A genuine question/realization)*: What do you do when rules stop working

JOHN: You rewrite them but

I'm not recommending that you rewrite this particular rule

SASHA *(Interrupting him)*: What's your apartment number

JOHN *(Backtracking is in order here)*: Now hold on a minute

(Sasha suddenly grabs the mail key out of John's hand as the Singer/ Songwriter gets up and stretches.)

SASHA *(Looking at his door)*: 3E

JOHN: as in

egalitarianism

SASHA: What's egalitarianism

JOHN: A dying art I'm afraid

(Sasha runs down the two flights of stairs to the mailboxes, checks John's mail and runs back upstairs, empty-handed. At the same time, the Singer/Songwriter sings some scales.)

SASHA: There was no mail
JOHN: The mailman's awfully late today
SASHA: She's a mailwoman
JOHN: Yes but she's still a mailman
    That's what you say
SASHA: She's a letter carrier
    That's what you say
JOHN: All right I will
SASHA: Do you have a pen
JOHN: Of course I have a pen
SASHA *(At last)*: You do
JOHN: Of course I have a pen
SASHA: Could I borrow it
JOHN: Of course you may borrow it but every child should
    have a pen of her own
SASHA: Of course every child should but this child lost hers
JOHN: Where did you lose it
SASHA: Why do people ask that question
    I just told you I lost my pen
    If I knew where I lost it my pen would be found
JOHN: Sometimes it helps to identify the general location of the loss
    For instance
    In the living room
    In the store
    In the park
    In the

(John gestures for Sasha to finish the sentence.)

SASHA: middle of a really bad day
JOHN: Why do you need a pen
SASHA: I've already explained this twice today
JOHN: I apologize for my absence from your previous explanations
SASHA: Was that slightly veiled sarcasm
JOHN: Absolutely not

(Sasha steals a look at John's watch.)

SASHA: I'm losing valuable time
JOHN: I'm ninety-nine years old
    Imagine how I feel

(Sasha sighs.)

SASHA *(Getting upset again)*: It's a research paper on the Brooklyn
Bridge
    It's very important
    I haven't started
JOHN: Why haven't you started
SASHA: I can't find a pen
JOHN: What's the real reason
SASHA: I can't find a pen
JOHN: What's the real reason
SASHA: I can't find a pen
JOHN: What's the real reason
SASHA: I don't know
    Yes I do
    I am in awe
JOHN: You are in awe
    of what
SASHA: That
    Bridge
JOHN: Ahh
SASHA: Awe
JOHN: Yes
    I see
SASHA: Yes
    Whatever I write will not live up to what I see
    That's the problem
    Does that sound silly
JOHN: It sounds precocious
SASHA: That sounds bad
JOHN: It's not
    in the long run
    How old are you

SASHA: I am ten years seven months six days and close to nineteen
hours old
JOHN: And able to articulate awe
    Awe is complex
SASHA: Haven't you ever felt awe
JOHN: Not since I lacked a name for it
SASHA: All I know is
    I have read too much and
    I can't figure out what matters
    except
    graduating to the sixth grade
JOHN: Is your graduation to the sixth grade
    in doubt
SASHA: Sorta
JOHN: What does sorta mean
SASHA: Sorta means yes
JOHN: I see
SASHA: I owe a lot of assignments
    but they had a meeting and
    decided I could graduate to
    the sixth grade if I did a really good
    job on my New York City research paper
JOHN: Why didn't you do your assignments Sasha
SASHA: John
    I did all my assignments
    (Pointing to her head) I did all my assignments John
    The problem was I did them all up here
    the problem was I
    didn't
    write
    them
    down
    (Getting upset again) and at my school they really hold that
against you
JOHN *(Hitting the arms of his wheelchair)*: You have a serious
condition
SASHA *(Alarmed)*: Is it as serious as *Sensus Lackus Ofus Timus*
JOHN: What's that

SASHA: Hard to explain
    You think I have a serious condition
JOHN: Clearly
    you can't commit
SASHA: I can't commit to what
JOHN: Paper
    I remember when you were born
SASHA *(Taken aback)*: You do
JOHN: Your parents brought you home in a cab
SASHA *(Excited)*: I took a cab
    (Back to being taken aback) Wait
    How do you know
JOHN: I look out the window a lot
SASHA *(Question before thought)*: Did my parents look
    happy

(Slight pause.)

JOHN *(Not at all)*: Very

(Slight pause.)

Let me go see about your pen

(John opens his door and wheels into his apartment. As he does so Talidia exits her apartment on the floor below, descends the stairs and walks out the front door of the building. Sasha waits, as the Singer/Songwriter plays a few bars. Suddenly, there is the sound of a lock unlocking in the Shadowy Figure's apartment. Sasha's instincts once again tell her to hide. She decides she doesn't have enough time to enter her apartment, so she runs into the stairway—between her floor and the one below. Only her eyes show as she watches from between the railing's vertical bars. The Shadowy Figure emerges from its apartment and crosses directly to the potted plant. It shakes its head in just-as-I-expected annoyance and moves the plant back to the position it—the Shadowy Figure—favors, commenting:)

SHADOWY FIGURE: Fdtkjtoijgnrjgrljeketcaekjfekjetcfdasf

(As the Shadowy Figure heads back into its apartment, four cables that connect the tops of the towers of the Bridge become visible. At the same time the Singer/Songwriter plucks four strings and sings:)

SINGER/SONGWRITER *(Sung)*:
    We're not waiting for anything

(And suddenly a man suspended by the cables and standing on a swing appears from offstage. His journey is a quick one that takes place in three parts, as he stops off at each of the "towers" and finally disappears out of view upstage right. Meanwhile, the elevator doors have opened to reveal a crowd of onlookers gazing up at the man's amazing journey. The crowd should be made up of as many people as can squeeze into the elevator, but their great cheers should sound like those of tens of thousands.

    Sasha, awaiting John's return, has been oblivious to the preceding event. Sam emerges from his apartment. As he locks the door he notices Sasha.)

SAM: Still no pen
SASHA: Trudi didn't have one so now
    John's looking
SAM: Who
SASHA: Trudi lives upstairs she moves money
    John lives there he moves on wheels
SAM: Oh I know her
    She's always in a hurry
SASHA: She has a recently diagnosed condition
SAM: And he's always recycling pizza boxes
    He must eat pizza every single day
SASHA: I wish I could eat pizza every single day
SAM: It's not good to do anything every single day
    except brush your teeth of course
SASHA: I don't have time to build a smile with you Sam so
    please don't ask
SAM: I don't have time to build smiles right now either
    I've got to get to school
    We have another test tonight

SASHA: What's the test on
SAM: Gum Disease
      Yesterday Today Tomorrow
SASHA: Yuck
SAM: I'll show you pictures
      You'll never forget to floss again

(We see the letter carrier enter the building. She crosses to the mailboxes and opens them as a pathetic meow emanates from Sam's apartment.)

Feline separation anxiety
SASHA: What's that
SAM: She don't want me to go
SASHA: Don't be blue Red
SAM: Bye Red
      Bye Sasha
SASHA: Bye Sam
SASHA AND SAM: Good luck

(Sam walks toward the elevator and then remembers:)

SASHA AND SAM: It's out of order
      again

(Sam disappears down the stairs. At the same time the letter carrier begins depositing mail in the mailboxes. At the same time there is another disconsolate meow from Sam's apartment.)

SASHA *(Whispers through the door)*: Red
      Here's what I'd recommend
      One
      Avoid waiting by the door
      A watched door never opens
      Two
      Take advantage of your time alone to do something a bit bad
      For instance go jump on the bed for a really long time
      Three

Curl up with a good book
or perhaps in your case you could
Curl up ON a good book
Most of all
Don't worry
He'll be back

(As Sasha awaits John's return with a pen she becomes conscious of the sound of the letter carrier closing the mailboxes. She then notices that she still holds John's mail key. In a hurry, instead of walking down the stairs, she slides down the banisters to the first floor as the letter carrier exits the building. Sasha arrives at the mailboxes and retrieves John's mail. She also removes the keys from around her neck and checks her own mail. She stops short when she sees the return address of a certain letter; she removes just that letter and leaves her keys as she rushes to the front door and exits the building. Waving the letter, she calls to the letter carrier, from the front stoop:)

(To letter carrier) 'SCUSE ME
    I NEED TO RETURN TO SENDER

(But the letter carrier is gone. Slowly, Sasha sinks down onto the front stoop, opens the envelope, takes out the letter, starts to unfold it and then folds it up again. Then she places it inside the envelope and suddenly takes it out again. Finally, she unfolds the letter, folds it up again, doesn't put it back in the envelope, but instead simply holds it. Meanwhile, there has been the sound, emanating through the window, of the Singer/Songwriter trying out another part of her song.)

SINGER/SONGWRITER *(Sung)*:
    Just when you thought you were alone in the room
    Rises the platinum arc of the moon
    Suspended patiently
    Waiting for

(Said) What

(At the same time the Other Shadowy Figure emerges from its apartment, crosses to the plant, restores it to its former position, grumbles—)

OTHER SHADOWY FIGURE: Therkjlejrolkejroiprretcmfekljetcmkd-jfetc

(—and retreats once more into its apartment. A moment later John emerges from his apartment, only to discover that Sasha is gone.)

JOHN: Drat

(John lingers for a minute before reentering his apartment and closing the door as Talidia, with a tremendous cart full of laundry, arrives at the front of the building from the street. If all times out as it should, Talidia's appearance coincides with the end of the singing and John's entry into his apartment. Talidia speaks with a Puerto Rican/Brooklyn accent.)

TALIDIA: Coming through

(Sasha, in a daze on the front stoop, doesn't move. Talidia is struggling under the weight of her cart.)

Ay
    Hello
    Chica
    Coming through
SASHA: Sorry

(Sasha moves to the right and then sits with her hands positioned at the side of her face like blinders, one hand still clutching the letter. Talidia searches through her pockets for her keys while balancing the cart.)

TALIDIA: *Ay*
    Ay
    Ay

(Slight pause.)

SASHA *(From behind the blinders)*: Is *Ay* your generation's expression of frustration

TALIDIA: It's my culture's expression of frustration

We say it every single time we go to the laundry and forget
our keys

Would you mind unlocking the door for me *chica*

SASHA *(From behind the blinders)*: I'm not allowed to let strangers
into the building

TALIDIA: That's not a problem since I'm not a stranger

I live in 2C

I've lived in 2C since before you were a single cell awaiting
division

(Sasha looks at Talidia for the first time.)

SASHA *(A single what awaiting what)*: Excuse me

TALIDIA: I was helping my son with his biology homework last
night

SASHA: You do look familiar but

I don't think I know you

TALIDIA: You don't

But we haven't known each other for a Very Long Time

That should count for something

SASHA *(Too tired to argue, reaching for her keys that habitually hang
from around her neck)*: If you say so

uh-oh

(To Talidia) I forgot my keys too

TALIDIA: *Ay*

SASHA: Ugh

(Talidia pulls back her cart so that it rests on solid ground.)

(Getting upset) I'm dead

TALIDIA: Don't say that

SASHA: But it's true

I'm dead

TALIDIA: Don't say that

SASHA: But it's true

I'm dead

TALIDIA: I don't like that kind of talk

SASHA: BUT YOU DON'T UNDERSTAND MY PREDICA-
MENT
TALIDIA: *Calme te calme te*
    Okay let's think
    Anyone you can buzz on the inside
SASHA *(I'm telling you It's True I'm Dead)*: My mother's at work
    You
TALIDIA: Frida has band practice
    Freddie's at the library
    Frankie's at the bowling alley
    Frannie's visiting her cousin
    Felix is doing his paper route
    Flora's riding her bike
    Fidelia's playing basketball
    My husband left eight years ago and
    the Super and I aren't speaking
SASHA: So what do we do
TALIDIA: We wait
    We fold

(Talidia takes out a clean sheet from her pile and silently coaxes Sasha to accept two corners of it. They fold the sheet and then another and another, but Sasha manages to hold on to the letter all the while.)

SASHA: Where did your husband go
TALIDIA: That's a funny question
SASHA: It's a simple question
TALIDIA: It's a simple question if it's a geography question but
    I don't think it's a geography question
SASHA: I don't think I know what you mean
TALIDIA: I mean it's a history question disguised as a geography
question
    I mean I can tell you that my husband went to Pittsburgh
    but that's not what you're asking
    You're asking why he went to Pittsburgh
    You're asking why he went
SASHA: Why did he

TALIDIA: Ask him
SASHA: He's not here
TALIDIA: Exactly
    Here's a towel for you
SASHA: It's still damp
TALIDIA: *Ay*
    Those dryers drive me crazy
    I'll have to hang it on the clothesline
SASHA: You have a lot of laundry
TALIDIA: I have a lot of children
SASHA: I see them sometimes
TALIDIA: They're hard to miss

(Slight pause.)

SASHA: You've lived in this building a long time
TALIDIA: I've lived in this building forever
SASHA: Did you know my father
TALIDIA: That's a strange question
SASHA: Do you call every question names before you answer it
TALIDIA: My mother used to do the same thing
    It buys you time to formulate your response
SASHA: It's a simple question
TALIDIA: It's a simple question if it's a yes or no question but
    I don't think it's a yes or no question
SASHA: Yes it is
TALIDIA: No it's not
    It's a complicated question disguised as a yes or no question
    I can tell you that I knew your father
    But that's not what you're asking
    You're asking me what your father was like
SASHA: What was he like
TALIDIA: I hardly remember him
SASHA: I don't remember him
TALIDIA: I knew him only
    to say hello to
SASHA: He said hello to you

TALIDIA: It's an expression
  When you know someone to say hello to it means
  you know them hardly at all
SASHA: So he didn't say hello to you
TALIDIA: Maybe he did
  I don't remember

(They fold.)

How long has he been gone
SASHA: Seven years five months three days and seven hours

(Sasha registers Talidia's surprise at her precision.)

Ish

(They fold.)

TALIDIA: How's school
SASHA: Ugh
TALIDIA: What
SASHA: People only say how's school when they don't know what
else to say

(They fold.)

TALIDIA: If a person's not allowed to say how's school how
  does a person find out how school is
SASHA: UGH
TALIDIA: *AY*
SASHA *(Said very quickly and with increasing upset)*: School is terrible
  I'm supposed to be writing a very important paper on the
Brooklyn Bridge and I don't have a pen because Sam and Trudi
didn't have one and even though John says he does have one that
does me no good because I'm locked out of the building and I'm
destined to remain in the fifth grade for the rest of my life expec-
tancy which for people my age is twenty-nine thousand seven

hundred and seventy-three more days but for me will probably be more like another couple of hours because I've somehow managed to lie to my mother about seven thousand times today and she doesn't find that sort of behavior charming but anyway I don't care what my mother thinks because

My Mother's Never Here

That's how school is

(Slightest pause.)

TALIDIA: Don't tell me you're trying to tell me that you haven't written your very important paper because you can't find a pen

Don't tell me you're trying to tell me that

SASHA: It's the truth

TALIDIA: Listen *chica*

I have seven children okay

Four with my husband two adopted one foster

I know when I'm being fed a preadolescent line

and for preadolescent lines I'm not hungry

SASHA: It's the truth

TALIDIA: No

It's an avoidance technique disguised as the truth

You might think you haven't written your very important paper because you can't find a pen

But that's not the real reason

So what's the real reason

(They fold.)

SASHA: That's the real reason

TALIDIA: So what's the real reason

SASHA: That's the real reason

TALIDIA: So what's the real reason

SASHA: That's the real reason well

okay that's Not the real reason but

I've already been through this with John I just

get overwhelmed when it comes to

Writing Things Down

TALIDIA: Why
SASHA: Because it makes me think about everything I'm
    NOT writing down
TALIDIA: But you can always erase what you write down and
    write something else down
SASHA: I could
    but that looks messy
TALIDIA: But you can get another piece of paper
SASHA: I could
    but that's a waste of paper
TALIDIA: But you can use a computer
SASHA: I could
    but I don't have a computer
TALIDIA: But you can go to the library
SASHA: I could
    but the library's closed
TALIDIA: *Ay*
    It's like talking to one of my kids
    Enough already
    Let's get to work

(Talidia digs around in her pocket and produces:)

Fidelia's chalk
    I confiscated it this morning
SASHA: You want me to write my research paper on the sidewalk
TALIDIA: You recite
    I'll write

(Sasha is cleaned out of excuses, so she paces.)

SASHA: The Brooklyn Bridge

(Sasha paces the other way.)

by Alexandra Trusotsky

(Sasha paces the other way, notices what Talidia has written and corrects her:)

317

"s" not "z"

(Sasha paces the other way.)

May 24, 2001

(Sasha paces the other way.)

Ms. Cohen's class

(Sasha paces the other way.)

P.S. 121

(Sasha paces the other way.)

Copyright 2001

(Sasha paces the other way.)

Brooklyn

(Sasha paces the other way.)

Comma

(Talidia shoots her a look. Sasha paces the other way.)

New York

(Sasha paces the other way.)

U.S.

(Sasha starts to pace the other way before turning to add:)

of A

(Sasha paces the other way.)

Northern Hemisphere

(Talidia REALLY shoots Sasha a look.)

TALIDIA: *AY*
  ¿Que voy a hacer contigo?

(Slightest pause.)

(Genuine curiosity) What's that paper you're clutching for dear life
SASHA: It's a letter from my father
TALIDIA: What does he say
SASHA: I haven't read it
TALIDIA: Why not
SASHA: He sends letters
  every year
  but the letters always arrive six months
  late

(Slight pause.)

You don't have a problem with the word Late
  do you
TALIDIA: No
SASHA: Good

(Sasha sits down on the front stoop.)

TALIDIA: So you haven't read the letter because it's
  late
SASHA: I'm not allowed to read the letters
TALIDIA: Does your mother read the letters
SASHA: In my mother's family when someone leaves they no longer exist
  My mother no longer exists for her mother
  My father no longer exists for my mother
  My father's not supposed to exist for me

(Talidia sits down next to Sasha. They are quiet.)

TALIDIA: The problem with people who no longer exist is that they
show up all the time

(Slight pause.)

SASHA: I'm not allowed to read the letters but I
read one once It was sitting on top of the trash
TALIDIA: What did it say
SASHA: I don't remember I just
remember lots and lots of
words

(Sasha carefully folds up the letter and puts it in her pocket.)

TALIDIA: Are you going to read it
SASHA: I don't know
TALIDIA: Does he ever try to see you
SASHA: I don't know but
how hard could it be
He knows where I
live
TALIDIA: Listen
I don't know your father
I don't know your mother
I don't know you
But I do know that the other thing about people who aren't
here
is that they lose their shape
Some become huge
Some become tiny
None resemble what they really are
What I'm saying is you can't trust what people's absences
turn them into
One funny-but-not-so-funny thing is that your mother's not
here
because she's working so YOU can be here

in this apartment building
in this country
in this other life that she wants you to have
Another funny-but-not-so-funny thing is that your father's
not here
but his words are
thousands and thousands of them
because for whatever reason they are all he has to give you
right now
Does it matter what those words are
I don't know
You have to decide
But I do know
that parents are exactly who they are
and even if they are not enough
they are what you have
You're not supposed to have to deal with such a fact at your
age
But for whatever reason life constantly asks us to deal with
all sorts
of age-inappropriate things

(Slight pause.)

Wait
There's one last thing I know
whatever your mother and father aren't able to do or be
whatever it is that you need that they can't give you
you must find it somewhere else
because it exists somewhere else
because everything we need exists somewhere
We just have to find where

(Slight pause.)

SASHA: My mother's a very sad person
TALIDIA: Why is that
SASHA: Because she's a very tired person

because she works very hard
And she's a very sad person
because she's a very smart person
who was a professor in Russia
who everybody listened to
But here nobody listens to her
because her English is broken
and she traded in a good life in a hard place
for a hard life in a good place
And she wonders why she did that
though she wants me to have a great life in a good place
And she wants me to be Russian
but she wants me to be American
but she wants me to be Russian
And she has no family around except me
and nothing feels truly familiar except me
except sometimes I think even I am becoming unfamiliar

(Slightest pause.)

My mother's a very sad person

(Slightest pause.)

And my father is
    I Don't Know Who My Father Is
    And I'm not sure I want to anymore
    And I'm not sure I feel bad about that
    Although I do feel sad about it

(They sit quietly for a long moment until Sasha remembers:)

John
TALIDIA: Who
SASHA: John can buzz us in

(Sasha walks over to the intercom and buzzes John's apartment.)

JOHN *(Through the intercom)*: Who's there
SASHA: Just Plain Nobody
JOHN *(Through the intercom)*: What are you doing out there
SASHA: I stepped outside and left my keys inside
JOHN *(Through the intercom)*: That was silly but
> you're in luck
> I've been expecting Just Plain Nobody

(The door buzzer sounds, unlocking the entryway. Sasha holds the door for Talidia and they both enter the building. As they do so, the Singer/Songwriter approaches the window carrying her guitar. She peeks around the side of the shade, apparently trying to spot someone in the street. Of her we see just eyes and a hand. The window is open but the shade is halfway lowered, so as the Singer/Songwriter perches on her windowsill with her guitar, her hips and hands are visible in full, while the upper part of her is seen in silhouette. She begins strumming. Meanwhile, Talidia and Sasha climb the stairs. Sasha helps Talidia haul her cart up the steps, one by one, and the sound the cart makes adds a percussive line to the Singer/Songwriter's strumming.

At the same time, the Bridge's suspenders and stays become visible; it looks as if a giant string instrument has three-dimensionally superimposed itself upon the building.

Talidia and Sasha reach the landing outside Talidia's apartment door.)

TALIDIA: *Ay*
SASHA: Ugh

(Talidia extends her hand.)

TALIDIA: Talidia
SASHA: Sasha
TALIDIA: Wait right here

(Talidia retreats into her apartment, leaving the cart of laundry in the hallway. The music stops and the Singer/Songwriter moves away from the window. Sasha suddenly remembers that she left John's mail out on the front stoop.)

SASHA: Oops

(Sasha runs downstairs, props open the door, grabs the mail and runs back up the stairs all the way to the third floor. John is waiting for her in the hallway.)

JOHN: I'm afraid I have good news and bad news
    Which would you like to hear first
SASHA *(Out of breath)*: The bad news
JOHN: My pen's run out of ink
SASHA: That's bad
JOHN: Yes I thought I named the news aptly
SASHA: What's the good news
JOHN: The good news is
    I have other pens
SASHA: That's good
JOHN: I'm just not exactly sure where they are at the moment
SASHA: That's bad
JOHN: I know I used at least three different pens yesterday
SASHA: That's good
JOHN: They just all seem to have evaporated
SASHA: That's bad
JOHN: However I am hopeful they will soon turn up
SASHA: That's good
JOHN: Although I'm unsure they will turn up tonight
SASHA: That's disastrous
JOHN: But the thing is

JOHN:	SASHA:
the pen's not your problem	the pen's not my problem

JOHN: You knew that

(Slight pause.)

SASHA: I don't know what to do
JOHN: That's easy
    Write your paper
SASHA: I can't

JOHN: You can
SASHA: I can't
JOHN: You can
SASHA: Can't
JOHN: Can
SASHA: Can't
JOHN: Can
SASHA: Can't
JOHN: Can
SASHA: Can't
JOHN: Can
SASHA: CAN'T CAN'T CAN'T CAN'T CAN'T
    keep yelling like this

(Slight pause.)

JOHN: Step into my office

(John starts to wheel himself into his apartment and Sasha starts to follow but then stops.)

SASHA: At what point is a person no longer a stranger
JOHN: That's an excellent question
SASHA: At what point does a stranger become a neighbor
JOHN: When your mother says so
SASHA: My mother insists that I turn around three times whenever I enter our apartment
JOHN: Why is that
SASHA: It's an old Russian superstition
    It's supposed to shake off any evil spirits that attached themselves to you while you were outside
JOHN: I'll have to try that

(Sasha moves behind John's wheelchair, pushes him into his apartment, and then spins around his wheelchair three times. Just then, Talidia emerges from her apartment.)

TALIDIA: So listen

(Talidia finds that Sasha is gone.)

Ay

(Talidia pushes her cart full of laundry into her apartment as John and Sasha become visible again; we see a window open and Sasha following John up a specially constructed ramp that allows him to wheel himself out onto the fire escape.)

SASHA: Nice office
JOHN: It's a little drafty in the winter months but
    you can't beat the view

(John produces two sets of binoculars. He passes one set to Sasha; they both look through the binoculars. Slight pause.)

(Through binoculars, to Sasha) I must tell you something
    Binocular to Binocular
    I am a Brooklyn Bridge Buff
SASHA *(Through binoculars, to John)*: I had no idea you were a
Brooklyn Bridge Buff
JOHN *(Through binoculars, to Sasha)*: I am a Brooklyn Bridge Buff
SASHA *(Through binoculars, to John)*: I also have no idea what a
Buff is
JOHN *(Through binoculars, to Sasha)*: A Buff is an enthusiast
    a fan
    one who is fascinated by a certain subject
SASHA *(Through binoculars, to John)*: Then we are Both Brooklyn
Bridge Buffs

(We see Talidia lean out her window as she hangs the damp towel on her clothesline. John now turns his binoculars in the "direction" of the Brooklyn Bridge, out to the audience, even though the Bridge actually appears at this moment to be diagonally bisected by the apartment building. Sasha, too, gazes through her binoculars at the Bridge; the two remain oriented this way through the entire following conversation.)

JOHN: It's time for a quiz
      What were the main phases of the Bridge's construction
SASHA: In order
JOHN: In order
SASHA: The sinking of the caissons
JOHN: And then
SASHA: The construction of the towers above them
JOHN: And then
SASHA: The building of the anchorages that would support the great cables
JOHN: And then
SASHA: The spinning of the great cables that would support the suspenders
JOHN: And then
SASHA: The hanging of the suspenders that would support the roadway
JOHN: And then
SASHA: The construction of the road and walkways that would support the traffic
JOHN: And then
SASHA: The placing of the diagonal stays that would support the support
JOHN: And then
SASHA: And then

(Slight pause.)

Opening Day

(Slight pause as the two gaze at the magnificent Bridge in silence.)

JOHN: Full length of the Bridge
SASHA: 5,989 feet
JOHN: Weight of the Bridge
SASHA: 14,680 tons
JOHN: Number of cables
SASHA: 4
JOHN: Number of suspenders

SASHA: 294

JOHN: Diameter of each cable

SASHA: Just under a foot and a quarter

JOHN: Length of wire in each cable

SASHA: 3,515 miles

JOHN: Did you say miles

SASHA: Miles

JOHN: Good

    Height of towers

SASHA: Above the roadway or above the water

JOHN: Water

SASHA: 276 feet 6 inches

JOHN: Length of time it took to build the Bridge

SASHA: 14 years

JOHN: First person to travel across the Bridge

SASHA: Before there was a road or after

JOHN: Both

(A change occurs from now on, as Sasha increasingly takes the reins of the Bridge narrative. As she does so, John laughs and nods his head and perhaps even vocalizes concurrence—basically, he delights in watching Sasha's knowledge insist on expression.)

SASHA: Before there was a road

    and to the great thrill of thousands of onlookers

    Master Mechanic E. F. Farrington traveled across on a sort of swing that was suspended by a wire rope that was strung between the towers

JOHN:	SASHA:
And after there was a roadway	And after there was a roadway the honor of the first official crossing was given to Emily Roebling wife of the Bridge's Chief Engineer who traveled by carriage across the Bridge in the company of a rooster signifying victory

JOHN: The Bridge's Chief
Engineer

SASHA *(Finishing his thought)*:
was plagued by a mysterious
medical condition Washington
Roebling suffered from caisson
disease later known as the bends
caused by a too rapid return to
normal air pressure from the
underwater environment of the
caissons

JOHN:
And as a result

SASHA:
And as a result
he was forced to oversee the
majority of the Bridge's
construction from the window
of his Brooklyn Heights
bedroom which luckily had an
excellent view of the Bridge and
where he would sit sometimes
for hours gazing out the window
through old-fashioned
binoculars which of course
weren't old-fashioned at the time

JOHN:
And as a result

SASHA:
And as a result
Washington Roebling's wife
Emily became instrumental in
the Bridge's progress acting as
her husband's spokesperson at
the work site and providing full
updates on the Bridge's progress
at home Emily in short became
Washington's right-hand man
except of course she was a woman

JOHN:
And as a result

SASHA:
And as a result
it was good for Washington
Roebling good for feminism
and especially good for those
who were awaiting an easier
means of crossing the East River

JOHN:
The Bridge's official name

SASHA:
The Bridge's official name
is The New York and Brooklyn
Bridge

JOHN:
The Bridge's nickname

SASHA:
The Bridge's nickname
is The Eighth Wonder of the
World

JOHN:
The Bridge's Opening Day date

SASHA:
The Bridge's Opening Day date
was May 24, 1883
(Said as a question to John) The
time *(But John is visibly stumped)*
was 2 o'clock P.M.

(John actually claps.)

SASHA: Highlights of the Bridge's Opening Day festivities
   included the following
   (Becoming more animated than we've ever seen her) President
Chester A. Arthur accompanied by other state and local officials
   crossed the Bridge by foot
   In the pictures it looks like a sea of top hats
   The crowd roared and military guns saluted
   Then when night fell there was the grandest festival of fire-
works anyone had ever seen
   But the best thing of all happened when light of a different
sort filled the sky

In a time when nobody had electricity in their homes imagine the feeling as they watched the Brooklyn Bridge
　become illuminated light by light along the promenade as if by scientific miracle

(John lowers his binoculars.)

JOHN: I believe you have accomplished something I thought not possible
　I believe I am in awe

(Slight pause.)

SASHA: But why
　Those are just a bunch of facts
　Facts are only part of the assignment
　The other part is having a point of view
　Taking a stand
　Deciding what's important
　The other part is what I'm missing

(Sasha lowers her binoculars. Slight pause.)

JOHN: Then it's high time for you to determine what you are left with
SASHA: Left with
JOHN: You've done your research
　You've gathered
　as you say
　your facts
　What are you left with
SASHA: What do you mean Left With
JOHN: There are facts and there is what matters
　and what matters is what you are left with
　So
　Sasha
　when you think about the Brooklyn Bridge what are you left with

(Sasha tries to pace in the limited area of the fire escape. Since there's no room she improvises and "paces" by climbing down and up the escape ladder.)

What are you doing
SASHA: Pacing
JOHN: Oh
    In that case carry on

(Sasha continues to "pace." Finally, she stops partway up the ladder and addresses John.)

SASHA: When I think about the Brooklyn Bridge
    I am left with what it cost
JOHN: $15,211,982.92
SASHA: I don't mean what it cost I mean what it
    Cost
    Besides money
JOHN: Besides money
SASHA: My mother says that SOME things cost money but EVERY-
THING costs something BESIDES money
JOHN: Such as
SASHA: Whole neighborhoods were demolished to make room for
the Bridge's anchorages
    Dozens of men lost their lives
    Others lost their health
JOHN: All worthwhile endeavor costs
    and even though we know this
    it is human nature to hope the price that's paid won't be
personal

(The two of them gaze at the Bridge without their binoculars, Sasha perching on the fire escape's ladder.)

SASHA: But the price WAS personal
JOHN: Yes
SASHA: And yet people stayed
    Almost all of them

who worked on the Bridge
They stayed
JOHN: Yes
SASHA: Even though it was very hard
JOHN: Yes
SASHA: Even though it would have been easier not to stay
JOHN: Yes
SASHA: Staying costs
JOHN: Yes yes yes
AND
I would argue that
considering Cost is another way of considering Worth
and trust me on this one
Worth is infinitely more satisfying to consider
SASHA: You think I should write about the Bridge's worth
JOHN: I think you should write about what you are left with
SASHA: That sounds like a riddle
JOHN: For some perhaps
but you're a girl whose awe is informed
SASHA: UGH
DRAT
AY

(Sasha paces some more, and then has an outburst:)

THE WORTH OF THE BRIDGE IS THAT IT WAS A FEAT
OF UNPARALLELED ENGINEERING
THE WORTH OF THE BRIDGE IS THAT IT WAS
THOUGHT NOT POSSIBLE
THE WORTH OF THE BRIDGE IS ITS ITS ITS
what's that word your generation uses for pretty in an important way
JOHN: Magnificence
SASHA: THE WORTH OF THE BRIDGE IS ITS MAGNIFICENCE
THE WORTH OF THE BRIDGE IS THAT IT LINKS
GEOGRAPHIES

THE WORTH OF THE BRIDGE IS THAT IT LINKS
POPULATIONS
THE WORTH OF THE BRIDGE IS THAT IT'S A
BRIDGE

(Pause.)

JOHN: YES
SASHA: THE BRIDGE IS A BRIDGE
JOHN: YES
SASHA: IT'S A BRIDGE JOHN
AND BRIDGES CONNECT THINGS
AND WHEN THINGS AREN'T ENOUGH IN ONE
PLACE
ALL YOU HAVE TO DO IS CROSS A BRIDGE
TO ANOTHER PLACE TO FIND THE THING THAT
WILL BE ENOUGH
THE BRIDGE IS A BRIDGE JOHN
AND BRIDGES ARE NECESSARY THINGS

(Slight pause.)

JOHN: A simple and elegant truth Sasha
Thank you for pointing it out

(Slight pause. Sasha is a bit exhausted.)

SASHA: Okay
but does ANYBODY in this universe have a pen

(At this moment a man wheeling a very large bass is buzzed in down-stairs. Over the next few minutes we will watch as he guides it over to the elevator, discovers that it's not working—)

MAN WITH BASS: Aargh

(—and begins the extremely arduous task of carrying the bass up the stairs, playing it as he climbs. The Singer/Songwriter also begins to play and sing da-da-da's, in counterpoint to the Man with Bass's

line. Meanwhile, John spins on his wheelchair and heads back into his apartment. Sasha follows. We see them disappear and then reappear in the hall. Wordlessly, they split up. Sasha heads first to the floor below and then to the floor above while John wheels himself down the hall. They each begin knocking on doors. Each time a door opens we won't be able to see the face of the tenant, only the door itself and the disappointed faces of John and Sasha, as each of their queries is apparently responded to in the negative. The language of their repeated questions is as follows:)

JOHN: I'm terribly sorry to bother you at this late hour
    but I wonder if I might trouble you for the temporary loan of a
    pen
SASHA: Do you have a pen I could borrow

(After a few minutes John has knocked on every door on their floor. As a terribly defeated Sasha descends the steps, a terribly exhausted Man with Bass ascends the steps. They cross paths on the bottom of the steps between Sasha's floor and the one above. Sasha impulsively grabs the Man with Bass's collar.)

GIMME YOUR PEN
MAN WITH BASS: Uh okay

(With his bass leaning against him, the Man with Bass searches through his pockets and produces a pen, which he hands over to Sasha, whose mood, momentarily, becomes positively positive. Sasha gives the Man with Bass an affectionate punch in the arm.)

SASHA: Thanks

(Sasha runs off to join John, holding her pen triumphantly as the Man with Bass continues on his way up to the floor above. At the same time, Trudi arrives at the front stoop, enters the building, and begins climbing the stairs.)

JOHN: I'll get you some paper

(John disappears into his apartment. Trudi emerges from the stairway just as Sam arrives at the front stoop. Sam enters the building and begins climbing the stairs through the following.)

SASHA: I thought you had a board meeting
TRUDI: I did
    but get this
    ALL the other board members
    got mixed-up and showed up for the meeting two hours BEFORE it was scheduled to start
    Can you imagine
SASHA: Are you in trouble
TRUDI: Trouble
    I can't help it if all eleven of them are compulsively early people
    Anyway
    I grabbed the president of the board's pen on my way out
SASHA: You did
TRUDI: I just have to find it

(Trudi begins riffling through her purse as Sam emerges from the stairway.)

SASHA: I thought you had an exam on
    Gum Disease
    Yesterday Today Tomorrow
TRUDI: Yuck
SAM: I did but the proctor had food poisoning so I had to drive him in my cab to the emergency room
    (To Trudi) I'll show you pictures
    You'll never forget to floss again
SASHA: I never get to take cabs
SAM: Anyway
    I grabbed the emergency room doctor's pen on my way out
SASHA: You did
SAM: But what did I do with it

(Sam searches his person for the pen. Talidia exits her apartment and walks up a flight of stairs to join the others.)

TALIDIA: There you are
    I grabbed a pen out of Felix's book bag
    It's got green ink is that all right
    Ay I just had it
    What did I do with it

(Talidia searches her person for the pen.)

SASHA: It's okay
    I don't need a pen

(Sam, Trudi and Talidia halt their searches.)

SAM, TRUDI AND TALIDIA *(Vague disappointment)*: Oh

(John emerges from his apartment with a large stack of paper, which he hands to Sasha.)

JOHN: That ought to do it

(All four grown-ups regard Sasha.)

SAM: She'll need a place to work

(The following four lines are said simultaneously and to each other:)

TRUDI:	JOHN:	SAM:	TALIDIA:
She should come to my place My apartment's got wonderful cross-ventilation	She should come to my place I have a desk and a desk chair with a pillow	She should come to my place I'll move my orthodontia textbooks over to the side	She should come to my place My kids will stay as quiet as proverbial church mice

(Sasha sits down in the hallway.)

SASHA: I'm perfectly comfortable right here
    Thank you though

(Simultaneously and to each other:)

TRUDI:	JOHN:	SAM:	TALIDIA:
She's fine right here	She's fine right here	She's fine right here	She's fine right here
Give the girl some space	What she needs is time to collect her thoughts	She doesn't need you breathing down her neck	Can't you see she wants to work in peace

SASHA: I'll let you know if I need anything

(Simultaneously and to each other:)

TRUDI:	JOHN:	SAM:	TALIDIA:
She'll let Me know if she needs anything	She'll let Me know if she needs anything	She'll let Me know if she needs anything	She'll let Me know if she needs anything

(The four grown-ups sort of wait around for a moment or two, not wanting to be the first to leave. Then, each of them reluctantly backs his or her way toward his or her apartment, enters, and closes the door. The last instant of this section is punctuated by a Saaaaaaaam meow from Red.

Sasha is alone. She picks up her pen and sits down on the floor in front of the stack of paper. She writes:)

SASHA: The Eighth Wonder of the World
    by Alexandra Trusotsky

(Behind the blind, in the Singer/Songwriter's apartment, we see the silhouette of the Man with Bass setting up his instrument. Suddenly the apartment doors of John, Talidia, Trudi and Sam open at once. All four look/listen to see how Sasha is faring, discern little, and then close their doors at once.

At the front of the building a Pizza Deliveryman is buzzed in. He, too, goes through the routine of attempting to call the elevator before realizing it is broken—)

PIZZA DELIVERYMAN: Rats

(—and then embarking on the trip up the stairs as Sasha continues writing. When the Pizza Deliveryman arrives at the third floor he steps over Sasha on the way to John's door. He knocks and John answers.)

Hello Mr. O'Hara
JOHN: SHHHHH
PIZZA DELIVERYMAN: What's the matter
JOHN *(Can't you see)*: She's thinking

(John hands the Pizza Deliveryman some cash and the Pizza Deliveryman hands John the pizza.)

PIZZA DELIVERYMAN: No kidding
    I used to do that all the time
    See you tomorrow Mr. O'Hara

(The Pizza Deliveryman leaves as John closes his door very quietly. As the Pizza Deliveryman exits the building, a guy stops the outside door from closing with his foot. He is trying, rather unsuccessfully, to simultaneously manage several containers that together make up his drum kit. As he goes through the comic motions of getting all his equipment inside the building, Sasha has a realization:)

SASHA: Oops

(Sasha knocks on John's door; he opens it.)

JOHN *(Whispering)*: I thought you were thinking
SASHA *(Whispering)*: I WAS thinking
    but then I thought of something
    Why are we whispering

JOHN *(Whispering)*: Because
   you're thinking
   (Normal voice) What did you think of
SASHA: The mail

(Sasha passes John his mail. John riffles through it.)

JOHN: Aha

(John has stopped at a particularly thick envelope, which he opens.)

SASHA: What is it
JOHN: For my collection
   An original Tiffany invitation to the
   New York and Brooklyn Bridge's Opening Day Ceremonies
SASHA: Can I see

(John shows her the invitation very briefly.)

JOHN: Now resume thinking

(John starts to wheel himself back into his apartment, but then changes his mind and gives Sasha the invitation before he goes inside and closes the door. Sasha goes back to her spot on the floor, holding the invitation, but then immediately gets up and crosses to the window in order to gaze at the Bridge again. She holds up the invitation as she gazes. The Man with Drums has by now made his way over, with difficulty, to the elevator. He realizes it is out of order.)

MAN WITH DRUMS: Yikes

(The Man with Drums embarks on a literally percussive and somewhat epic journey up the stairs. The Singer/Songwriter and the Man with Bass provide a bassline and counterpoint to the Man with Drums' sounds.

   At the same time, the doors of the broken-down elevator open to reveal the Victorian bedroom of Washington and Emily Roebling, who just now have their field glasses trained not on the Bridge, but on

Sasha looking at the Bridge. Throughout the rest of the play they will remain focused on Sasha.

Perhaps the next section should approximate the experience of watching time-lapse photography, perhaps not; it should, in any case, feel rhythmically distinct, and symphonic.

Sasha writes.

John appears, hands Sasha a piece of pizza and then disappears.

Sasha lies down on her stomach with her knees bent and feet in the air, thinking as she chews on her pen.

Sam appears, hands Sasha a toothbrush, starts to disappear, but then pulls the pen out of her mouth before he does.

Talidia appears, leaves Sasha with a blanket and then disappears.

Trudi appears, leaves Sasha with an alarm clock and then disappears.

The Man with Drums steps over Sasha on his way up the stairs as Sasha continues to write.

As the Man with Bass begins to warm up, the Man with Drums spills into the Singer/Songwriter's apartment and begins to set up his kit; Sasha continues to write.

Even as the Shadowy Figure emerges from its apartment, steps over Sasha on its way to moving the potted plant and remarks:)

SHADOWY FIGURE: Fdfldkjfsdketcdfkfaetcdffdfdgfg

(Sasha continues to write.

Even as the Other Shadowy Figure emerges from its apartment, steps over Sasha on its way to moving the potted plant and remarks:)

OTHER SHADOWY FIGURE: Gettirjoetcfkgrltjrketckjteltjeltkjtl

(Sasha continues to write.

Even as the two Shadowy Figures engage in a direct battle of plant placement scored by grunts and the tuning of a drum set, Sasha continues to write.

Now the trio of musicians is all set up and stands in silhouette behind the blind in the Singer/Songwriter's apartment. And at last we hear the song—which up to now we've come to know only in bits and drafts as the Singer/Songwriter labored over its composition. We hear the song.

At the same time Talidia, John, Sam and Trudi emerge from their apartments, cross to hall windows with Bridge views and simultaneously bring binoculars up to their eyes. The Shadowy Figures do the same.

As Sasha continues to scribble away, and as the Roeblings continue to gaze at her, we see a sea of Men in Top Hats moving across the Bridge that has encroached upon the building. The Men in Top Hats move from downstage right to upstage left, so that we watch their backs.

This live view of the Men in Top Hats' (perhaps slow and stylized) progression is offered a counterpoint by a projection of a historical photograph of the Men in Top Hats from the front.

As the Men in Top Hats continue to cross, we see a projection of the Opening Day Faces in the Crowd.

As the Men in Top Hats continue to cross we see a projection of fireworks.

As the Men in Top Hats continue to cross we see a projection of Opening Day Faces in the Crowd that include the faces of the play's characters, i.e, the play's characters see their own faces in the crowd.

And then the Men in Top Hats have disappeared from view.

And then Sasha has stopped writing.

And then the musicians have stopped playing.

And then Sasha and the musicians have picked up binoculars and joined the others in gazing at the Bridge.

And even the Roeblings have turned their gazes on the Bridge.

And the Bridge is lit up for the first time, light by light.

And perhaps at the same time we see a projection of the Bridge being lit up for the first time.

The point is, whatever it takes, as we and the characters gaze at the Bridge we understand that naming it the Eighth Wonder of the World was no hyperbole, for it is a beautiful thing.)

END

"Wire Wings"

Words and music by Barbara Brousal

Sheltered by its wire wings
They come with offerings
Steamboats sigh, tugboats sing

A long list of wishes and dreams
Are set here by the sea
Take a moment there's a perfect view for free

Just when you thought you were alone in the room
Rises the platinum arc of the moon
Suspended patiently
Waiting for you to turn your head and see

Here's the Bridge, here's the water, here's the gift
Here's my time, my words, here's my blanket
Here's what you've been telling me all along

We're not waiting for anything
Just lean back into the wind

We're not missing anything
If I lean, you'll hold me

MELISSA JAMES GIBSON's recent plays include *What Rhymes with America* and *Current Nobody*. Her work has been produced and/or developed at Playwrights Horizons, Center Theatre Group, Soho Rep, La Jolla Playhouse, Children's Theatre Company, Steppenwolf Theatre Company, Adirondack Theatre Festival, Woolly Mammoth Theatre Company, Seattle Rep and the Sundance Institute Theatre Lab, among others, regionally and internationally. Recent commissions include Atlantic Theater Company, Manhattan Theatre Club/Sloan and Second Stage Theatre. Honors include: Obie Award, Guggenheim Fellowship, Steinberg Playwright Award, Kesselring Prize, Whiting Writers' Award, Lucille Lortel Foundation Playwrights' Fellowship, Lilly Award, Jerome Fellow, MacDowell Colony Fellow, NEA/TCG Theatre Residency Program for Playwrights and Susan Smith Blackburn Prize finalist. She received an MFA from Yale School of Drama and is a graduate of New Dramatists. She has lectured in the Program in Theater at Princeton University. Film credits include the screenplay for *Almost Christmas*, starring Paul Giamatti, Paul Rudd and Sally Hawkins, which was directed by Phil Morrison and premiered at the 2013 Tribeca Film Festival. She is a writer for the FX series *The Americans*, created by Joe Weisberg.